The Finance (No 2) Act 2005

Contributors

Charles Barcroft, CTA

Giles Clarke, MA, PhD, Barrister

David Bertram, FCA, CTA

Sarah Bradford, BA(Hons), ACA, CTA

John Clube, MA, CA, CTA

Colin Davis, MA, FCA, FTII

Mark Downey

Jon Golding, TEP, ATT

Gareth Green, Managing Director, Transfer Pricing Solutions Ltd

Andrew Hubbard, BMus, PhD, CTA, ATT

Jonathan Kandel, MA (Cantab), Solicitor, Clifford Chance LLP

Zigurds Kronbergs, MA, BSc, ARCS, ACA, FCCA

Mark McLaughlin, CTA(Fellow), ATT, TEP

Robert Murgatroyd, formerly one of HM Inspectors of Taxes

Richard Pincher, FTII, AIITP, LLB(Hons), Barrister

Gary Richards, MA, LLB, ATII, Solicitor

Members of the LexisNexis Group worldwide

United Kingdom	LexisNexis Butterworths, a Division of Reed Elsevier (UK) Ltd, Halsbury House, 35 Chancery Lane, LONDON, WC2A 1EL, and RSH, 1–3 Baxter's Place, Leith Walk EDINBURGH EH1 3AF
Argentina	LexisNexis Argentina, BUENOS AIRES
Australia	LexisNexis Butterworths, CHATSWOOD, New South Wales
Austria	LexisNexis Verlag ARD Orac GmbH & Co KG, VIENNA
Canada	LexisNexis Butterworths, MARKHAM, Ontario
Chile	LexisNexis Chile Ltda, SANTIAGO DE CHILE
Czech Republic	Nakladatelství Orac sro, PRAGUE
France	Editions du Juris-Classeur SA, PARIS
Germany	LexisNexis Deutschland GmbH, FRANKFURT and MUNSTER
Hong Kong	LexisNexis Butterworths, HONG KONG
Hungary	HVG-Orac, BUDAPEST
India	LexisNexis Butterworths, NEW DELHI
Ireland	LexisNexis, DUBLIN
Italy	Giuffrè Editore, MILAN
Malaysia	Malayan Law Journal Sdn Bhd, KUALA LUMPUR
New Zealand	LexisNexis Butterworths, WELLINGTON
Poland	Wydawnictwo Prawnicze LexisNexis, WARSAW
Singapore	LexisNexis Butterworths, SINGAPORE
South Africa	LexisNexis Butterworths, DURBAN
Switzerland	Stämpfli Verlag AG, BERNE
USA	LexisNexis, DAYTON, Ohio

© Reed Elsevier (UK) Ltd 2005

Published by LexisNexis Butterworths

A CIP Catalogue record for this book is available from the British Library.

ISBN 1405709006

Typeset by Letterpart Ltd, Reigate, Surrey

Printed and bound in Great Britain by CPI Bath Press, Bath

Visit LexisNexis Butterworths at www.lexisnexis.co.uk

CONTENTS

RELEVANT DATES AND ABBREVIATIONS

Budget statement	16 March 2005
Finance Bill published	26 May 2005
Royal Assent	20 July 2005

The following abbreviations are used in this book—

ACT	=	Advance Corporation Tax
BGDA	=	Betting and Gaming Duties Act
BPRA	=	Business Premises Renovation Allowances
CA	=	Companies Act
CAA	=	Capital Allowances Act
CEMA	=	Customs and Excise Management Act 1979
CCL	=	Climate Change Levy
CFC	=	Controlled Foreign Company
CGT	=	Capital Gains Tax
CRCA	=	Commissioners for Revenue and Customs Act 2005
CTSA	=	Corporation Tax Self-Assessment
Ch	=	Chapter (of a part of an Act)
cl	=	clause
cll	=	clauses
EC	=	European Communities
ECJ	=	European Court of Justice (Court of Justice of the European Communities)
EIS	=	Enterprise Investment Scheme
ESOP	=	Employee Share Ownership Plan
EU	=	European Union
FA	=	Finance Act
F(No 2)A	=	Finance (No 2) Act
HMRC	=	Her Majesty's Revenue and Customs
IHTA	=	Inheritance Tax Act
ITEPA	=	Income Tax (Earnings and Pensions) Act 2003
ITMA	=	Income Tax Management Act
IT-TOIA	=	Income Tax (Trading and Other Income) Act 2005
OTA	=	Oil Taxation Act
para	=	paragraph (of a Schedule to an Act)
PCTA	=	Provisional Collection of Taxes Act 1968
PRT	=	Petroleum Revenue Tax
reg	=	regulation (of an SI)
s	=	section (of an Act)
SAYE	=	Save as you Earn
Sch	=	Schedule (to an Act)
SDTS	=	Simon's Direct Tax Service
SI	=	Statutory Instrument (since 1948)
SR&O	=	Statutory Rule and Order
ss	=	sections
sub-cl	=	subclause
sub-para	=	sub-paragraph
sub-s	=	subsection
SDTS	=	Simon's Direct Tax Service
SWTI	=	Simon's Weekly Tax Intelligence
TA	=	Income and Corporation Taxes Act 1988
TCGA	=	Taxation of Chargeable Gains Act 1992

T&IA	= Tribunal and Inquiries Act 1992
TMA	= Taxes Management Act 1970
VATA	= Value Added Tax Act 1994
VCT	= Venture Capital Trust

FINANCE (NO 2) ACT 2005

INTRODUCTION

PART 1
VALUE ADDED TAX

Goods subject to warehousing regime: place of acquisition or supply HMRC is given power to specify by regulation circumstances in which the normal rule for warehoused goods (that the supply takes place outside the UK) is not to apply (s 1).

Cars: determination of consideration for fuel supplied for private use From a day to be appointed, the Treasury may substitute for the present scale charge a system based on the carbon dioxide emission figure of the car (s 2).

Credit for, or repayment of, overstated or overpaid VAT Under current law, HMRC may refuse a claim to refund excess VAT to the extent that it would unjustly enrich the claimant, but only where the excess represents VAT paid that was not due. With respect to claims made after 25 May 2005, the unjust-enrichment defence may be invoked to refuse a claim for credit or repayment of VAT that the taxable person has accounted for to an excessive degree or where he has been assessed to an excessive amount of VAT (without there needing to have been a payment). The three-year limitation period will apply in all cases (s 3). Consequential amendments are made to VATA 1994 ss 78 (interest in cases of official error), 80A (arrangements for reimbursing customers), 80B (assessments of amounts due under s 80 arrangements) and 83 (appeals) (s 4).

Reverse charge: gas and electricity valuation With respect to supplies made after 16 March 2005, supplies of gas and electricity treated as made by the recipient under the reverse-charge provisions will be valued on the basis of the full consideration payable (s 5).

Disclosure of value added tax avoidance schemes From a day to be appointed, the disclosure provisions will be extended to include instances where the tax advantage lies in the reduction of a person's irrecoverable VAT. Where a new scheme is designated, there will be no requirement to notify again where notification of that scheme has already been made previously or its details otherwise disclosed (s 6 and Sch 1).

PART 2
INCOME TAX, CORPORATION TAX AND CAPITAL GAINS TAX

Chapter 1 Personal taxation

Social security pension lump sums Where a person exercises his or her right under the Pensions Act 2004 to defer a state pension in exchange for the receipt of a lump sum ('the social security pension lump sum'), the lump sum will not form part of that person's total income for the applicable year of assessment but be taxable at the highest rate of income tax on the person's other income for that year of assessment (s 7). Which year is to be the applicable year of assessment for the charge under s 7 is defined (s 8). Terms in ss 7 and 8 are defined and they are to commence with the 2006–07 year of assessment (s 9). Consequential amendments are made to ITEPA 2003 (s 10).

Gift aid The circumstances in which a right of admission to a property given in recognition of a charitable donation by an individual will not be treated as denying tax relief are extended with effect for gifts made after 5 April 2006 (s 11).

Employee securities Amendments are made by Sch 2 to ITEPA 2003 Part 7 to counter avoidance schemes designed to avoid the tax and NIC charge on employment-related securities. Rights under contracts of insurance (other than excluded contracts) are included in the definition of securities in ITEPA 2003 s 420, and excluded contracts are defined (Sch 2 para 2). Part 7 Chapter 2, which deals with restricted securities, is amended to include as restricted securities employment-related securities that are or represent an interest in redeemable securities. A new ITEPA 2003 s 431B provides that where the right or opportunity to acquire restricted securities or an interest therein is part of a tax-avoidance arrangement, the employer and employee are deemed to have made an election under ITEPA 2003 s 431(1) to disregard restrictions and tax the unrestricted market value of the securities at the time of acquisition (Sch 2 paras 3–7). Part 7 Chapter 3, which deals with convertible securities, is amended to disapply ITEPA 2003 s 437(1) where the right or opportunity to acquire the securities is part of a tax-avoidance arrangement, with the result that the market value of the securities on acquisition on which the employee is taxed will be computed without disregarding the right to convert (Sch 2 paras 8–11). Part 7 Chapter 3C, which deals with securities acquired for less than market value, is amended, most significantly by the addition of ITEPA 2003 s 446UA, which ensures that where securities to which the Chapter applies are acquired under a tax-avoidance arrangement, there is no deemed notional loan, as would otherwise be the case under ITEPA 2003 ss 446S–446U, but the amount that would otherwise be the initial amount of that loan is to be treated as employment income of the year of acquisition (Sch 2 paras 12–16). ITEPA 2003 s 447, which is part of Part 7 Chapter 4, which deals with post-acquisition benefits from securities, is amended to remove the exemption from a charge under that Chapter where income tax is otherwise chargeable on the benefit concerned in cases where anything that has been done that affects the securities is part of a tax-avoidance arrangement. A similar amendment is made to ITEPA 2003 s 449, which exempts certain shares from Chapter 4 (Sch 2 paras 17–19). Purpose tests in the Chapters affected are generally more closely aligned (Sch 2 variously). Minor and consequential amendments are made to FA 2003 Sch 23, which provides for relief from corporation tax where shares are provided to employees (Sch 2 para 20). The amendments generally have effect for events occurring after, things done after or securities acquired after, 1 December 2004, except for Sch 2 para 15 (which, inter alia, inserts ITEPA 2003 s 446UA), which has effect from 20 July 2005. The amendments made to FA 2003 generally have effect from 20 July 2005 (s 12 and Sch 2).

Chapter 2 Scientific research organisations

The exemption under TA 1988 s 508 from corporation tax available to scientific research organisations is extended to associations having the undertaking of research and development as their object. The definition of 'research and development' is that contained in TA 1988 s 837A, which applies for tax purposes generally. As with the earlier narrow definition, the aim of the qualifying activity must be to lead to or facilitate an extension of any class or classes of trade. The requirement to seek annual retrospective approval from the Secretary of State for Trade and Industry is removed. The amendments are to have effect from a date to be appointed (s 13). Consequential amendments are made to ITTOIA 2005 s 88, which provides for an income tax deduction for payments made to research associations (s 14), and to TA 1988 s 82B, which provides for a parallel corporation tax deduction (s 15).

Chapter 3 Authorised investment funds etc

A special rate of corporation tax, equal to the lower rate of income tax (currently 20 per cent), is to apply to open-ended investment companies (OEICs). Where an OEIC is an 'umbrella company' (broadly, an OEIC that operates a number of separate investment pools for different groups of investors) the special rate is to apply to each pool separately as if it were an OEIC (s 16). Various existing provisions relating to authorised investment trusts and OEICs are repealed. Further changes may be made by regulation (s 17). The type and purpose of such changes is specified (s 18). These provisions are to have effect from a day to be appointed (s 19).

Statutory effect is given to Extra-Statutory Concession D17, under which units temporarily held in a 'box' by the managers of an unauthorised unit trust following disposal by one investor pending their disposal to another investor are ignored in determining whether the condition in TCGA 1992 s 100(2) for the trust's gains not to be chargeable gains is met. Additionally, where units are held by an insurance company or a friendly society, the fact that a charge to corporation tax on the gains arising from the disposal of those units may arise is not to cause the condition in TCGA 1992 s 100(2) to fail. The section has effect from 2005–06 (s 20).

Statutory effect is given to an HMRC practice whereby under certain conditions, sums reinvested in a unit trust on a unitholder's behalf in respect of his accumulation units are to qualify as deductions within TCGA 1992 s 38(1)(b) in computing any chargeable gain or loss on the disposal of the units. The section has effect for disposals made after 15 March 2005 (s 21).

For payments made after 5 April 2005, a person liable to corporation tax need only satisfy itself that the payment is being made to a PEP or ISA manager in order to make a payment of interest gross (ie without deduction of tax). By virtue of SI 2004/1450 reg 24(c), the same rule applies to payments by an authorised investment fund to a Child Trust Fund provider (s 22).

Minor defects in the offshore funds legislation (TA 1988 Part XVII Chapter V) are corrected (s 23).

Chapter 4 Avoidance involving tax arbitrage

This Chapter, consisting of ss 24–31 and Sch 3, consists of a package of anti-avoidance measures aimed at cross-border tax avoidance involving certain hybrid instruments or hybrid entities. The legislation has effect for both deductions that companies seek to make and to receipts that would otherwise escape the charge to tax. It applies only where a direction is given by HMRC.

In the case of deductions, four conditions must be satisfied (in the reasonable belief of HMRC) before a direction may be issued. Those conditions are: that there exists a 'qualifying scheme' to which the company is a party; that as a result of the scheme the company will claim or will have claimed a deduction or set-off in computing its profits for the purposes of corporation tax; that the main purpose or one of the main purposes of the scheme is to achieve a 'UK tax advantage' for the company; and that the amount of that advantage is more than minimal. What is minimal is not defined in the legislation, but it is believed that amounts of less than £50,000 will be considered minimal. A company falls within these provisions only if it is UK-resident or is otherwise within the charge to UK corporation tax (ie because it is carrying on a trade in the UK through a permanent establishment) (s 24).

Where a direction in the prescribed form has been given, the company must compute or recompute its liability to corporation tax according to a rule 'A' and where appropriate, also to a rule 'B'. Rule A requires that no deduction shall be allowed for corporation tax purposes where the same expense is allowed for the purposes of any other tax (including foreign tax), except for petroleum revenue tax and the special charge under TA 1988 s 501A(1) in respect of ring-fence trades. Rule A also applies where the expense would have been allowed twice (a 'double dip') but for the operation of any UK or foreign rule having the same effect as Rule A. Rule B applies where as a result of the qualifying scheme, there is a payment that creates a deduction or allowance for the payer or another party to the scheme (in respect of UK or foreign tax) but where the recipient is not taxable on the receipt or has his liability to tax reduced as a result. Recipient entities that are generally exempt from tax in the UK or abroad (eg because they are charities) are excluded. Where Rule B applies, the deduction is disallowed altogether (if the recipient is not to liable to tax at all on the associated receipt) or reduced in proportion to the recipient's non-liability (s 25).

Schedule 3 defines what is a 'qualifying scheme'. A qualifying scheme will be one involving a 'hybrid entity' (Sch 3 Part 2), a 'hybrid effect' (Sch 3 Part 3) or a 'hybrid effect' and connected persons (Sch 3 Part 4) (para 1).

A 'hybrid entity' is an entity that is recognised as a [legal] person for the tax purposes of any jurisdiction but whose profits are also taxable in the hands of another person for the purposes of UK income tax or corporation tax or of any similar tax in any other jurisdiction. For this purpose, CFC rules in another jurisdiction are disregarded (paras 2 and 3).

A scheme has a 'hybrid effect' if it involves an 'instrument of alterable character', shares subject to conversion, securities subject to conversion or debt instruments treated as equity (para 4). An instrument is of alterable character if any party to the instrument may elect in any jurisdiction to alter a 'relevant characteristic' of that instrument (para 5). A scheme involves shares subject to conversion if it includes the issue by a company of such shares or an amendment of rights attaching to shares to make them convertible (para 6). Parallel provisions apply in respect of convertible securities (para 7). A scheme involves a debt instrument treated as equity if it includes a debt instrument issued by a company that is treated as equity in that company under generally accepted accounting practice (para 8).

A scheme involves a hybrid effect and connected persons if it either includes the issue to a connected person of shares not conferring a 'qualifying beneficial entitlement' or the transfer between connected persons of rights under a security (para 9). Broadly, shares confer a qualifying beneficial entitlement if they are fully paid ordinary shares conferring a right to a relevant proportion of distributable profits and assets available for distribution on a winding-up (para 10). A scheme involves the transfer of rights under a security if the transferor transfers rights to receive a payment under a security or otherwise secures that a payment to which he would otherwise be entitled arises to one or more other persons (para 11).

The second arm of the anti-arbitrage measures concerns so-called 'receipts cases'. HMRC will issue a direction where it has reasonable grounds for believing that all of five conditions are or may be satisfied in relation to a UK-resident company. Those conditions are: (A) that there is a scheme involving the company and another person ('the payer') making a payment to that company; (B) that the payment is a 'qualifying payment'; (C) that the payer is entitled in the UK or in any other jurisdiction to an allowable deduction in respect of that payment; (D) that at least a part of the amount received by the company in respect of the payment is neither taken into account in computing the company's profits or gains chargeable to UK corporation tax or taken into account as income in computing another UK-resident company's liability to UK corporation tax; and (E) that on entering into the scheme both the company and the payer expected that a benefit would arise as a result of condition D. Some exceptions are provided in respect of condition C. A 'qualifying payment' is a payment that increases the capital of the recipient company (s 26). Where a direction is issued in the prescribed form, the company on which it is served must compute or recompute its liability to corporation tax as if the 'relevant part' of the qualifying payment were income chargeable under Schedule D Case VI. The 'relevant part' is that part (which may be the whole) of the payment in respect of which conditions C and D of s 26 are satisfied (s 27). Provisions are made to determine when a direction under ss 24 or 26 may be made and what the consequences may be (s 28). Consequential amendments are made to the corporation tax self-assessment provisions of FA 1998 Sch 18 (s 29). There are interpretation provisions (s 30). The provisions in respect of deduction cases have effect for accounting periods beginning after 15 March 2005. Those in respect of receipts cases have effect with respect to contributions to capital made after 15 March 2005. There are transitional provisions for straddling periods in respect of deduction cases (s 31).

Chapter 5 Chargeable gains

Residence, location of assets etc Sections 32 to 34 comprise a set of anti-avoidance provisions designed to prevent CGT avoidance involving exploitation of non-residence. TCGA 1992 s 10A imposes a charge to capital gains tax on individuals in the year of assessment in which they return to the UK after a temporary period of non-residence ('the intervening years') in respect of assets they have disposed of during the intervening years. Excluded from this charge are assets acquired while the individual was neither resident nor ordinarily resident in the UK. The exclusion is extended to assets acquired when the individual was dually resident but treated as not resident in the UK under the terms of a double tax treaty. Similarly, an individual is not to be regarded as having returned to the UK in any year if he or she is treated as not resident in the UK for the purposes of a double tax treaty. However, where a year becomes an intervening year as a result of these changes, they are not to have effect to postpone a charge under any of TCGA 1992 ss 13 (attribution of gains made by a non-resident company), 86 (attribution of gains of non-resident settlement to the settlor), 87 (attribution of gains of non-resident settlement to beneficiaries) or 89(2) (attribution of gains of migrant settlement to beneficiaries). Furthermore, nothing in a double tax treaty (allocation of the right to tax the gain to the treaty partner, for example) is to be taken as exempting the individual from a charge to tax under TCGA 1992 s 10A (s 32). A new TCGA 1992 s 83A is introduced to prevent avoidance of capital gains tax in connection with a settlement whose trustees are both resident and non-resident in a particular year of assessment. This is aimed primarily at so-called 'sunset schemes' under which trustees who are UK-resident at some time in the year of assessment dispose of trust assets at a time when they are not so resident, and under the operation of a double tax treaty, little or no foreign tax is paid on the gain, which is also exempt from UK tax. The operation of TCGA 1992 s 77 is such that a settlor with an interest in the settlement escapes a charge to capital gains tax to which he would otherwise be liable. New TCGA 1992 s 83A provides that nothing in the terms of a double tax treaty is to prevent a charge to tax from arising in these circumstances on either the trustees or any other person (eg the settlor). This provision applies to disposals made after 15 March 2005 (s 33). It should be noted that both ss 32 and 33 seek to override terms of the UK's international agreements, which is a questionable measure in international law.

Section 34 introduces Sch 4, which provides new rules to determine the situs of assets for the purposes of capital gains tax. The main aim of these new rules is to prevent avoidance of capital gains tax by UK-resident but non-domiciled individuals on the disposal of assets linked to the UK but deemed to be situated abroad at the time of disposal. Such gains are exempt from UK capital gains tax if they are not directly or indirectly remitted to the UK. An example of an asset affected is bearer shares in a UK company, which common law deems to be situated where they are physically located. The existing TCGA 1992 s 275, which provides where certain assets are situated for the purposes of capital gains tax, is amended to include several further provisions. Thus, a new s 275(1)(da) provides that shares or debentures of a UK-incorporated company are situated in the UK, subject to the existing exceptions in s 275(1)(d) (Sch 4 para 4). A new TCGA 1992 s 275A provides primarily for the situs of futures or options. It provides first that if any intangible asset is subject to UK law at the time of its creation, it is deemed always to be situated in the UK. Further, where the underlying subject matter of a future or option is or includes an intangible asset, then, broadly, if that intangible asset is situated in the UK at the time of its creation, the future or option is treated as situated in the UK, even if it was actually situated elsewhere at the time of its own creation (Sch 4 para 5). A new TCGA 1992 s 275C provides that where there are co-owners (owning either jointly or in common) of an asset, then their interest in that asset is situated where the asset is situated (Sch 4 para 6). Schedule 4 Part 2 makes minor amendments to align certain provisions of TCGA 1992 with earlier amendments introduced when references to a company's trading in the UK through a branch or agency were replaced by references to trading through a permanent establishment (Sch 4 paras 7–9). The amendments generally have effect from 16 March 2005 (Sch 4 para 10) (s 34 and Sch 4).

Miscellaneous Section 35 introduces Sch 5, which makes amendments to the treatment of options for the purposes of capital gains tax. The existing rule in TCGA 1992 s 144ZA disapplies the market-value rule on the exercise of options where they are granted or otherwise acquired by way of a transaction at arm's length but exercised otherwise than at arm's length or vice versa. It was introduced by FA 2003 to counter certain avoidance schemes but may itself be exploited for avoidance purposes, for example where the exercise price of a call option exceeds the value of the underlying subject matter at the time of exercise or where the exercise price of a put option is less than the value of the underlying subject matter at the time of exercise. The provisions of Sch 5, which amend s 144ZA and introduce TCGA 1992 ss 144ZB, 144ZC and 144ZD, are intended to counter such avoidance schemes. Section 144ZA is amended so that, when in the circumstances described in the section the market-value rule is displaced, it is the exercise price, and not the actual value, that is substituted (Sch 5 para 1). New s 144ZB applies (subject to certain exclusions) where the exercise of the option is 'non-commercial' (as defined in new s 144ZC) and s 144ZA would otherwise apply. Where s 144ZB applies, s 144ZA does not apply and in the case of a put option, both the acquisition cost of what the grantor buys and the value of the consideration for the disposal of what the grantor buys on exercise is equated to the market value of what is bought. Similarly, for a call option, both the value of the consideration for the disposal of what the grantor sells and the cost to the person exercising the option of acquiring what is sold on exercise is the market value of what is sold. These provisions thus restore the market-value rule in the circumstances described in the section. New s 144ZC defines a non-commercial exercise as one in which, for a put option, the exercise price is less than the open market price of the underlying subject matter of the option, whereas for a call option, the exercise is non-commercial if the exercise price is greater than the open market price of the underlying subject matter. Rules for determining the open market price are provided. Finally, new s 144ZD defines five circumstances in which s 144ZB is not to apply even where the exercise of the option is non-commercial (Sch 5 para 2). Schedule 5 Part 2 makes miscellaneous amendments to TCGA 1992 ss 105A (election for alternative treatment for shares acquired on same day), 149A (share-option schemes) and 288 (interpretation) (Sch 5 paras 3–5). The amendments made by Sch 5 paras 1–3 have effect for options exercised after 1 December 2004 and the amendments made by Sch 5 paras 4 and 5 have effect for options granted after 1 December 2004 (Sch 5 para 6) (s 35 and Sch 5).

TCGA 1992 s 171A allows members of a group to elect for a deemed transfer of an asset to have been made from one company to another before its disposal outside the group, thus obviating the need for an actual transfer while still benefiting from the no-gain no-loss rule on intra-group transfers. Where the deemed transferee company is a non-resident trading in the UK through a permanent establishment, s 171A is amended to deem the non-resident to have acquired the asset for the purposes of the permanent establishment. This enables the disposal out of the group of that asset to remain within the charge to capital gains tax, so that the non-resident company may set the gain or loss against its other losses or gains. The amendment has effect for disposals made after 15 March 2005 (s 36).

Chapter 6 Miscellaneous

Accounting practice and related matters Section 37 introduces Sch 6, which contains further provisions to cater for the adoption of International Financial

Reporting Standards (IFRS) and their predecessors, International Accounting Standards (IAS). The main purpose is to correct for legislation enacted in FA 2005, which HMRC has accepted after consultation goes further than intended.

ITTOIA 2005 s 227 provides the circumstances in which Part 2 Chapter 17 of that Act applies to changes in the basis on which profits of a trade, profession or vocation are computed for the purposes of income tax. Section 227(4) is amended so that Chapter 17 also applies to a change from UK generally accepted accounting practice (UK GAAP) to IAS (Sch 6 para 2). A new definition of 'statutory insolvency arrangement' (in ITTOIA 2005 s 259) is provided to match that applying for corporation tax (Sch 6 para 3). A new FA 1996 Sch 9 para 4A, which provides for a charge to tax (a deemed release of liability) where a debt is transferred from one company to another and the new creditor is connected with the debtor immediately after the transfer, is substituted, so that it no longer applies in two unintended situations – where the old creditor and the new creditor are connected at any time in the period of account in which the transfer takes place (where they are members of the same group, for example) or where the new creditor pays less than the face value of the debt solely because it was issued at a discount (Sch 6 para 5). The deadline for an election for a company not accounting under FRS 26 or IAS 39 to elect for bifurcated treatment under FA 1996 s 94A of loan relationships is extended from 31 July 2005 to 31 December 2005, with the possibility of a later election in some circumstances; such elections are now to be made under F(No 2)A 2005 Sch 6 para 7 and not under FA 2005 Sch 4 para 28(3), (4), which is repealed (Sch 6 para 7). Provisions are made to repeal FA 1996 s 84A, which provides for exchange gains and losses on loan relationships to be disregarded in certain circumstances from an appointed day should attempts to reconcile its interaction with FA 2002 Sch 26 para 16 (which is the like provision for derivative contracts, and may also be repealed) and the Disregard Regulations (SI 2004/3256) not be resolved. See also the Loan Relationships and Derivative Contracts (Disregard and Bringing into Account of Profits and Losses) (Amendment) Regulations, SI 2005/2012 (Sch 6 paras 9–11) (s 37 and Sch 6).

Financial avoidance Annuities and other annual payments are removed from the class of payments in TA 1988 s 338A that are treated as charges on income. The Government is still consulting on abandoning the concept of charges on income altogether as part of its mooted corporation tax reform, but has taken this step in reaction to avoidance schemes that have been disclosed to HMRC. For payments made after 15 March 2005, relief for annuities and other annual payments will be given by way of a deduction for management expenses under TA 1988 ss 75 or 76, which impose a business purpose test. There are transitional provisions for payments made before 16 March 2005 in an accounting period straddling that date (s 38).

Section 39 introduces Sch 7, which contains anti-avoidance provisions against schemes involving the use of financial products and arrangements, and is another example in this Act of measures taken as a direct result of disclosures made under the disclosure rules of FA 2004 Part 7. The 15-year limit on the application of TA 1988 ss 43A–43G, which provide for a charge to tax on lump sums received under rent-factoring schemes, is repealed with respect to schemes entered into after 15 March 2005, so that schemes in which the obligation to divert the rents lasts for a period of more than 15 years no longer automatically escape the charge under the legislation (Sch 7 para 1). TA 1988 s 730, which taxes transfers of the rights to income from securities where the title to the securities themselves is not transferred ('strips'), is amended to apply from 2 December 2004 to dividend strips only (Sch 7 para 2). Interest strips are now dealt with by new TA 1988 s 775A (see Sch 7 para 4 below). TA 1988 ss 768B–768E are designed to prevent the carry-over of non-trading losses where there are circumstances (e g a major change in the nature or conduct of the business within three years before or after a change of ownership) similar to those in TA 1988 s 768, which deals with trading losses. Amendments are made to TA 1988 ss 768B and 768C, which deal specifically with investment companies, and to TA 1988 Sch 28A to prevent the carry-forward of non-trading loan-relationship deficits where there is a 'relevant change of ownership' of an investment company. The new provisions apply to changes of ownership after 9 February 2005 (Sch 7 para 3). New TA 1988 s 775A is introduced to charge to tax 'annuity strips' where any sale or transfer of the right to receive an annual payment is made where the consideration for the sale or transfer would not otherwise be chargeable to tax (whether income tax or corporation tax). The charge is on the market value of the right transferred, is made on the transferor, and applies in the accounting period or tax year in which the sale or transfer is made. Exceptions are made for annual payments under life annuities, pension income, and annual payments by individuals that are not charges on income and are not chargeable to income tax. The new section applies to sales or transfers made after 15 March 2005 (Sch 7 para 4). Amendments are made to TA 1988 s 807A consequent on the introduction by Sch 7 para 10 of new provisions treating certain shares as loan relationships, in order that no foreign tax credit may be claimed in respect of distributions received when the company in question did not hold such a share (Sch 7 para 5). Amendments are made to the manufactured interest provisions of TA 1988 Sch 23A to ensure that they interact fully with the accrued income scheme (Sch 7 para 6).

TCGA 1992 s 48 provides that when computing the gain on a disposal, there is no discount for deferred consideration. A new TCGA 1992 s 48(2) overrides that provision in respect of any part of the consideration which consists to any extent of rights under a creditor relationship to which a company becomes a party as a result of the disposal (as in the case of a money debt). This provision is consequent on the amendment of FA 1996 s 100 by Sch 7 para 12 (Sch 7 para 7).

A new TCGA 1992 s 151D is inserted to prevent the creation of an allowable loss under any tax-avoidance scheme (including a scheme to create such a capital loss) as the consequence of a payment that is not made in respect of the acquisition or disposal of a corporate strip (Sch 7 para 8). It has the same effect as new FA 1996 Sch 13 para 13D, inserted by Sch 7 para 21, with which it must be read.

TCGA 1992 s 171 (no-gain no-loss transfers of assets within a group) is amended consequent upon the introduction of FA 1996 s 91A (see under Sch 7 para 10 below) so that where a share within that section is transferred intra-group by a third party holding the obligations with respect to that share without a transfer of the obligations, s 171 does not apply to that transfer (Sch 7 para 9).

New FA 1996 ss 91A–91G, introduced by Sch 7 para 10, provide for certain shares to be treated as if they were loan relationships. The object is to prevent the conversion of what would otherwise be interest income to a tax-exempt dividend, a capital gain or a 'tax nothing'. Where a company ('the investing company') holds a share (of the 'issuing company') that is subject to outstanding third-party obligations and the share is an 'interest-like' investment, it is to be treated as a creditor loan relationship, and any distribution in respect of the share is treated as if it were not a distribution falling within TA 1988 s 209(2)(a) or (b), and hence not exempt from corporation tax. Fair-value accounting is to be used to determine the debits and credits to be brought into account by the investing company. Outstanding third-party obligations are yet-to-be-discharged obligations held by persons other than the investing company to meet unpaid calls or to make a contribution to the capital of the issuing company which could affect the value of the share. An 'interest-like investment' is a share such that its fair value is likely to increase at a rate representing a return on an investment at a commercial rate of interest and is unlikely to deviate substantially from that rate of increase (FA 1996 s 91A). A further instance where the provisions are to have effect to recharacterise shares as loan relationships is provided by new FA 1996 s 91B. That section applies where the investing company holds shares in the issuing company which are 'non-qualifying shares' and those shares are neither treated as creditor loan relationships under FA 1996 Sch 10 para 4 (non-qualifying investments in unit trusts etc) nor under FA 1996 s 91A. Non-qualifying shares are shares not falling within TA 1988 s 95 (shares held by dealers etc) which satisfy any one or more of the conditions in FA 1996 ss 91C–91E. Again, distributions from such shares are not exempt from corporation tax and fair-value accounting must be used in determining the debits and credits to be taken into account under the loan-relationship legislation. FA 1996 s 91C sets out the first of the conditions referred to in FA 1996 s 91B. That condition is that the fair value of the shares is likely to increase at a rate representing a return on an investment at a commercial rate of interest and is unlikely to deviate substantially from that rate of increase. It is also a condition that neither the whole nor substantially the whole of the assets (measured by their fair value) of the issuing company be income-producing. Assets that are income-producing are defined in FA 1996 s 91C(3). The second condition referred to in FA 1996 s 91B is given by FA 1996 s 91D. This condition is that the share is redeemable, is designed to produce a return that equates in substance to the return on an investment of money at a commercial rate of interest and is not an 'excepted' share. Excepted shares are (a) shares publicly issued to independent persons and such that less than 10 per cent of that issue are held by the investing company or connected persons; (b) shares 'mirroring' a public issue or (c) shares held by the investing company for a purpose that is not an 'unallowable' purpose. The circumstances in which shares mirror a public issue are set out in FA 1996 s 91D(7)–(8). An 'unallowable' purpose is (broadly) a tax-avoidance purpose. The third condition referred to in FA 1996 s 91B is contained in FA 1996 s 91E. That condition is that there exists a scheme or arrangement under which the share and one or more associated transactions are together designed to produce a return that equates in substance to the return on an investment of money at a commercial rate of interest. Shares that would satisfy one of the other conditions or would do so but for the income-producing assets exclusion in FA 1996 s 91C or the excepted shares exclusion in FA 1996 s 91D are excluded. The Treasury is given the power to add, vary or remove conditions (FA 1996 s 91F). Rules are provided for treatment of shares that begin or cease to be subject to either FA 1996 s 91A or 91B (ie begin or cease to be treated as if they were creditor loan relationships) without an associated change of ownership, and there are transitional provisions for shares coming within the rules on the day of commencement – 16 March 2005 (FA 1996 s 91G).

The restriction contained in FA 1996 s 97 which limits the debits and credits to be taken into account in a loan relationship where a company has a right to receive manufactured interest to those that are related to that interest is repealed, with effect for related transactions after 15 March 2005 (Sch 7 para 11).

FA 1996 s 100 brings within the loan-relationships rules amounts of interest and exchange gains and losses on debts (eg money debts) that are not themselves loan relationships. Profits from disposals of interest and all discounts are now added to the types of profit included in FA 1996 s 100 as are profits from any related transactions (within the meaning of FA 1996 s 84) in respect of the right to receive interest. Particular instances are given of when a discount arises (Sch 7 para 12).

What is a commercial rate of interest for these provisions is defined (Sch 7 para 13).

Capital redemption policies are no longer to be excluded from the loan-relationships legislation, as they have been under FA 1996 Sch 9 para 1A(1)(b) (Sch 7 para 14). This is to prevent the manufacture of an artificial allowable loss from the holding of capital redemption bonds by companies. See also under Sch 7 para 20 below.

FA 1996 Sch 9 para 10A deems a company ceasing to be resident in the UK to have disposed of and immediately reacquired for their fair value all its assets and liabilities representing loan relationships. Following the enactment of FA 1996 Sch 9 para 12A (see Sch 7 para 18 below), a double charge could arise under both provisions on the same event. The charge under para 12A is to have priority (Sch 7 para 15).

FA 1996 Sch 9 para 11 provides that where any disposal or acquisition in whole or in part of rights or liabilities under a loan relationship ('a related transaction') is not at arm's length, the debits and credits that are to be brought into account are nevertheless those appropriate to an arm's length transaction (ie their fair values). However, transactions between groups of companies have hitherto been excluded from the operation of this paragraph. This general exclusion is removed in favour of one that excludes the rule in Sch 9 para 11 only where Sch 9 para 12 applies (for the effect of that paragraph as now amended, see under Sch 7 para 17 below) or would apply but for the fact that the transferor uses fair-value accounting already (Sch 7 para 16).

FA 1996 Sch 9 para 12 broadly provides that where as the result of a related transaction, one company ('the transferee company') directly or indirectly replaces another company ('the transferor company') in the same group as a party to a loan relationship, the transferee company is to 'stand in the shoes' of the transferor company for all the purposes of the loan-relationships legislation. The paragraph is now amended to provide instead that the transferor is treated as having entered into the transaction for a consideration equal to the 'notional carrying value' of the loan relationship. For the transferee, the transferor's carrying value is deemed to be the acquisition cost. The 'notional carrying value' is the amount that would have been shown in the transferor's balance sheet for the relationship if financial statements had been drawn up at the date of the transfer. The result is that the transaction is effectively treated to be one that takes place at 'no gain no loss' (Sch 7 para 17).

A degrouping charge, contained in new FA 1996 Sch 9 para 12A, is introduced. It provides that where there has been an intra-group transaction to which FA 1996 Sch 9 para 12 has applied and within six years, the transferee company ceases to be a member of the same group, the transferee company is deemed to have assigned the loan relationship for its fair value immediately before the transfer and to have reacquired it for that same amount immediately after the transfer. However, either one of two conditions must be satisfied as a result of applying the rule for it to be applied at all. The first condition is that as a result of applying the rule, the transferee company would have to bring a credit into account. The second condition is that, where the first condition does not apply, the result of the rule is that the transferee company would have to bring a debit into account in respect of that loan relationship but a credit in respect of a hedging derivative contract (Sch 7 para 18). The provisions of this paragraph should be read in conjunction with those of Sch 7 para 22 below.

FA 1996 Sch 9 para 15 provides that where a loan relationship is acquired under a repo or stock-lending transaction, disposals or acquisitions of loan relationships under such transactions are not 'related transactions' and therefore do not give rise to a charge under FA 1996 Sch 9, except for credits in respect of interest. This provision is amended so that only the first transfer and the last transfer back are not to be treated as related transactions. Furthermore, the charge to tax on intermediate transactions is to include all credits arising, not only interest. The amendments apply to loan relationships acquired after 1 December 2004 (Sch 7 para 19).

Consequent on the changes made by Sch 7 para 14, FA 1996 Sch 9 para 11 is amended to ensure that when the 'I minus E' basis of computing the profits of a life assurance business is applied, no debits or credits are to be brought into account in respect of a debtor relationship that is a capital redemption policy. This amendment applies after 9 February 2005 (Sch 7 para 20).

Schedule 7 paras 21 and 25 extend the relevant-discounted securities regime of FA 1996 Sch 13 to all strips of bonds other than gilts, which are already subject to special rules. The aim is to bring into the charge to income tax strips of corporate bonds that are not discounted securities when issued and hence have not fallen within FA 1996 Sch 13 or its successor for income tax purposes, ITTOIA 2005 Part 4 Chapter 8. FA 1996 Sch 13 ceased to have effect for income tax purposes after 5 April 2005. However, amendments are needed to both sets of provisions to ensure that the targeted transactions are brought into the charge to tax. New paragraphs 13A–13D are inserted into FA 1996 Sch 13. Paragraph 13A defines a 'corporate strip' and what constitutes the conversion of an interest-bearing corporate security into a corporate strip of that security. Paragraph 13B provides that every corporate strip is a relevant discounted security and that where a person converts an interest-bearing corporate security into corporate strips, he is deemed to have paid in respect of each strip an amount that bears the same proportion to the acquisition cost of the corporate security as the market value of the corporate strip bears to the aggregate value of all the separate assets resulting from the conversion. Paragraph 13C applies where there is a tax-avoidance scheme in respect of corporate strips and provides that in such a case market value is to be substituted in any case where the acquisition cost of the corporate strip is more than its market value or the redemption or disposal proceeds are less than market value. Paragraph 13D provides that where as part of any tax-avoidance scheme (including a scheme aimed at producing a capital loss), a capital loss accrues to any person that loss is to be disregarded for the purposes of capital gains tax (Sch 7 para 21).

Parallel amendments to those made by Sch 7 para 17 above to FA 1996 Sch 9 para 12 are made to the derivative-contracts legislation, by amendment to FA 2002 Sch 26 para 28. They effectively provide for no-gain no-loss treatment where a derivative contract is transferred intra-group (Sch 7 para 22). A minor consequential amendment is made to FA 2004 Sch 26 para 30 (Sch 7 para 23).

Provisions parallel to those of Sch 7 para 18, which introduced FA 1996 Sch 9 para 12A (providing for a degrouping charge when a company leaves a group within six years of being the recipient of an intra-group transfer of a loan relationship), are introduced into the derivative-contracts legislation, by means of the insertion of FA 2002 Sch 26 para 30A (Sch 7 para 24).

Parallel amendments to those made by Sch 7 para 21, which extend the relevant-discounted securities regime to all corporate strips under FA 1996 Sch 13, are made to the successor provisions of ITTOIA 2005 Part 4 Chapter 8 to extend the deeply discounted securities regime contained there to provide for a charge to income tax where appropriate in respect of all corporate strips. New ITTOIA 2005 s 452A provides that all corporate strips are to be treated as deeply discounted securities. New ITTOIA 2005 s 452B defines what is meant by an 'interest-bearing corporate security'. New ITTOIA 2005 s 452C defines what constitutes the conversion of an interest-bearing corporate security into a corporate strip. New ITTOIA 2005 s 452D extends the new regime to strips of the separate assets obtained as the result of an earlier strip ('lower-level conversions'). New ITTOIA 2005 s 452E defines what is meant by a corporate strip. New ITTOIA 2005 s 452F provides that a person who converts an interest-bearing corporate security into corporate strips is deemed to have acquired each strip for an amount that bears the same proportion to the acquisition cost of the converted corporate security as the market value of the corporate strip bears to the aggregate market values of all the separate assets resulting from the conversion. Finally, new ITTOIA 2005 s 452G applies where there is a tax-avoidance scheme in respect of corporate strips and provides that in such a case market value is to be substituted in any case where the acquisition cost of the corporate strip is more than its market value, the amount payable on a transfer of the corporate strip is less than its market value or where the amount payable on redemption of the corporate strip is less than market value (Sch 7 para 25).

Financing of companies etc Section 40 introduces Sch 8, which contains amendments to the transfer-pricing legislation in TA 1988 Sch 28AA and the loan-relationships legislation of FA 1996 Sch 9. The intention is to extend the transfer-pricing rules to parties who do not currently come within the ambit of those rules but who have acted together in relation to financing a business and who collectively could exercise control over that business. A new TA 1988 Sch 28AA para 4A provides that a person (P) is to be treated as indirectly participating in the management, control or capital of another person (A) in relation to financing arrangements between them if A is a company or partnership, P has acted together with other persons in relation to those financing arrangements and P could have control of A if the rights and powers of each of those other persons were to be attributed to P. The result is that transactions between P and A in respect of those financial arrangements must be stated at market value. The definition is extended similarly to the situation where the same person or persons is deemed to be indirectly participating in the management, control or capital of each of the persons between whom the rules are to apply. A new TA 1988 Sch 28AA para 4B extends the application of the transfer-pricing rules to financing arrangements made up to six months before a relationship exists between the parties concerned (Sch 8 para 1).

Changes are also made to the loan-relationships rules of FA 1996 Sch 9. FA 1996 Sch 9 para 2 defers the deduction for interest paid under a loan relationship between connected persons where the creditor is outside the charge to corporation tax and the interest is not paid within 12 months of the accounting period in which it accrues to the time that the interest is actually paid. However, where the debtor is a collective investment scheme, an exception is made to this rule in certain circumstances. The paragraph is amended so as to include a person who controls a company participator, an associate of such a person and a company controlled by such a person to those creditors who are regarded as connected to the debtor company. Further amendments limit the exclusion to cases where the debtor is a small or medium-sized enterprise and the creditor is not resident in a tax haven or other non-qualifying territory for the purposes of TA 1988 Sch 28AA para 5E (Sch 8 para 2). Similar amendments are made to FA 1996 Sch 9 para 18, which defers the debits to be brought into account in respect of a discounted security issued by a close company to a connected person in defined circumstances to the period in which the security is redeemed. There are parallel exclusions where the creditor is a collective investment scheme (Sch 8 para 3). The amendments generally have effect for accounting periods beginning after 3 March 2005 (Sch 8 para 4).

Intangible fixed assets A number of amendments are made to the intangible fixed assets regime for companies contained in FA 2002 Sch 29. FA 2002 Sch 29 para 92 provides that transfers of intangible assets between a company and a related party are to be treated as made at market value, subject to two exceptions. Two further exceptions are now added. The first new exception applies where (a) an intangible fixed asset is transferred from a company to a related party at less than market value or from a related party to a company for more than market value; (b) the related party is not a company or where it is a company, the asset is not an intangible asset to which Sch 29 applies and (c) the transfer gives rise or would give rise to a charge to tax on account of a distribution under TA 1988 s 209 or earnings or benefits under ITEPA 2003 Part 3. The second new exception applies where a related party transfers an asset to a company, that asset falls within Sch 29 in the company's hands and holdover relief for gifts of business assets is claimed under TCGA 1992 s 165 in respect of the transfer. The definition of 'related party' in FA 2002 Sch 29 para 95 is extended. Payment entitlements under the EU single payment scheme for farmers are added to the classes of intangible fixed asset for which rollover relief is not available under FA 2002 Sch 29 para 132 (s 41).

Insurance companies etc Section 42 introduces Sch 9, which makes detailed amendments to the provisions dealing with the taxation of insurance companies. Like most of the provisions of this Act, the amendments are largely of an anti-avoidance nature.

Only the major themes of the amendments will be discussed below. Changes consequent on the adoption by the Financial Services Authority of the so-called Integrated Prudential Sourcebook for insurers are made to TA 1988 s 76 (expenses of insurance companies), TA 1988 s 431 (interpretation of the insurance companies legislation), TA 1988 s 432A (apportionment of income and gains), TA 1988 s 444BA (equalisation reserves for general business), FA 1989 s 82B (unappropriated surplus on valuation), TA 1988 s 431A (Treasury's power to amend provisions) and FA 2003 s 156 (overseas life insurance companies) (Sch 9 paras 1–4, 9, 10, 17). Further anti-avoidance provisions are introduced in relation to the transfer of insurance business to close off three particular schemes designed to exclude profits from tax. The amendments concerned are those to TA 1988 s 444AA (deemed periodical returns on transfers of business), TA 1988 s 444AC (transfers with excess liabilities), FA 1989 s 82C (relevant financial reinsurance contracts) and TA 1988 s 432E (apportionments of participating funds under TA 1988 s 432B). A new TA 1988 s 444ACA is inserted, to cover cases where shares in the transferor company form part of the transferee company's long-term insurance fund and the transactions in securities provisions of TA 1988 ss 703–709 do not apply (Sch 9 paras 5–8, 11). A change is made to the definition of 'notional income' in FA 1989 s 83 (profits to be taken into account when computing the profits of a life insurance business under Schedule D Case I) (Sch 9 para 20).

International matters To allow for full implementation into UK law of the amendments made to the EC Parent Subsidiary Directive (90/435/EEC) by Directive 2005/19/EC, TA 1988 s 801, which gives tax relief for UK and underlying third-country taxes in respect of a dividend paid by a foreign company to a UK-resident company or the UK permanent establishment of a foreign company, is amended so as to substitute a share-capital test for a voting-power test in determining whether the requisite minimum 10 per cent holding subsists for the underlying tax relief to be given. The amendment has effect from 1 January 2005, the final date for implementation of the amended Directive. UK law already complies without further amendment to the Parent Subsidiary Directive as amended (s 43).

The UK's controlled foreign company (CFC) rules apply in respect only of controlled companies subject to a 'lower level of taxation' in their jurisdiction of residence. A 'lower level of taxation' exists, as provided in TA 1988 s 750, where the tax paid by the controlled company on its profits is less than 75 per cent of what the UK corporation tax payable by the company would be if it were resident in the UK and the assumptions set out in TA 1988 Sch 24 held good. In order to counter schemes that exploit these tests as they currently stand, TA 1988 s 750 is amended to provide that where there is income or expenditure of the controlled company that is taken into account in determining the tax paid locally but would not be taken into account in determining what its chargeable profits would be in the UK, the local tax taken into account in applying the 75 per cent test is reduced to what it would be in the absence of that income or expenditure. A further amendment reduces the local tax paid that is taken into account for the 75 per cent test where a connected repayment of local tax is made to some other person. The amendments have effect for accounting periods beginning or deemed to begin after 1 December 2004 (s 44).

Miscellaneous The basic provisions for assessing and collecting tax from individual members of Lloyd's are contained in FA 1993 s 173 and Sch 19. These provisions are extended to corporate members of Lloyd's by FA 1994 s 221. Provision is made for repealing these provisions and making consequential amendments to other provisions from a date to be appointed, when they are to be replaced by regulations (s 45).

Following changes made by the Energy Act 2004 and the Health Protection Agency Act 2004, certain exemptions and other provisions relating to the United Kingdom Atomic Energy Authority (UKAEA), the National Radiological Protection Board and pension schemes operated by the UKAEA have become redundant. They are repealed generally with effect from 1 April 2005 (s 46).

PART 3
STAMP TAXES

Stamp duty land tax Provisions relating to registration of land transactions in the stamp duty land tax (SDLT) legislation in FA 2003 and related Scottish legislation are amended so as to allow for the introduction of conveyancing and registration by electronic means (s 47).

A new FA 2003 s 78A is introduced to allow information contained in land transaction returns (the basic SDLT returns) to be passed to the Valuations Office Agency and the equivalent Northern Ireland agency. This is information that was formerly contained in Particulars Delivered forms under the stamp duty regime. With the replacement of stamp duty by SDLT on 1 December 2003, the statutory permission for disclosure of this information lapsed and the equivalent permission now provided for was not enacted in its place. The new section comes into effect on a day to be appointed (s 48).

Section 49 introduces Sch 10, which makes miscellaneous amendments to the SDLT legislation. These are of a mixed nature; some merely regulate the interaction of various reliefs while others are also anti-avoidance measures.

FA 2003 s 45 (subsales, assignments and other transfers of rights) is amended to ensure that the exemption available in certain circumstances to intermediate purchasers is withdrawn where the transaction with the ultimate purchaser benefits from relief under FA 2003 s 73 (which applies where land is sold to a financial institution and then resold to an individual) (Sch 10 para 2). Changes are made to the group relief provisions of FA 2003 Sch 7. Where group relief is withdrawn under FA 2003 Sch 7 para 3 from a previously eligible transaction that took the form of the grant of a lease, rent passing under the lease is to be taken into account in determining the chargeable consideration. There is currently no withdrawal under FA 2003 Sch 7 para 3 where the vendor leaves the group; the definition of leaving the group is amended. Group relief is now to be withdrawn in certain circumstances when a transferee company has claimed group relief and there is a change of control of the transferee within three years of the transfer (Sch 10 paras 3–7). Acquisition relief under FA 2003 Sch 7 para 8 is to be restricted to cases where the undertaking or part-undertaking acquired has a trade as its main activity and that trade does not consist wholly or mainly of dealing in land (Sch 10 paras 8, 9). A land transaction is to be deemed to have taken place in certain circumstances where there is a transfer of land into a partnership and within three years of that transfer, there is a withdrawal of money from the partnership or a loan made to the partnership by the person who made the transfer or a person connected to that person is repaid (Sch 10 para 10). The provision attributing the acts and interests of a bare trustee to the beneficiary (FA 2003 Sch 16 para 3) is to be disapplied where the transaction is the grant of a lease by or to a bare trustee. A consequential amendment is made to FA 2003 Sch 17A para 11 (assignment of lease to be treated as grant (Sch 10 paras 11, 12). The charge to tax under FA 2003 Sch 17A para 15A on the reduction of rent payable under a lease or a reduction of the lease term is extended (Sch 10 para 13). A new FA 2003 Sch 17A para 18A is inserted to treat the amount of a loan or deposit made on the grant or assignment of a lease and contingently repayable on an act or omission by the lessee or assignee as chargeable consideration in the prescribed circumstances (Sch 10 para 14). A consequential amendment is made to FA 2003 s 80, which provides for repayments of tax in circumstances where the occurrence or non-occurrence of a contingency reduces the tax already paid (Sch 10 para 15). Commencement provisions are made for Sch 10 Part 1, which is to have effect for transactions the effective date of which is after 19 May 2005 (Sch 10 para 16).

Changes are made to the definition of 'company' in FA 2003 s 66 (public bodies) (Sch 10 para 18). Group relief is not to be available in respect of a transaction forming part of a tax-avoidance scheme (Sch 10 para 19). Similarly, acquisition relief is not to be available in respect of a transaction forming part of a tax-avoidance scheme (Sch 10 para 20). There is to be no charge to stamp duty under FA 2003 Sch 15 para 33 on the transfer of a partnership interest unless the 'relevant partnership property' (as defined) includes stock or marketable securities (Sch 10 para 21). The amendments made by Sch 10 Part 2 (paras 17–22) are to have effect from Royal Assent, subject to transitional provisions (Sch 10 para 22 (s 49 and Sch 10).

Stamp duty and stamp duty reserve tax Power is given to the Treasury to make regulations to extend the exemptions from stamp duty and stamp duty reserve tax under FA 1986 ss 80A, 80C, 88A and 89AA for intermediaries and stock lending to members of a specified multilateral trading facility as defined in the EC Markets in Financial Instruments Directive (2004/39/EC) which is not a recognised exchange under the provisions mentioned (s 50).

PART 4
EUROPEAN COMPANY STATUTE

Sections 51 to 65 amend legislation relating to various taxes to accommodate the creation of the European Company (*Societas Europaea* – SE) as provided in Council Regulation (EC) No. 2157/2001 of 8 October 2001. They relate to circumstances in which an SE is formed by the cross-border merger of two or more companies resident in more than one Member State.

Three new sections are inserted into TCGA 1992. The overarching condition for any of the new sections to apply is that an SE is formed by the merger of two or more companies resident between them in at least two Member States (a 'cross-border merger'). They do not apply, therefore, when all the merging companies are resident in the same Member State. Section 140E provides that certain transferred assets acquired by an SE and left within the charge to UK tax are to be treated as transferred at no gain and no loss. The SE must be resident in the UK at its formation or have a permanent establishment in the UK through which it carries on a trade and the asset must be a chargeable asset of that permanent establishment immediately after the transfer. The transferor must be resident in the UK at the time of the transfer (or be a non-resident trading through a UK permanent establishment immediately before the transfer and the asset must be a chargeable asset of that permanent establishment). The section is analogous to TCGA 1992 s 140A, which provides similar relief where a UK trade is transferred between two companies resident in different Member States.

Section 140F applies where an SE is formed by a merger during which a UK-resident company transfers a business it has carried on in another Member State through a permanent establishment to a company resident in another Member State. It is a further condition that the aggregate chargeable gains accruing to the UK transferor company as a result of the transfer exceed its aggregate losses from the transfer. Where the section applies, the transfer is to be treated as giving rise to a single chargeable gain of the net amount. This section is analogous to TCGA 1992 s 140C, which provides similar relief to the transfer of a non-UK trade by a UK-resident company to a company resident in another Member State. New TCGA 1992 s 140G provides that a merger involving the formation of an SE which would not otherwise be treated as a scheme of reconstruction within TCGA 1992 s 136 is to be so treated. This has the result that where securities in an SE are issued in proportion to the holdings of the existing shareholders of the merging companies, the holdings in the SE are to be equated for the purposes of capital gains tax to the original holdings. It is a further condition of all three sections that they apply only where the formation of the SE is carried out for bona fide commercial reasons and not as part of a tax-avoidance scheme. All have effect for formations of an SE taking place after 31 March 2005 (s 51).

Where, as part of a cross-border merger forming an SE, intangible fixed assets falling within the corporate intangibles regime of FA 2002 Sch 29 are transferred, then, provided that FA 2002 Sch 29 para 84 (company reconstruction involving transfer of business) does not apply, the transfer of the intangible fixed assets is to be tax-neutral. This relief applies only if the formation of the SE is carried out for bona fide commercial reasons and not as part of a tax-avoidance scheme. Pre-transaction clearances may be obtained (s 52, inserting FA 2002 Sch 29 para 85A).

Where a non-UK trade is transferred by a UK-resident company to a company resident in another Member State as part of a cross-border merger involving the formation of an SE, and the assets transferred include intangible fixed assets of the transferor immediately before the transfer, any tax that would have been chargeable in the Member State in which the trade is situated in respect of the transfer of those intangible fixed assets but for the operation of the EC Mergers Directive (90/43/EEC) is to be treated for the purposes of UK double tax relief as if it had been charged. Again, this relief is not available where the formation of the SE is not effected for bona fide commercial reasons or takes place as part of a tax-avoidance scheme (s 53, introducing FA 2002 Sch 29 para 87A).

Where an SE is formed as part of a cross-border merger and either the SE is resident in the UK and within the charge to UK corporation tax immediately after its formation or it is at that time within the charge to UK corporation tax because it is carrying on a trade in the UK through a UK permanent establishment, any transfer of loan relationships involved in the merger is to be disregarded for the purposes of a charge to tax under the loan-relationships legislation of FA 1996 Sch 9, subject to two exceptions, and the transferor and transferee companies in relation to the loan relationship are to be treated as one and the same company. Again, the formation of the SE must be carried out for bona fide commercial reasons and not as part of a tax-avoidance scheme (s 54, introducing FA 1996 Sch 9 para 12B). An analogous provision is made for the derivative-contracts legislation of FA 2002 Sch 26. Where an SE is formed as part of a cross-border merger and either the SE is resident in the UK and within the charge to UK corporation tax immediately after its formation or it is at that time within the charge to UK corporation tax because it is carrying on a trade in the UK through a UK permanent establishment, any transfer of rights and liabilities under a derivative contract involved in the merger is to be disregarded for the purposes of a charge to tax under the derivative-contracts legislation, subject to two exceptions, and the transferor and transferee companies in relation to the derivative contract are to be treated as one and the same company. Again, the formation of the SE must be carried out for bona fide commercial reasons and not as part of a tax-avoidance scheme (s 55, introducing FA 2002 Sch 26 para 30B).

Where a qualifying asset is transferred as part of a cross-border merger in the course of forming an SE, and that merger is one to which new TCGA 1992 s 140E applies (for which see under s 51 above), the transfer is not to give rise to any allowances or charges under the Capital Allowances Act 2001. Assets are qualifying if they qualify for the capital gains relief in TCGA 1992 s 140E (s 56, introducing CAA 2001 s 561A).

Securities issued or raised by an SE with its registered office in the UK are to be chargeable securities for the purposes of stamp duty reserve tax, regardless of whether the SE was originally incorporated in the UK or indeed whether it had a registered office in the UK at the time when the securities were issued or raised. However, securities issued or raised by an SE are not chargeable securities if at the relevant time the SE does not have its registered office in the UK and they are stocks, shares, loan capital, interests in or in dividends or other rights arising out of stocks, shares or loan capital or rights to allotments of or to subscribe for or options to acquire stocks, shares or loan capital (s 57).

An SE that has transferred its registered office outside the UK is not to constitute a 'body corporate incorporated in the UK' for the purposes of stamp duty and stamp duty reserve tax on bearer securities under FA 1986 s 90(3C)(a) or (3E)(a). This means that a UK bearer instrument issued by such an SE is not a chargeable security for stamp duty reserve tax even if it satisfies the other conditions of those subsections (s 58). Amendments consequential to ss 51 to 58 are made (s 59).

An SE that transfers its registered office to the UK is to be regarded from the time of its registration as a UK-resident company for the purposes of the Taxes Acts, regardless of the contrary effect of any other rule of law, and continues to be so resident even after any subsequent transfer of its registered office abroad. However, where an SE is dually resident but regarded for the purposes of a double tax treaty as resident in the other jurisdiction, then it is also to be regarded as non-resident in the UK for all purposes of the Taxes Acts (s 60, introducing FA 1998 s 66A and amending FA 1994 s 249(3)).

Where a UK company ceases to be UK-resident in the course of a merger forming an SE outside the UK or, having been transformed into an SE, transfers its registered office to another Member State, any liabilities to tax or matters arising before that time will continue to be assessable to UK corporation tax or subject to the self-assessment machinery of FA 1998 Sch 18. The same continuity rule applies where an SE that has its registered office in the UK transfers its registered office abroad and ceases to be UK-resident. This provision is subject to the rule in FA 1998 s 66A, described under s 60 above, regarding SEs that have previously transferred their registered office to the UK (s 61).

Where a principal company of a UK capital gains group either becomes an SE by being the acquiring company in the formation of an SE through a merger by acquisition, or becomes a subsidiary of a holding SE or becomes an SE by transformation, that group and any other group of which the SE is a member on its formation are to be regarded as one and the same group for the group provisions of TCGA 1992 ss 171–181 (s 62). Exactly the same provisions are to apply for the purposes of the intangible fixed assets regime of FA 2002 Sch 29 (s 63, introducing FA 2002 Sch 29 para 51A).

TCGA 1992 s 140(4) brings into charge the gain deferred under that section on the transfer of a non-UK trade by a UK company to a company resident in another Member State if and when the UK company disposes of all or part of any of the securities it received as consideration for the transfer. Where, as part of a cross-border merger forming an SE to which new TCGA 1992 s 140E applies (see under s 51 above), securities are transferred to the SE by a transferor company, the transfer is to be disregarded for the purposes of TCGA 1992 s 140(4), so that the transfer does not produce a charge on the deferred gain. Similarly, where a gain is rolled over under TCGA 1992 s 154 on the replacement of a business asset by a depreciating asset, then the transfer of the depreciating asset or of shares in a company holding the depreciating asset to an SE as part of a merger forming that SE and to which TCGA 1992 s 140E (see under s 51 above) applies is not to be an event triggering a charge to tax under TCGA 1992 s 154(2) on the gain held over. Where as part of a merger forming an SE and to which TCGA 1992 s 140E applies, a company that is a member of a group ceases to exist and as a consequence, assets or shares in one or more companies that were also members of the group are transferred to the SE, that company is not to be treated as having left the group so as to give rise to a crystallised gain under TCGA 1992 s 179 following an asset transfer at no gain and no loss in the preceding six years (s 64). The restrictions contained in TCGA 1992 Sch 7A on the set-off of losses incurred before a company becomes a member of a group ('pre-entry losses') are extended to cover losses accruing before entry on an asset held before entry where the asset in question was transferred to an SE as part of its formation in a merger by acquisition (s 65). Sections 51 to 65 generally apply in respect of events occurring after 31 March 2005 (ss 51–65, passim).

PART 5
MISCELLANEOUS MATTERS

Vehicle excise duty The circumstances under which the liability to pay late renewal supplement under the Vehicle Excise and Registration Act 1994 are extended (s 66).

Reorganisation of water and sewerage services in Northern Ireland The Treasury may make regulations to deal with the tax consequences of the establishment of a new company to operate water services in Northern Ireland (s 67).

Notifications under the EC Mutual Assistance Directive HMRC is empowered to serve documents on behalf of the tax authorities of another Member State to a UK-resident taxpayer in relation to a tax liability of that taxpayer in that other Member State. This is a requirement of the Mutual Assistance Directive (77/799/EEC) as amended, particularly by Directive 2004/56/EC, and applies to requests for assistance received after 31 December 2004 (s 68).

Abolition of statutory adjudicator for National Savings and Investments The post of statutory adjudicator under the Friendly Societies Act 1992 in disputes with the department of National Savings and Investments is abolished from 1 September 2005. In future, disputes will be arbitrated by the Financial Ombudsman Service (s 69).

PART 6
SUPPLEMENTARY PROVISIONS

Repeals are provided for by Sch 11 (s 70). The interpretation and short-title provisions (ss 71 and 72) take their usual form.

FINANCE (NO 2) ACT 2005

(2005 Chapter 22)

ARRANGEMENT OF SECTIONS

PART 1

VALUE ADDED TAX

PART 2

INCOME TAX, CORPORATION TAX AND CAPITAL GAINS TAX

CHAPTER 1

PERSONAL TAXATION

Social security pension lump sums

Gift aid

Employee securities

CHAPTER 2

SCIENTIFIC RESEARCH ORGANISATIONS

CHAPTER 3

AUTHORISED INVESTMENT FUNDS ETC

CHAPTER 4

AVOIDANCE INVOLVING TAX ARBITRAGE

CHAPTER 5

CHARGEABLE GAINS

Residence, location of assets etc

Miscellaneous

CHAPTER 6

MISCELLANEOUS

Accounting practice and related matters

Financial avoidance etc

Financing of companies etc

Intangible fixed assets

Insurance companies etc

International matters

Miscellaneous

PART 3

STAMP TAXES

Stamp duty land tax

Stamp duty and stamp duty reserve tax

PART 4

EUROPEAN COMPANY STATUTE

An Act to Grant certain duties, to alter other duties, and to amend the law relating to the National Debt and the Public Revenue, and to make further provision in connection with finance.

[20 July 2005]

PART 1

VALUE ADDED TAX

1 Goods subject to warehousing regime: place of acquisition or supply

In section 18 of VATA 1994 (goods subject to warehousing regime: place and time of acquisition or supply), after subsection (1) insert—

"(1A) The Commissioners may by regulations prescribe circumstances in which subsection (1) above shall not apply."

GENERAL NOTE

VATA 1994 s 18(1) provides relief for goods imported from a third country direct to the UK or via another EU member state. In broad terms, the acquisition (in the latter case) or an onward supply of the goods (in either case) is not charged to VAT in the UK if the goods are warehoused at the material time. The goods are merely charged to import VAT at the time when a customs debt is incurred (if the goods are chargeable to customs duty) or the time when such a debt would have been incurred (if no customs duty is chargeable) (see VATA 1994 s 15). The value of the goods is determined in accordance with customs rules (see VATA 1994 s 21).

This relief has been exploited for avoidance purposes. The scheme has been described in the following terms. X purchases goods for £10,000 in the US, imports them into the UK, lodges them in a customs warehouse, resells them to Y and Z (who are not taxable persons) for £30,000 and removes them from the warehouse on behalf of Y and Z. X is aware of the price paid for the goods. He can therefore declare a value of £10,000. Y and Z therefore incur VAT based on a value of £10,000 (the price paid by X) rather than £30,000 (the price at which they purchased the goods). The loss to the Exchequer is VAT based on a value of £20,000 (see *Explanatory Notes to Finance Bill 2005* (HM Treasury, May 2005)).

This section inserts a new VATA 1994 s 18(1A). The Commissioners may make regulations disapplying the relief in prescribed circumstances.

2 Cars: determination of consideration for fuel supplied for private use

(1) Section 57 of VATA 1994 (determination of consideration for fuel supplied for private use) is amended as follows.

(2) After subsection (4) (power of Treasury by order to substitute a different Table for Table A) insert—

"(4A) The power conferred by subsection (4) above includes power to substitute for Table A a Table (whether or not of the same or a similar configuration) where any description of vehicle may be by reference to any one or more of the following—

(a) the CO_2 emissions figure for the vehicle;
(b) the type or types of fuel or power by which the vehicle is, or is capable of being, propelled;
(c) the cylinder capacity of the engine in cubic centimetres.

(4B) The provision that may be included in any such Table includes provision for the purpose of enabling the consideration to be determined by reference to the Table—

(a) by applying a percentage specified in the Table to a monetary amount specified in the Table, or
(b) by any other method.

(4C) Table A, as from time to time substituted by virtue of subsection (4A) above, may be implemented or supplemented by either or both of the following—

(a) provision in Rules inserted before the Table, prescribing how the consideration is to be determined by reference to the Table;
(b) provision in Notes inserted after the Table in accordance with the following provisions of this section.

(4D) The provision that may be made in Notes includes provision—

(a) with respect to the interpretation or application of the Table or any Rules or Notes;
(b) with respect to the figure that is to be regarded as the CO_2 emissions figure for any vehicle or any particular description of vehicle;
(c) for treating a vehicle as a vehicle with a particular CO_2 emissions figure;
(d) for treating a vehicle with a CO_2 emissions figure as a vehicle with a different CO_2 emissions figure;
(e) for or in connection with determining the consideration appropriate to vehicles of any particular description (in particular, vehicles falling within any one or more of the descriptions in subsection (4E) below).

(4E) The descriptions are—

(a) vehicles capable of being propelled by any particular type or types of fuel or power;
(b) vehicles first registered before 1st January 1998;
(c) vehicles first registered on or after that date which satisfy the condition in subsection (4F) below (registration without a CO_2 emissions figure).

(4F) The condition is that the vehicle is not one which, when it is first registered, is so registered on the basis of—

(*a*) an EC certificate of conformity that specifies a CO_2 emissions figure, or

(*b*) a UK approval certificate that specifies such a figure.

(4G) Any Rules or Notes do not form part of the Table, but the Treasury, by order taking effect from the beginning of any prescribed accounting period beginning after the order is made, may—

(*a*) insert Rules or Notes,

(*b*) vary or remove Rules or Notes, or

(*c*) substitute any or all Rules or Notes.".

(3) In subsection (5) (fuel supplied for 2 or more vehicles)—

(*a*) in paragraph (*a*), for "Table A above, that Table" substitute "Table A above or any Notes, that Table and those Notes";

(*b*) in paragraph (*b*), after "that Table", in both places, insert "or those Notes".

(4) In subsection (7) (cubic capacity of internal combustion engine with reciprocating pistons) after "for the purposes of Table A above" insert "and any Notes".

(5) In subsection (8) (cubic capacity in other cases) after "for the purposes of Table A above" insert "and any Notes".

(6) After subsection (8) insert—

"(9) In this section—

"CO_2 emissions figure" means a CO_2 emissions figure expressed in grams per kilometre driven;

"EC certificate of conformity" means a certificate of conformity issued by a manufacturer under any provision of the law of a Member State implementing Article 6 of Council Directive 70/156/EEC, as from time to time amended;

"Notes" means Notes inserted by virtue of subsection (4C)(*b*) above;

"Rules" means Rules inserted by virtue of subsection (4C)(*a*) above;

"UK approval certificate" means a certificate issued under—

(*a*) section 58(1) or (4) of the Road Traffic Act 1988, or

(*b*) Article 31A(4) or (5) of the Road Traffic (Northern Ireland) Order 1981.

(10) If the Treasury consider it necessary or expedient to do so in consequence of—

(*a*) the form or content of any Table substituted or to be substituted by virtue of subsection (4A) above, or

(*b*) any provision included or to be included in Rules or Notes,

they may by order amend, repeal or replace so much of this section as for the time being follows subsection (1) and precedes Table A and relates to the use of that Table.".

(7) The amendments made by this section come into force on such day or days as the Treasury may appoint by order made by statutory instrument; and different days may be so appointed for different purposes.

GENERAL NOTE

The fuel scale charge systems for VAT and direct taxes were originally based on the type of engine and its cylinder capacity in cubic centimetres. However, the direct tax system was changed to a system based on carbon dioxide emissions with effect from April 2003. The Pre-Budget Report announced that, subject to Commission approval and informal consultation with businesses, the VAT fuel scale charge (see VATA 1994 ss 56, 57) will be aligned with the company car benefit (see ITEPA 2003 ss 149–153): see *Opportunity for All: The Strength to Take the Long-term Decisions for Britain* (Cm 6408, December 2004) para 7.44. For the discussion paper referred to, see *Proposed Changes to VAT Fuel Scale Charges System* (HM Customs and Excise, undated). This section amends VATA 1994 s 57 (sub-s (1)) to enable the VAT fuel charge system to be changed by statutory instrument if a final decision to that effect is made.

The consideration for fuel supplied for private use is currently determined in accordance with Table A in VATA 1994 s 57(3), as substituted by VAT (Fuel Provided for Private Use) Order 2005, SI 2005/722. Sub-section (2) inserts new VATA 1994 s 57(4A)–(4G). These provisions enable HM Treasury to substitute a new Table A by order so that the consideration for fuel for private use is determined by reference to any one or more of:

(a) the carbon dioxide emissions figure for the vehicle;

(b) the type(s) of fuel or power used to propel the vehicle; and

(c) the cylinder capacity of the engine in cubic centimetres.

Sub-section (6) insets a new VATA 1994 s 57(9) setting out definitions relevant to the new Table A. It also inserts a new VATA 1994 s 57(10) enabling HM Treasury to amend, appeal or replace VATA 1994 s 57(1A), (2), (3) in so far as they relate to the use of the current Table A. Sub-sections (3)–(5) make corresponding amendments to VATA 1994 s 57(5), (7), (8).

The current VAT fuel charge system derogates from Directive 77/388/EEC arts 5(6), 17(6) (the Sixth Directive). It is authorised by Decision 86/356/EEC (OJ L212/35, 3.8.86). A further Decision is necessary before the foregoing changes can take effect. Sub-section (7) accordingly provides that the amendments made by this section come into force on a day to be appointed by statutory instrument.

3 Credit for, or repayment of, overstated or overpaid VAT

(1) Section 80 of VATA 1994 (recovery of overpaid VAT) is amended as follows.

(2) For subsection (1) (liability of Commissioners to repay overpaid VAT) substitute—

"(1) Where a person—

(*a*) has accounted to the Commissioners for VAT for a prescribed accounting period (whenever ended), and

(*b*) in doing so, has brought into account as output tax an amount that was not output tax due,

the Commissioners shall be liable to credit the person with that amount.

(1A) Where the Commissioners—

(*a*) have assessed a person to VAT for a prescribed accounting period (whenever ended), and

(*b*) in doing so, have brought into account as output tax an amount that was not output tax due,

they shall be liable to credit the person with that amount.

(1B) Where a person has for a prescribed accounting period (whenever ended) paid to the Commissioners an amount by way of VAT that was not VAT due to them, otherwise than as a result of—

(*a*) an amount that was not output tax due being brought into account as output tax, or

(*b*) an amount of input tax allowable under section 26 not being brought into account,

the Commissioners shall be liable to repay to that person the amount so paid.".

(3) In subsection (2) (Commissioners only liable to repay an amount on a claim) before "repay" insert "credit or".

(4) After subsection (2) insert—

"(2A) Where—

(*a*) as a result of a claim under this section by virtue of subsection (1) or (1A) above an amount falls to be credited to a person, and

(*b*) after setting any sums against it under or by virtue of this Act, some or all of that amount remains to his credit,

the Commissioners shall be liable to pay (or repay) to him so much of that amount as so remains.".

(5) In subsection (3) (defence of unjust enrichment) for "under this section, that repayment" substitute "under this section by virtue of subsection (1) or (1A) above, that the crediting".

(6) For subsection (3A) (cost of payment borne for practical purposes by third party) substitute—

"(3A) Subsection (3B) below applies for the purposes of subsection (3) above where—

(*a*) an amount would (apart from subsection (3) above) fall to be credited under subsection (1) or (1A) above to any person ("the taxpayer"), and

(*b*) the whole or a part of the amount brought into account as mentioned in paragraph (*b*) of that subsection has, for practical purposes, been borne by a person other than the taxpayer.".

(7) In subsection (3B) (loss or damage to be disregarded) in paragraph (*a*), for "repayment" substitute "crediting".

(8) For subsection (4) (time limit on claims) substitute—

"(4) The Commissioners shall not be liable on a claim under this section—

(*a*) to credit an amount to a person under subsection (1) or (1A) above, or

(*b*) to repay an amount to a person under subsection (1B) above,

if the claim is made more than 3 years after the relevant date.

(4ZA) The relevant date is—

(*a*) in the case of a claim by virtue of subsection (1) above, the end of the prescribed accounting period mentioned in that subsection, unless paragraph (*b*) below applies;

(*b*) in the case of a claim by virtue of subsection (1) above in respect of an erroneous voluntary disclosure, the end of the prescribed accounting period in which the disclosure was made;

(*c*) in the case of a claim by virtue of subsection (1A) above in respect of an assessment issued on the basis of an erroneous voluntary disclosure, the end of the prescribed accounting period in which the disclosure was made;

(*d*) in the case of a claim by virtue of subsection (1A) above in any other case, the end of the prescribed accounting period in which the assessment was made;

(*e*) in the case of a claim by virtue of subsection (1B) above, the date on which the payment was made.

In the case of a person who has ceased to be registered under this Act, any reference in paragraphs (*b*) to (*d*) above to a prescribed accounting period includes a reference to a period that would have been a prescribed accounting period had the person continued to be registered under this Act.

(4ZB) For the purposes of this section the cases where there is an erroneous voluntary disclosure are those cases where—

(*a*) a person discloses to the Commissioners that he has not brought into account for a prescribed accounting period (whenever ended) an amount of output tax due for the period;

(*b*) the disclosure is made in a later prescribed accounting period (whenever ended); and

(*c*) some or all of the amount is not output tax due.".

(9) For subsections (4A) and (4B) (recovery of excess repayments) substitute—

"(4A) Where—

(*a*) an amount has been credited under subsection (1) or (1A) above to any person at any time on or after 26th May 2005, and

(*b*) the amount so credited exceeded the amount which the Commissioners were liable at that time to credit to that person,

the Commissioners may, to the best of their judgement, assess the excess credited to that person and notify it to him.".

(10) For subsection (7) (no other liability of Commissioners to repay VAT not due) substitute—

"(7) Except as provided by this section, the Commissioners shall not be liable to credit or repay any amount accounted for or paid to them by way of VAT that was not VAT due to them.".

(11) The side-note to the section accordingly becomes "Credit for, or repayment of, overstated or overpaid VAT".

(12) Section 4 contains consequential and supplementary provision.

GENERAL NOTE

This section modifies VATA 1994 s 80 to ensure that the defence of unjust enrichment applies to all claims for repayment of overpaid output tax. In summary:

(a) it replaces s 80(1) with new s 80(1)–(1B); s 80(4) with new s 80(4)–(4ZB); and s 80(4A), (4B) with new s 80(4A) (sub-ss (2), (8), (9));

(b) it inserts a new s 80(2A) (sub-s (4));

(c) it substitutes new ss 80(3A), (7) (sub-ss (6), (10)); and

(d) it amends s 80(2), (3), (3B) and the side-note to s 80 (sub-ss (3), (5), (7), (11)).

Consequential and supplementary provisions are set out in s 4 below (sub-s (12)). In particular, s 4(6) below provides that this section applies to claims made after 25 May 2005.

Credit for output tax

The Commissioners are liable to credit a person who, in accounting to the Commissioners for VAT for a prescribed accounting period, has brought into account as output tax an amount that was not output tax (substituted s 80(1)). The person must claim the credit (amended s 80(2)) in accordance with s 80(6) and VAT Regulations 1995, SI 1995/2518, reg 37. The claim must be made no more than three years after the end of the prescribed accounting period in which the disclosure was made (if a voluntary disclosure was made) or three years after the end of the prescribed accounting period concerned (in other cases) (substituted s 80(4), (4ZA)(a) and (b)).

The Commissioners are liable to credit a person if, in assessing him to VAT for a prescribed accounting period, they have brought into account as output tax an amount that was not output tax (substituted s 80(1A)). The person must claim the credit (amended s 80(2)) in accordance with s 80(6) and VAT Regulations 1995, SI 1995/2518, reg 37. The claim must be made no more than three years after the end of the prescribed accounting period in which the disclosure was made (if the assessment was issued on the basis of an erroneous voluntary disclosure) or three years after the end of the prescribed accounting period in which the assessment was made (in other cases) (substituted s 80(4), (4ZA)(c) and (d)).

If, in either case, the credit exceeds any sums set against it (ie in accordance with s 81), the Commissioners are liable to pay (or repay) the excess to the claimant (new s 80(2A)).

The Commissioners can invoke the defence of unjust enrichment in relation to a claim for credit if all or part of the amount brought into account as output tax in either case has, for practical purposes, been borne by a person other than the claimant (amended s 80(3)). The provisions of s 80(3B) and (3C) apply to claims for unjust enrichment. They are unchanged except for a change of terminology in s 80(3B).

A voluntary disclosure is defined as a disclosure to the Commissioners made in one prescribed accounting period that he has not brought an amount of output tax into account for an earlier period (substituted s 80(4ZB)).

Repayment of VAT not due

The Commissioners are liable to repay a person who, in relation to a prescribed accounting period, has paid an amount by way of VAT (not being output tax or input tax) that was not VAT due to them (substituted s 80(1B)). An amount would fall within this description if, for example, it was a tax liability paid twice. The person must claim repayment (amended s 80(2)) in accordance with s 80(6) and VAT Regulations 1995, SI 1995/2518, reg 37. The claim must be made no more than three years after the date on which the payment was made (substituted s 80(4), (4ZA)(e)).

4 Section 3: consequential and supplementary provision

(1) In consequence of the amendments made by section 3, VATA 1994 is amended as follows.

(2) In section 78 (interest in certain cases of official error) in subsection (1)(*a*) (overstated output tax) for "and which they are in consequence liable to repay to him" substitute "and, as a result, they are liable under section 80(2A) to pay (or repay) an amount to him,".

(3) In section 80A (arrangements for reimbursing customers)—

(*a*) in subsection (2)(*a*), for "repayment" substitute "crediting";
(*b*) in subsection (2)(*b*), for "the cost of the original payment of that amount to the Commissioners" substitute "the amount brought into account as mentioned in paragraph (*b*) of subsection (1) or (1A) of that section";
(*c*) in subsection (3)(*a*), for "repayment" substitute "crediting of the amount";
(*d*) for subsection (3)(*b*) substitute—
    "(*b*) provision for cases where an amount is credited but an equal amount is not reimbursed in accordance with the arrangements;";
(*e*) in subsection (3)(*c*), for "repaid" substitute "paid (or repaid)";
(*f*) in subsection (4)(*a*), for "to make the repayments to the Commissioners that they are required to make" substitute "to make the repayments, or give the notifications, to the Commissioners that they are required to make or give";
(*g*) in subsection (7)—
    (i) for "repayment", in the first place, substitute "credit";
    (ii) for "the making of any repayment" substitute "the crediting of any amount".

(4) In section 80B (assessment of amounts due under section 80 arrangements) after subsection (1) (person liable to pay an amount) insert—

"(1A) Where—

(*a*) an amount ("the gross credit") has been credited to any person under subsection (1) or (1A) of section 80,

(*b*) any sums were set against that amount, in accordance with subsection (2A) of that section, and

(*c*) the amount reimbursed in accordance with the reimbursement arrangements was less than the gross credit,

subsection (1B) below applies.

(1B) In any such case—

(*a*) the person shall cease to be entitled to so much of the gross credit as exceeds the amount so reimbursed, and

(*b*) the Commissioners may, to the best of their judgement, assess the amount due from that person and notify it to him,

but an amount shall not be assessed under this subsection to the extent that the person is liable to pay it to the Commissioners as mentioned in subsection (1) above.

(1C) In determining the amount that a person is liable to pay as mentioned in subsection (1) above, any amount reimbursed in accordance with the reimbursement arrangements shall be regarded as first reducing so far as possible the amount that he would have been liable so to pay, but for the reimbursement of that amount.

(1D) For the purposes of this section, nil is an amount.

(1E) Any reference in any other provision of this Act to an assessment under subsection (1) above includes, if the context so admits, a reference to an assessment under subsection (1B) above.".

(5) In section 83 (appeals)—

(*a*) in paragraph (t) (repayment of amounts under section 80 etc) before "repayment" insert "crediting or";

(*b*) in paragraph (ta) (assessments under section 80B(1) etc) after "80B(1)" insert "or (1B)".

(6) The amendments made by section 3 and this section have effect in any case where a claim under section 80(2) of VATA 1994 is made on or after 26th May 2005, whenever the event occurred in respect of which the claim is made.

GENERAL NOTE

This section amends VATA 1994 ss 78, 80A, 80B and 83 (sub-ss (2)–(5)) as a consequence of the amendments made by s 3 above (sub-s (1)). It provides that the amendments made by ss 3 and 4 apply to claims under VATA 1994 s 80(2) (as amended by s 3(3) above) made after 25 May 2005 (sub-s (6)).

Interest in cases of official error (sub-s (2))

VATA 1994 s 78(1)(a) requires the Commissioners to pay interest to a person who, due to an error by the Commissioners, has accounted to them for an amount of output tax that was not due. Sub-section (2) amends s 78(1)(a) to provide that interest runs on the amount paid or repaid to the person under s 80(2A) (as inserted by s 3(4) above) rather than the amount credited to him under s 80(1) or (1A) (as substituted by s 3(2) above). Thus, no interest runs on the amount set of by the Commissioners under s 80(2A)(b) (as so inserted).

Reimbursement arrangements (sub-s (3))

In principle, a person claiming credit under VATA 1994 s 80(1) or (1A) (as substituted by s 3(2), above) is not regarded as being unjustly enriched if he enters into 'reimbursement arrangements' in accordance with regulations made under s 80A. For the regulations currently in force, see VAT Regulations 1995, SI 1995/2518, regs 43A–43H (as inserted by VAT (Amendment) Regulations 1998, SI 1998/59).

VATA 1994 s 80A is amended to provide that the reimbursement arrangements made by regulations relate to the credit claimed under s 80(1) or (1A) (as so substituted) rather than to the amount paid or repaid by the Commissioners under s 80(2A) (as inserted by s 3(4) above).

VATA 1994 s 80A(4) is amended to enable regulations to impose an obligation to notify the Commissioners if the amount reimbursed is less than the aggregate of the amount credited under s 80(1) or (1A) (as so substituted) and any interest paid thereon (i e under s 78(1)(a) as amended by sub-s (2)).

The 1995 Regulations will be amended in due course to reflect these changes.

Assessments (sub-s (4))

VAT Regulations 1996, SI 1995/2518, reg 43D (as inserted by VAT (Amendment) Regulations 1998, SI 1998/59) currently requires a person to repay all or part of the amount *paid* to him by the Commissioners in respect of a claim made under VATA 1994 ss 78 and 80 if a lesser sum is passed on to his customers under reimbursement arrangements. VATA 1994 s 80B(1), (2) provide that the Commissioners can assess the amount concerned and that interest runs on the amount so assessed.

As regards claims under s 80(1) or (1A) (as substituted by s 3(2) above) made after 25 May 2005, the amount *paid* on such a claim may be less than the amount *credited* because an amount due to the Commissioners has been set off in accordance with s 80(2A) (as inserted by s 3(4) above). As the amount to be reimbursed to customers is the amount *credited*, it follows that a new power of assessment is necessary until such time as the 1995 Regulations have been amended to reflect the concept of credit rather than payment.

The necessary power is set out in new VATA 1994 s 80B(1A)–(1D). A person ceases to be entitled to all or part of a credit given by the Commissioners under VATA 1994 s 80(1) or (1A) (as so substituted) if a lesser sum is reimbursed to customers in accordance with the reimbursement arrangements. The Commissioners may assess the part of the credit to which the person has ceased to be entitled.

A new s 80B(1E) provides that identical provisions apply to assessments under s 80B(1) and (1B) in relation to the manner in which interest runs and assessments are made. These provisions are prescribed by s 80B(2), which is unchanged. In brief, assessments are governed by s 78A(2)–(5) and (8). Interest runs as if the amounts had been assessed under s 73 (rather than s 80B(1), (1B)) and ss 74, 76, 77 apply for this purpose in the modified form prescribed by s 78A(6), (7).

Appeals (sub-s (5))

VATA 1994 s 83(t) and (ta) are amended to give a right of appeal to a VAT and Duties Tribunal in relation to:

(a) a claim for credit under s 80(1) or (1A) (as substituted by s 3(2) above); and

(b) an assessment made under s 80B(1B) (as inserted by sub-s (4)).

5 Reverse charge: gas and electricity valuation

(1) In paragraph 8 of Schedule 6 to VATA 1994 (valuation in case of reverse charge)—

    (*a*) after "8" insert ", or any supply of goods is treated by virtue of section 9A,", and

    (*b*) after "the services" insert "or goods".

(2) This section has effect in relation to supplies made on or after 17th March 2005.

GENERAL NOTE

FA 2004 s 21 inserted a new VATA 1994 s 9A introducing a reverse charge for gas and electricity supplied by persons outside the UK from 1 January 2005. Due to an oversight, the new s 9A did not prescribe how the supply was to be valued. This section rectifies the omission by extending the scope of VATA 1994 Sch 6 para 8 (sub-s (1)) in relation to supplies made after 16 March 2005 (sub-s (2)).

The value of a supply of gas or electricity deemed to be made by the recipient in accordance with VATA 1994 s 9A is the consideration for the supply made by the person outside the UK (if the consideration is money) or an amount in money equal to that consideration (in other cases).

6 Disclosure of value added tax avoidance schemes

(1) Schedule 1 (which contains amendments of Schedule 11A to VATA 1994) has effect.

(2) Subsection (1) and Schedule 1 shall come into force on such day as the Treasury may by order made by statutory instrument appoint.

(3) An order under subsection (2) may—

(*a*) appoint different days for different purposes, and
(*b*) contain transitional provisions and savings.

GENERAL NOTE

This section introduces Sch 1 (sub-s (1)). Sub-section (1) and Sch 1 come into force on a day to be appointed by statutory instrument (sub-ss (2), (3)).

PART 2
INCOME TAX, CORPORATION TAX AND CAPITAL GAINS TAX

CHAPTER 1
PERSONAL TAXATION

Social security pension lump sums

7 Charge to income tax on lump sum

(1) A charge to income tax arises where a person becomes entitled to a social security pension lump sum.

(2) For the purposes of the Tax Acts (including subsection (5)) a social security pension lump sum—
(*a*) is to be treated as income, but
(*b*) is not to be taken into account in determining the total income of any person.

(3) The person liable to a charge under this section is the person ("P") entitled to the lump sum, whether or not P is resident, ordinarily resident or domiciled in the United Kingdom.

(4) The charge is imposed on P for the applicable year of assessment (see subsection (6)).

(5) A charge under this section is a charge in respect of the amount of the lump sum at the following rate—
(*a*) if P's total income for the applicable year of assessment is nil, 0%;
(*b*) if P's total income for that year of assessment is greater than nil but does not exceed the starting rate limit for that year, the starting rate for that year;
(*c*) if P's total income for that year of assessment exceeds the starting rate limit but does not exceed the basic rate limit for that year, the basic rate for that year;
(*d*) if P's total income for that year of assessment exceeds the basic rate limit for that year, the higher rate for that year.

(6) Section 8 makes provision as to the meaning of "the applicable year of assessment" for the purposes of this section.

(7) Section 9 contains further definitions and makes provision as to commencement.

(8) Section 10 contains consequential amendments.

GENERAL NOTE

The Pensions Act 2004 introduced rewards for those who defer their state pension from April 2005. The reward can be paid either as an increase in the weekly pension or as a one-off taxable lump sum. The minimum deferral period before a lump can be claimed is 12 months. This means that the first time that a charge to tax could arise in respect of such a lump sum is in 2006–07.

The lump sum is taxable. However, to prevent a person being denied age-related personal allowances as a result of receiving such a lump sum, special rules apply.

A tax charge arises when a person becomes entitled to a social security pension lump (sub-s (1)). The lump sum is treated as income, but is not taken into account in determining total income (sub-s (2)). This means that although the sum is taxable, it is ignored for determining whether a person is entitled to age-related personal allowances.

The lump sum is taxable irrespective of whether the person is receipt of the lump sum is resident, ordinarily resident or domiciled in the UK. The rate at which the lump sum is charged to tax depends on the person's total income for the year as set out in the table below (sub-s (5)). It should be noted that the person's total income for these purposes is exclusive of the lump sum.

Total income for the applicable year of assessment	Rate at which lump sum is taxed
Nil	0%
Greater than nil but not exceeding the starting rate limit	The starting rate for the applicable year of assessment
Exceeds the starting rate limit but does not exceed the basic rate limit	The basic rate of tax for the applicable year of assessment
Exceeds the basic rate limit	The higher rate of tax for the applicable year of assessment

PAYE regulations are to be made to enable the Department for Work and Pensions to deduct tax at the appropriate rate.

The rules apply for 2006–07 and subsequent tax years (s 9(4)).

For details of the meaning of 'the applicable year of assessment', see s 8.

8 Meaning of "applicable year of assessment" in section 7

(1) For the purposes of section 7 "the applicable year of assessment" has the meaning given by this section.

(2) Subject to subsections (5) to (7), the applicable year of assessment is—

(*a*) the year of assessment in which the first benefit payment day falls, or

(*b*) if P dies before the beginning of that year of assessment, the year of assessment in which P dies.

(3) For the purposes of subsection (2) "the first benefit payment day" is, subject to subsection (4), the day as from which P's—

(*a*) Category A or Category B retirement pension,

(*b*) shared additional pension, or

(*c*) graduated retirement benefit,

becomes payable following the period of deferment by virtue of which P's entitlement to the lump sum arises.

(4) But where—

(*a*) the lump sum is a state pension lump sum to which P is entitled under paragraph 7A of Schedule 5 to SSCBA 1992 or paragraph 7A of Schedule 5 to SSCB(NI)A 1992 or a graduated retirement benefit lump sum to which P is entitled under a provision corresponding to either of those paragraphs, and

(*b*) at the time of S's death, P was entitled to a Category A or Category B retirement pension or (as the case may be) graduated retirement benefit,

the first benefit payment day is the day on which S died; and for this purpose "S" is the person by virtue of whose period of deferment P's entitlement to the lump sum arises.

(5) Subsections (6) and (7) apply where social security regulations make provision enabling the making of an election for a social security pension lump sum to be paid in the year of assessment ("the later year of assessment") next following that given by subsection (2).

(6) If such an election is made by P and is not revoked, the applicable year of assessment is—

(*a*) the later year of assessment, or

(*b*) if P dies before the beginning of that year of assessment, the year of assessment in which P dies.

(7) If—

(*a*) P dies after the beginning of the later year of assessment,

(*b*) by the time of P's death, P has not notified the Secretary of State as to whether or not P wishes to make such an election,

(*c*) social security regulations make provision enabling the making of such an election in such a case by the personal representatives of P, and

(*d*) P's personal representatives make such an election in accordance with the regulations,

the applicable year of assessment is the later year of assessment.

(8) For the purposes of determining the applicable year of assessment, it does not matter when the lump sum is actually paid.

(9) In this section—

"Category A or Category B retirement pension" means Category A or Category B retirement pension under Part 2 of SSCBA 1992 or Part 2 of SSCB(NI)A 1992;

"graduated retirement benefit" means graduated retirement benefit under section 36 or 37 of NIA 1965 or section 35 or 36 of NIA(NI) 1966;

"shared additional pension" means shared additional pension under Part 2 of SSCBA 1992 or Part 2 of SSCB(NI)A 1992;

"social security regulations" means any regulations under—

 (*a*) the Social Security Administration Act 1992 (c. 5), or

 (*b*) the Social Security Administration (Northern Ireland) Act 1992 (c. 8).

(10) This section is to be construed as one with section 7.

GENERAL NOTE

A social security pension lump sum is charged to tax in the applicable year of assessment (see s 7). The applicable year of assessment is either the year of assessment in which the first benefit payment falls, or if the person entitled to the lump sum has died before the start of that year of assessment, the year of assessment in which the death occurs (sub-s (2)). For these purposes, the first benefit day is the day as from which the category A or category B retirement pension, shared additional pension or graduated retirement pension becomes payable following the period of deferment by virtue of which the entitlement to the lump sum arises (sub-s (3)).

A category A or category b retirement pension is a category A or category B retirement pension under SSCBA 1992 Pt 2 and a graduated retirement benefit is one under NIA 1965 ss 36, 27. A shared additional pension is one under SSCBA 1992 Pt 2 (sub-s (9)).

However, if the lump sum is a state pension lump sum to which entitlement arises under SSCBA 1992 Sch 5 para 7A or Northern Ireland equivalent or a graduated lump to which entitlement arises under a corresponding provision and at the deceased's death, the surviving spouse was entitled to a category A or category B retirement pension or graduated retirement benefit, the first benefit day is the day on which the deceased died (sub-s (4)).

Regulations are to be made to allow a pensioner who has taken up his or her pension following a deferment of 12 months or more and who chooses the lump sum reward, the option of taking the lump sum either at the time that the social security pension is claimed or, on making an election, in the following tax year. Where election is made to take the lump sum in the following tax year, the applicable year of assessment is the later year of assessment, unless the person dies before the beginning of that year of assessment, in which the case the applicable year of assessment is the one in which death occurs (sub-ss (5),(6)).

However, if the person dies after the beginning of the later year of assessment and by the time of the person's death, he or she has not made such an election but the social security regulations enable the personal representatives to make the election and they have done so, the applicable year of assessment is the later year of assessment (sub-s (7)).

For the purposes of determining which year is the applicable year of assessment, it does not matter when the lump sum is actually paid (sub-s (8)).

This section has effect for 2006–07 and subsequent tax years.

9 Interpretation and commencement

(1) In sections 7 and 8 "social security pension lump sum" means—

 (*a*) a state pension lump sum,

 (*b*) a shared additional pension lump sum, or

 (*c*) a graduated retirement benefit lump sum.

(2) In section 8 and this section—

"graduated retirement benefit lump sum" means a lump sum payable under—

 (*a*) section 36 or 37 of NIA 1965, or

 (*b*) section 35 or 36 of NIA(NI) 1966;

"shared additional pension lump sum" means a lump sum payable under—

 (*a*) section 55C of, and Schedule 5A to, SSCBA 1992, or

 (*b*) section 55C of, and Schedule 5A to, SSCB(NI)A 1992;

"state pension lump sum" means a lump sum payable under—

 (*a*) section 55 of, and Schedule 5 to, SSCBA 1992, or

(*b*) section 55 of, and Schedule 5 to, SSCB(NI)A 1992.

(3) In section 8 and this section—

"NIA 1965" means the National Insurance Act 1965 (c. 51);

"NIA(NI) 1966" means the National Insurance Act (Northern Ireland) 1966 (c. 6 (N.I.));

"SSCBA 1992" means the Social Security Contributions and Benefits Act 1992 (c. 4);

"SSCB(NI)A 1992" means the Social Security Contributions and Benefits (Northern Ireland) Act 1992 (c. 7).

(4) Sections 7 and 8 and this section have effect in relation to the year 2006–07 and subsequent years of assessment.

GENERAL NOTE

For the purposes of ss 7, 8, a 'social security pension lump sum' is a state pension lump sum, a shared additional pension lump sum or a graduated retirement pension lump sum (sub-s (1)).

A state pension lump sum is a lump sum payable under SSCBA 1992 s 55 and Sch 5, or Northern Ireland equivalent. A shared additional pension lump sum is a lump sum payable under SSCBA 1992 s 55C and Sch 5A or Northern Ireland equivalent and a graduated retirement benefit lump sum payable under NIA 1965 s 36, 37 or Northern Ireland equivalent.

This section and ss 7 and 8 have effect for 2006–07 and subsequent tax years.

10 Consequential amendments

(1) ITEPA 2003 is amended as follows.

(2) In section 577 (UK social security pensions) after subsection (1) insert—

"(1A) But this section does not apply to any social security pension lump sum (within the meaning of section 7 of F(No.2)A 2005).".

(3) In section 683 (PAYE income) in subsection (3) (meaning, subject to subsection (4), of "PAYE pension income") in the opening words, for "subsection (4)" substitute "subsections (3A) and (4)".

(4) In that section, after subsection (3) insert—

"(3A) "PAYE pension income" for a tax year also includes any social security pension lump sum (within the meaning of section 7 of F(No.2)A 2005) in respect of which a charge to income tax arises under that section for that tax year.".

(5) In section 686 (meaning of "payment") in subsection (1) (rules as to when payment of, or on account of, PAYE income is to be treated as made for the purposes of PAYE regulations) at the end of the subsection insert—

"But this is subject to subsection (5) (PAYE pension income: social security pension lump sums).".

(6) In that section, after subsection (4) insert—

"(5) For the purposes of PAYE regulations, a payment of, or on account of, an amount which is PAYE pension income of a person by virtue of section 683(3A) (social security pension lump sums) is to be treated as made at the time when the payment is made.".

(7) In Schedule 1 (abbreviations and defined expressions) in Part 1 (abbreviations of Acts and instruments) insert at the end—

"F(No.2)A 2005   The Finance (No. 2) Act 2005 (c.)".

GENERAL NOTE

As a result of the provision introducing a charge to tax on a social security pension lump sum (see ss 7–9), consequential amendments are made to ITEPA 2003 (sub-s (1)). The consequential amendments ensure that a social security pension lump sum is treated as PAYE and provide for the Department of Work and Pensions to withhold income tax at the point of payment.

New ITEPA 2003 s 577(1A) excludes the social security pension from the definitions in s 577(1). The effect of this is that the lump sum is not part of taxable pension income or total income chargeable to income tax (sub-s (2)).

New ITEPA 2003 s (3A) and amended s 683(3) ensure that the social security pension lump sum is treated as PAYE income. This enables tax to be withheld on payment under a PAYE-type arrangement (sub-ss (3), (4)).

New ITEPA s 686(5) and amended s 686(1) provide that a payment of or on account of a PAYE pension is treated as made at the time as when the payment is made (sub-ss (5), (6)). This ensures that the Department for Work and Pensions cannot deduct the tax until the lump sum is paid.

The abbreviation F(No.2)A 2005 meaning the Finance (No.2) Act 2005 is added to the list of abbreviation and defined expressions in ITEPA 2005 Sch 1 (sub-s (7)).

The consequential amendments are effective from the date of Royal Assent to F(No.2)A 2005.

Gift aid

11 Donations to charity by individuals

(1) For section 25(5E) to (5G) of FA 1990 (donations to charity by individuals: benefits: disregard of certain rights of admission) substitute—

"(5E) In determining whether a gift to a charity is a qualifying donation the benefit of any right of admission received in consequence of the gift shall be disregarded if subsections (5F) to (5H) are satisfied in relation to the right.

(5F) This subsection is satisfied if the opportunity to make a gift and to receive the right of admission in consequence is available to the public.

(5G) This subsection is satisfied if the right of admission is a right granted by the charity for the purpose of viewing property preserved, maintained, kept or created by a charity in pursuance of its charitable purposes, including, in particular—

(*a*) buildings,
(*b*) grounds or other land,
(*c*) plants,
(*d*) animals,
(*e*) works of art (but not performances),
(*f*) artefacts, and
(*g*) property of a scientific nature.

(5H) This subsection is satisfied if—

(*a*) the right of admission applies, during a period of at least one year, at all times at which the public can obtain admission, or
(*b*) a member of the public could purchase the same right of admission and the amount of the gift is greater by at least 10% than the amount which he would have to pay.

(5I) In subsection (5E) "right of admission" means a right of admission—

(*a*) of the person who makes the gift or of that person and one or more members of his family (whether or not the right must be exercised by all those persons at the same time),
(*b*) to premises or property to which the public are admitted on payment of an admission fee, and
(*c*) without payment of the admission fee or on payment of a reduced fee;

and in the application of subsection (5H)(*b*) "the same right of admission" means a right relating to the same property, classes of person and periods of time as the right received in consequence of the gift.

(5J) For the purposes of subsection (5H)(*a*) a right of admission shall be treated as applying at all times at which the public can obtain admission despite the fact that the right does not apply on days specified by the charity, being days on each of which an event is to take place on the premises to which the right relates; provided that no more than 5 days are specified for that purpose in relation to—

(*a*) the period during which the right applies, in the case of a period of one year, or
(*b*) each calendar year during all or part of which the right applies, in the case of a right applying for a period of more than one year."

(2) This section shall have effect in relation to gifts made on or after 6th April 2006.

GENERAL NOTE

The Gift Aid legislation contained within FA 1990 s 25 is amended to correct an unintended effect of changes made to the scheme by FA 2000. The changes have effect in relation to gifts made on or after 6 April 2006.

The Gift Aid scheme provides relief for gifts to charity by individuals where the gifts are qualifying gifts. Improvements were made to the scheme by FA 2000 in order to encourage new donations to charity. However, an unintended effect of these improvements was that a payment for admission could become eligible for Gift Aid if the right of admission granted met certain conditions. Charities are able to offer free admission to sites where an entrance fee is normally required provided a payment is made that is at least equal to the entrance fee on which Gift Aid can be reclaimed. Although this is not the intended purpose of Gift Aid the existing rules do not prevent it. However, under the provisions as amended by FA 2000 it is only those charities whose sole or main object is the preservation of heritage property or the conservation of wildlife who are allowed to disregard the benefit of any right of admission received in consequence of making the gift in determining whether the gift to charity is a qualifying donation for gift aid purposes.

As many other types of charities allow visitors to pay to view property it is not considered fair that heritage and conservation charities benefit from special treatment.

To correct this anomaly, new FA 1990 s 25(5E)–(5J) are substituted for FA 1990 s 25(5E)–(5G) (sub-s (1)).

New FA 1990 s 25(5E) provides that in determining whether a gift to charity is a qualifying donation for gift aid purposes, any right of admission received in consequence of the gift is disregarded if new sub-ss (5F)–(5H) are satisfied in relation to the gift.

New sub-s (5F) is satisfied if the opportunity to make a gift and to receive the right of admission in consequence is available to the public.

New sub-s (5G) is satisfied if the right of admission is a right granted by the charity for the purpose of viewing property preserved, maintained, kept or created by a charity in pursuance of charitable purposes, including:

(a) buildings;

(b) grounds or other land;

(c) plants;

(d) animals;

(e) works of art (but not performance);

(f) artefacts; and

(g) property of a scientific nature.

New sub-s (5H) is satisfied if either the right of admission applies during a period of at least one year, at all times at which the public can obtain admission, or a member of the public could purchase the same right of admission and the amount of the gift is greater by at least 10% than the amount by which he would have to pay.

For the purposes of new sub-s (5E), 'right of admission' means a right of admission of the person who makes the gift or of that person and one or more members of his family (whether or not the right must be exercised by all those persons at the same time) to premises or to property to which the public are admitted on the payment of an admission fee and without payment of the admission fee or on payment of a reduced fee. In new sub-s (5H)(b), 'the same right of admission' means a right relating to the same property, classes of person and periods of time as the right received in consequence of the gift (new sub-s (5I)).

For the purposes of new sub-s (5H)(a), a right of admission is treated as applying at all times at which the public can obtain admission despite the fact that the right does not apply on days specified by the charity. These are days on which an event takes place on the premises, subject to a limit of five days during the period in relation to which the right applies in the case of a period of one year, or each calendar year during all or part of which the right applies in the case of a right applying for a period of more than one year (new sub-s (5J)).

Employee securities

12 Employee securities: anti-avoidance

Schedule 2 contains amendments relating to employee securities.

GENERAL NOTE

This section introduces Schedule 2.

CHAPTER 2

SCIENTIFIC RESEARCH ORGANISATIONS

GENERAL NOTE

Sections 13–15 are all concerned with scientific research organisations (SROs). SROs are, broadly, bodies which are formed to undertake research for the mutual benefit of their members. They are exempt from corporation tax in a similar way to charities. These sections modernise the framework for this tax exemption and remove certain regulatory barriers.

13 Corporation tax exemption for organisations

(1) Section 508 of ICTA (tax exemption for scientific research organisations) is amended as follows.

(2) In subsection (1) (Associations undertaking scientific research and approved by Secretary of State), for paragraph (*a*) substitute—

"(*a*) an Association has as its object the undertaking of research and development which may lead to or facilitate an extension of any class or classes of trade; and".

(3) In that subsection, for ", be allowed in the case of the Association" substitute "in relation to any accounting period, be allowed in the case of the Association for that accounting period".

(4) After that subsection insert—

"(1A) The Treasury may by regulations prescribe circumstances in which the conditions in subsection (1) above shall be deemed not to be complied with.

(1B) The Treasury may by regulations make provision specifying for the purposes of paragraph (*a*) of that subsection—

(*a*) what shall be deemed to be, or not to be, an Association,

(*b*) circumstances in which an Association shall be deemed to have, or not to have, the undertaking of research and development as its object,

(*c*) circumstances in which the undertaking of research and development shall be deemed to be, or not to be, capable of leading to or facilitating an extension of a class of trade, or

(*d*) what shall be deemed to be, or not to be, a class of trade."

(5) For subsection (3) (meaning of "scientific research") substitute—

"(3) Section 837A (meaning of "research and development") applies for the purposes of subsection (1)(*a*) above.

(4) Regulations under subsection (3) of that section (power to prescribe activities which are, or are not, research and development) may make provision for the purposes of that section as it applies by virtue of subsection (3) of this section which is additional to, or different from, the provision made otherwise for the purposes of that section."

(6) This section has effect in relation to accounting periods beginning on or after such day as the Treasury may by order made by statutory instrument appoint.

GENERAL NOTE

Under the current rules in TA 1988 s 508 a SRO has to have as its object the undertaking of scientific research. The test is now modernised and requires instead that the SRO should have as its object the undertaking of research and development. The requirement that annual retrospective approval from the Secretary of State for Trade and Industry was necessary in order to qualify for the tax exemption has been dropped. Relief in future is now to be claimed from HMRC in the same way as a charity claims relief from tax.

The Treasury is empowered to make regulations to determine what is and is not an SRO and what conditions must be met to meet the qualifying requirements.

Research and development takes the same meaning as it does for the purpose of R&D tax credits and regulations may be made to define what is research and development for the purposes of s 508 relief. These do not have to be identical to the regulations which operate for the purposes of R&D tax credits.

The new rules operate from a day to be appointed by statutory instrument.

14 Income tax deduction for payments to organisations

(1) Section 88 of ITTOIA 2005 (income tax deduction for payments to research associations etc.) is amended as follows.

(2) In subsection (1) (conditions for deduction), for the words from the beginning of paragraph (*a*) to "research" in paragraph (*b*) substitute—

"(*a*) pays any sum to an Association in the case of which exemption may be claimed under section 508 of ICTA and which has as its object the undertaking of research and development which may lead to or facilitate an extension of the class of trade to which the trade carried on by the person belongs, or

(*b*) pays any sum to be used for scientific research related to that class of trade".

(3) In subsection (4), omit paragraph (*a*) (meaning of "approved" in relation to scientific research association).

(4) In subsection (5) (references to scientific research related to a class of trade), for "references in this section" substitute "reference in subsection (1)(*b*)".

(5) This section has effect in relation to sums paid to an Association during any accounting period of the Assocation beginning on or after the day appointed under section 13(6).

GENERAL NOTE

Income tax relief is given for payments to SROs under ITTOIA 2005 s 88. Section 14 amends the language of s 88 to take account of the changes in s 13. There are no substantive changes to the way relief is given.

15 Corporation tax deduction for payments to organisations

(1) Section 82B of ICTA (corporation tax deduction for payments to research associations etc.) is amended as follows.

(2) In subsection (1) (conditions for deduction), for the words from the beginning of paragraph (*a*) to "above" in paragraph (*b*) substitute—

"(*a*) pays any sum to an Association in the case of which exemption may be claimed under section 508 and which has as its object the undertaking of research and development which may lead to or facilitate an extension of the class of trade to which the trade carried on by the company belongs, or

(*b*) pays any sum to be used for scientific research related to that class of trade".

(3) In subsection (3) (reference to scientific research related to a class of trade), for "this section" substitute "subsection (1)(*b*) above".

(4) This section has effect in relation to sums paid to an Association during any accounting period of the Assocation beginning on or after the day appointed under section 13(6).

GENERAL NOTE

This is a parallel provision to s 14 above which applies for the purposes of corporation tax relief. Again there are no substantive changes to the way that relief is given.

CHAPTER 3

AUTHORISED INVESTMENT FUNDS ETC

16 Open-ended investment companies

After section 468 of ICTA (authorised unit trust schemes) insert—

"468A Open-ended investment companies

(1) In relation to an open-ended investment company the rate of corporation tax for the financial year 2005 and subsequent financial years shall be deemed to be the rate at which income tax at the lower rate is charged for the year of assessment which begins on 6th April in the financial year concerned (and sections 13, 13AA and 13AB shall not apply).

(2) In this section "open-ended investment company" means a company incorporated in the United Kingdom to which section 236 of the Financial Services and Markets Act 2000 (c. 8) applies.

(3) Each of the parts of an umbrella company shall be regarded for the purposes of this section as an open-ended investment company and the umbrella company as a whole shall not be so regarded (and shall not, unless an enactment expressly provides otherwise, be regarded as a company for any other purpose of the Tax Acts).

(4) In subsection (3) "umbrella company" means an open-ended investment company—

(*a*) in respect of which the instrument of incorporation provides arrangements for separate pooling of the contributions of the shareholders and the profits or income out of which payments are to be made to them, and

(*b*) the shareholders of which are entitled to exchange rights in one pool for rights in another,

and a reference to part of an umbrella company is a reference to a separate pool."

GENERAL NOTE

This section introduces new TA 1988 s 468A, which provides definitions of an open-ended investment company (OEIC) and an umbrella company. These definitions were previously in the Open-ended Investment Companies (Tax) Regulations 1997, SI 1997/154.

TA 1988 s 468A(1) sets a special rate of corporation tax, chargeable on the whole of an OEIC's income, equal to the lower rate of income tax for the tax year beginning on 6 April in the financial year concerned. This means that the corporation tax starting rate, the rate applicable to small companies and the non-corporate distribution rate do not apply to an OEIC. This rule has previously been in regulations and keeps the tax treatment of an OEIC in line with that of an authorised unit trust (AUT).

17 Authorised unit trusts and open-ended investment companies

(1) The following provisions shall cease to have effect—

(*a*) sections 468H to 468Q of ICTA (authorised unit trusts),

(*b*) paragraphs 2A and 2B of Schedule 10 to FA 1996 (authorised unit trusts and open-ended investment companies: loan relationships),

(*c*) paragraphs 32 and 33 of Schedule 26 to FA 2002 (collective investment schemes: derivative contracts),

(*d*) section 373(4) and (6) of ITTOIA 2005 (open-ended investment company: interest distributions), and

(*e*) section 376(4) and (6) of ITTOIA 2005 (authorised unit trust: interest distributions).

(2) In this Chapter "authorised investment funds" means—

(*a*) authorised unit trust schemes, and

(*b*) open-ended investment companies.

(3) The Treasury may, by regulations—

(*a*) make provision about the treatment of authorised investment funds for the purposes of an enactment relating to taxation;

(*b*) provide for the modification of an enactment relating to taxation in its application in relation to—

(i) authorised investment funds,

(ii) shareholders or unit holders in authorised investment funds, or

(iii) transactions involving authorised investment funds;

(*c*) impose requirements on persons responsible for the management of an authorised investment fund in relation to the provision of information, the form of accounts, the keeping of records or other administrative matters.

(4) For the purposes of this Chapter—

(*a*) "unit trust scheme" has the meaning given by section 237 of the Financial Services and Markets Act 2000 (c. 8),

(*b*) a unit trust scheme is authorised in relation to an accounting period if an order under section 243 of the Financial Services and Markets Act 2000 is in force in relation to that scheme during the whole or part of that accounting period,

(*c*) "unit holder" means a person entitled to a share of the investments subject to the trusts of a unit trust scheme, (*d*) a reference to a shareholder or unit holder includes a person beneficially entitled to shares or units (and a reference to owning units or shares shall be construed accordingly),

(*e*) "open-ended investment company" means a company incorporated in the United Kingdom to which section 236 of the Financial Services and Markets Act 2000 applies,

(*f*) "associate" has the meaning given by section 417 ICTA,

(*g*) "net asset value" means the value of the assets of the authorised investment fund, after the deduction of specified liabilities,

(*h*) a reference to a distribution includes investing an amount on behalf of a unit holder or shareholder in respect of his accumulation units or accumulation shares,

(*i*) "distribution accounts" means accounts showing—

(i) the total amount available for distribution to unit holders or shareholders, and
(ii) how that amount is computed,

(*j*) the "distribution date" for a distribution period in relation to an authorised investment fund means—

(i) the date specified by or in accordance with the terms of the trust or the instrument of incorporation of the company for any distribution for that distribution period, or
(ii) if no date is specified, the last day of that distribution period,

(*k*) "distribution period" in relation to an authorised investment fund means a period by reference to which the total amount available for distribution to unit holders or shareholders is ascertained,

(*l*) "umbrella company" has the meaning given by section 468A of ICTA,

(*m*) "umbrella scheme" has the meaning given by section 468 of ICTA, and

(*n*) section 839 of ICTA (connected persons) applies.

GENERAL NOTE

This section, along with ss 18 and 19, rationalises the existing tax regime for AUTs and OEICs, which are collectively called 'authorised investment funds' (AIFs) (s 2).

Subsection (3) authorises the Treasury to make regulations:

(a) governing the taxation treatment of AIFs;

(b) modifying enactments relating to taxation of investors in AIFs;

(c) governing transactions in which AIFs are involved; and

(d) requiring fund managers to supply information and keep records.

This authority is in very broad terms, but s 18 specifies in more detail what the regulations may include.

These regulations, when made, will supersede parts of the existing legislation, listed in sub-s (1), and these will then be repealed.

The intention is to have most of the rules in the form of regulations so that they can be updated without having to wait for the next Finance Act.

Subsection (4) contains definitions which apply to ss 17–23.

18 Section 17(3): specific powers

(1) Regulations under section 17(3)(*a*) or (*b*) may make provision about distributions which may, in particular—

(*a*) require an authorised investment fund to comply with prescribed rules for determining (whether by reference to a formula or otherwise) what proportion of an amount shown in distribution accounts as available for distribution is to be distributed by way of dividends and what proportion is to be distributed by way of yearly interest;

(*b*) permit persons responsible for the management of an authorised investment fund to elect to distribute entirely by way of dividends;

(*c*) require distribution accounts to show the amount available for distribution—

(i) by way of dividends;
(ii) by way of yearly interest;

(*d*) allow a distribution of yearly interest for a distribution period to be deducted, in the prescribed manner, in computing the profits of the authorised investment fund for the accounting period in which the last day of that distribution period falls;

(*e*) make provision for determining the distribution date in relation to a distribution period of an authorised investment fund;

(*f*) permit distributions to be made, in prescribed circumstances, to or for the benefit of a person not ordinarily resident in the United Kingdom without deducting tax;

(*g*) permit distributions to be made without deducting tax, in prescribed circumstances, to a person ordinarily resident in the United Kingdom who is unlikely to be liable to pay an amount by way of income tax for the year of assessment in which the distribution is made;

(*h*) include provision, in respect of a unit holder or shareholder who is within the charge to corporation tax, about—

    (i) the liability to corporation tax resulting from receipt of a distribution, and

    (ii) the method of computing that liability.

(2) Regulations under section 17(3)(*a*) or (*b*) may, in particular—

(*a*) make special provision for loan relationships held by an authorised investment fund;

(*b*) make special provision for derivative contracts held by an authorised investment fund;

(*c*) modify the meaning of "relevant holding" for the purposes of—

    (i) paragraph 4 of Schedule 10 to FA 1996 (loan relationships), and

    (ii) paragraph 36 of Schedule 26 to FA 2002 (derivative contracts);

(*d*) make special provision in relation to the treatment of umbrella companies and umbrella schemes (or shareholders or unit holders in umbrella companies or umbrella schemes);

(*e*) prohibit action which favours a class of unit holders or shareholders.

(3) Regulations under section 17(3)(*a*) or (*b*) may, in particular—

(*a*) make special provision in relation to a person who, alone or together with associates or connected persons, owns (otherwise than as a nominee) units or shares, in a fund designated by the Financial Services Authority as a Qualified Investor Scheme, which represent 10% or more (or such other percentage as the regulations may specify) of the net asset value of the fund;

(*b*) include exceptions from provision made by virtue of paragraph (*a*) above including, in particular, an exception relating to units or shares held—

    (i) by a charity (within the meaning of section 506(1) of ICTA),

    (ii) by a registered pension scheme (within the meaning of section 150 of FA 2004),

    (iii) by an insurance company (within the meaning of section 431(2) of ICTA) as assets of its long-term insurance fund (within the meaning of that section), or

    (iv) by such other persons, in such circumstances, as the regulations may specify.

(4) Regulations under section 17(3)(*c*) may, in particular, require persons responsible for the management of an authorised investment fund to supply information to, and make available books, documents and other records for inspection by, the Commissioners for Her Majesty's Revenue and Customs.

(5) Regulations under section 17(3) may in particular—

(*a*) amend a reference in an enactment to a provision repealed by section 17(1);

(*b*) make different provision for different circumstances;

(*c*) make incidental, consequential, supplemental or transitional provision.

GENERAL NOTE

This section contains a detailed list of matters which the Treasury may include in regulations.

Most of these matters are already dealt with in existing legislation or regulations, but the intention is to rewrite the rules completely. Provision is made for special taxation treatment of investors in a special type of AIF known as a Qualified Investor Scheme available to a limited class of investors; the special treatment is not to apply to charities, pension schemes and insurance companies.

19 Section 17: commencement and procedure

(1) Section 17(1) shall come into force on such day as the Treasury may appoint by order.

(2) An order under subsection (1) may—

(*a*) commence only a specified repeal;

(*b*) commence different repeals at different times;

(*c*) commence a repeal at different times for different purposes;

(*d*) include savings.

(3) Regulations under section 17(3) shall be subject to annulment by a resolution of the House of Commons.

(4) But the first set of regulations under section 17(3) may not be made unless a draft has been laid before and approved by resolution of the House of Commons.

GENERAL NOTE

The repeals in s 17(1) apply from a date to be appointed by order of the Treasury (sub-s (1)). Such an order may provide for the repeals to take effect on different dates and may include exceptions (sub-s (2)).

The first set of regulations made under s 17(3) can only be made if a draft has been approved by a resolution of the House of Commons; further regulations do not require a resolution but may be annulled by a resolution (sub-ss (3), (4)).

20 Unauthorised unit trusts: chargeable gains

(1) Section 100 of TCGA 1992 (exemption for authorised unit trusts, &c.) shall be amended as follows.

(2) After subsection (2) insert—

"(2A) In determining whether subsection (2) applies no account shall be taken of units in a scheme which—

(*a*) have been disposed of by a unit holder, and

(*b*) are held by the managers of the scheme (in that capacity) pending disposal.

(2B) In determining whether subsection (2) applies no account shall be taken of the possibility of a charge to corporation tax on income in respect of a gain accruing on a disposal by—

(*a*) an insurance company (within the meaning given by section 431 of the Taxes Act), or

(*b*) a friendly society (being an incorporated friendly society or registered friendly society within the meaning given by section 466(2) of the Taxes Act)."

(3) This section shall have effect for the year 2005–06 and subsequent years of assessment.

GENERAL NOTE

An unauthorised unit trust is not exempt from tax on its capital gains. However, exemption is given by TCGA 1992 s 100(2) where all the units are held by exempt bodies such as pension funds, charities and local authorities In the past, exemption has been given by concession if units were temporarily held by the trust managers pending re-sale. This section inserts new TCGA 1992 s 100(2A) which gives statutory effect to that concession.

The section also introduces new TCGA 1992 s 100(2B) which does not deny the exemption because units are held by an insurance company, an incorporated friendly society or a registered friendly society which might be subject to corporation tax (sub-s (2)).

These changes have effect for 2005–06 onwards (sub-s (3)).

21 Unit trusts: treatment of accumulation units

(1) In Chapter III of Part III of TCGA 1992 (collective investment schemes, &c.) after section 99A insert—

"99B Calculation of the disposal cost of accumulation units

(1) For the purposes of computing the gain accruing on a disposal by a unit holder of units in a unit trust scheme and for the purposes of all other provisions of this Act, an amount shall be treated as expenditure falling within section 38(1)(*b*) if—

(*a*) it represents income from the investments subject to the unit trust scheme,

(*b*) it has been reinvested in respect of the units on behalf of the unit holder (without an issue of new units), and

(*c*) it is either—

    (i) charged to income tax as income of the unit holder (or would be charged to income tax as his income but for a relief which has effect in respect of it) for the purposes of the Income Tax Acts, or

    (ii) taken into account as a receipt in calculating profits, gains or losses of the unit holder for the purposes of the Income Tax Acts.

(2) Where an amount is treated as expenditure by virtue of subsection (1), the expenditure shall be treated for the purposes of this Act as having been incurred—

    (*a*) in relation to an authorised unit trust, on the distribution date for the distribution period in respect of which the amount is reinvested, and

    (*b*) in relation to any other unit trust scheme, on the date on which the amount is reinvested.

(3) In subsection (2)(*a*) "distribution date" and "distribution period" shall have the meaning given by section 468H of the Taxes Act."

(2) This section shall have effect in relation to a disposal of units on or after 16th March 2005.

GENERAL NOTE

This section introduces new TCGA 1992 s 99B which has effect for disposals after 15 March 2005 (sub-s (2)). It gives statutory effect to a Revenue practice.

New TCGA 1992 s 99B

Where a unit trust distributes income from its investments to unit holders, the unit holders are chargeable to income tax or corporation tax in respect of those distributions. Where a unit trust has accumulation units, the income from those units is not distributed but is reinvested on behalf of the unit holders. No new units are issued to the unit holders, so that the value of the existing units is increased. The unit holders are charged to income tax or corporation tax on the amount reinvested.

This section provides that, in calculating the chargeable gain realised by the holder when he sells an accumulation unit, he may deduct as 'enhancement expenditure' any amounts which have been charged to tax in respects of income reinvested (sub-s (1)).

In the case of an AUT, the enhancement expenditure is deemed to have been incurred on the distribution date for the distribution period in which the income was reinvested. In any other unit trust scheme, the enhancement expenditure is deemed to have been incurred on the date when the income was reinvested (sub-s (3)).

22 Section 349B ICTA: exemption for distributions to PEP/ISA managers

(1) Section 349B(4) of ICTA (requirement for individual to be entitled to income tax exemption) shall be amended as follows.

(2) In paragraph (*a*) after "of a plan" insert "of a kind to which regulations under Chapter 3 of Part 6 of ITTOIA 2005 (income from individual investment plans) apply".

(3) Paragraph (*b*) shall cease to have effect.

(4) This section shall have effect in relation to payments made on or after 6 April 2005.

GENERAL NOTE

An individual investment plan (IIP) means a personal equity plan (PEP) or an individual savings account (ISA). Under TA 1988 ss 349A, 349B(4), a company is not required to deduct income tax from interest paid to the manager of an IIP if it reasonably believes that payment is in respect of investments of the IIP and that the investor in the IIP is exempt from tax on the interest he receives from the IIP.

This section removes the need for the company to be concerned with the tax exempt status of the investor. The change also applies to payment of interest to Child Trust Fund Providers. It applies to payments of interest after 5 April 2005.

23 Offshore funds

(1) In section 761 of ICTA (charge on offshore income gain)—

    (*a*) in subsection (2)—

        (i) for "sections 2(1) and 10" substitute "sections 2(1), 10 and 10B", and

(ii) for "section 11(2)(*b*)" substitute "section 11(2A)(*c*)", and
(*b*) in subsection (3)—
(i) for "section 10" substitute "sections 10 and 10B",
(ii) for "subsection (1) of that section" substitute "subsection (1) of section 10", and
(iii) for the words "and subsection (3) of that section (which makes similar provision in relation to corporation tax) shall have effect with the omission of the words "situated in the United Kingdom"" substitute "and paragraphs (*a*) and (*b*) of subsection (1) of section 10B (which make similar provision in relation to corporation tax) shall have effect with the omission of the words "situated in the United Kingdom and"".

(2) For paragraph 1(1)(*d*) of Schedule 27 to ICTA (distributing funds) substitute—
"(*d*) the form of the distribution is such that—
(i) if any sum forming part of it were received in the United Kingdom by an individual resident there and did not form part of the profits of a trade, profession or vocation, that sum would fall to be chargeable to tax under a provision specified in section 830(2) of ITTOIA 2005, or
(ii) if any sum forming part of it were received in the United Kingdom by a company resident there and did not form part of the profits of a trade, profession or vocation, that sum would fall to be chargeable to tax in accordance with section 18 of ICTA (Schedule D)—
(*a*) under Case III of Schedule D in respect of income arising from securities out of the United Kingdom or from possessions out of the United Kingdom, or
(*b*) under Case V of Schedule D;".

(3) For paragraph 3(1)(*a*) of that Schedule (distributing funds) substitute—
"(*a*) the holders of interests in the fund who are individuals domiciled and resident in the United Kingdom—
(i) are chargeable to tax under a provision specified in section 830(2) of ITTOIA 2005 in respect of such of those sums as are referable to their interests; or
(ii) if any of that income is derived from assets within the United Kingdom, would be so chargeable had the assets been outside the United Kingdom;
(aa) the holders of interests in the fund which are companies resident in the United Kingdom—
(i) are chargeable to tax under Case III of Schedule D in respect of income arising from securities out of the United Kingdom or from possessions out of the United Kingdom;
(ii) are chargeable to tax under Case V of Schedule D; or
(iii) if any of that income is derived from assets within the United Kingdom, would have been chargeable under sub-paragraph (i) or (ii) had the assets been outside the United Kingdom; and".

(4) In paragraph 3(1)(*b*) of that Schedule (distributing funds) for "sub-paragraph (i) or (ii)" substitute "paragraph (*a*) or (aa)".

GENERAL NOTE

This section corrects minor defects in the legislation dealing with the taxation of income and gains arising from offshore income gains.

Subsection (1) inserts cross-references to additional provisions which were included in FA 2003.

Subsections (2) and (3) insert cross-references:

(a) for income tax, to provisions in ITTOIA 2005 which replace Schedule D Cases IV and V;
(b) for corporation tax, to Schedule D Case III in the case of income under a loan relationship.

CHAPTER 4

AVOIDANCE INVOLVING TAX ARBITRAGE

GENERAL NOTE

The provisions of this chapter are designed to counteract UK tax avoidance through the use of hybrid entities or hybrid instruments (as defined in Sch 3).

Clearance procedure

Her Majesty's Revenue and Customs (HMRC) have agreed to operate an informal clearance procedure, by way of requests for advice about the legislation, including whether the legislation will apply to a planned series of transactions that may constitute a scheme. Where possible, they will give a decision whether any notice will be issued in respect of the disclosed transactions, and will consider themselves bound by a clearance given in accordance with that procedure. Annex C of their guidance notes gives further details of the arrangements for obtaining clearance.

24 Deduction cases

(1) If the Commissioners for Her Majesty's Revenue and Customs consider, on reasonable grounds, that conditions A to D are or may be satisfied in relation to a transaction to which a company falling within subsection (2) is party, they may give the company a notice under this section.

(2) A company falls within this subsection if—

(*a*) it is resident in the United Kingdom, or

(*b*) it is resident outside the United Kingdom but is within the charge to corporation tax.

(3) Condition A is that the transaction to which the company is party forms part of a scheme that is a qualifying scheme.

(4) Condition B is that the scheme is such that for the purposes of corporation tax the company is in a position to claim or has claimed an amount by way of deduction in respect of the transaction or is in a position to set off or has set off against profits in an accounting period an amount relating to the transaction.

(5) Condition C is that the main purpose, or one of the main purposes, of the scheme is to achieve a UK tax advantage for the company.

(6) Condition D is that the amount of the UK tax advantage in question is more than a minimal amount.

(7) A notice under this section is a notice—

(*a*) specifying the transaction in relation to which the Commissioners consider that conditions A to D are or may be satisfied,

(*b*) specifying the accounting period in relation to which the Commissioners consider that condition B is or may be satisfied as regards the transaction, and

(*c*) informing the company that as a consequence section 25 (rules relating to deductions) has effect in relation to the transaction.

(8) Nothing in this section prevents the Commissioners from giving a company falling within subsection (2) a notice under this section as regards two or more transactions.

(9) Schedule 3 makes provision about what constitutes a qualifying scheme.

GENERAL NOTE

The deductions rules apply where a scheme involving a hybrid entity or hybrid instrument increases a UK tax deduction or deductions to more than they would otherwise have been in the absence of the scheme. Where the legislation applies, the effect will be to limit tax deductions as far as is necessary to cancel the increase in UK tax deductions attributable to the scheme.

The deductions rules apply if all of the following conditions are met:

(1) the transaction giving rise to the deduction is part of a scheme involving the use of a hybrid entity or hybrid instrument;

(2) the scheme is a 'qualifying scheme' (as defined in Sch 3) that allows the hybrid entity or hybrid instrument to create either a double deduction or a deduction not matched by a taxable receipt;

(3) the main purpose or one of the main purposes of the scheme is to obtain a UK tax advantage; and

(4) the UK tax advantage is more than a minimal amount.

If HMRC believe the above conditions are met they will issue a notice giving effect to the legislation. The company must then take account of the legislation in its self-assessment, 'which should reflect its own view of whether the legislation applies, and if so what effect it has' (per HMRC guidance notes).

25 Rules relating to deductions

(1) The following provisions of this section apply in relation to a transaction if—

    (*a*) a notice specifying the transaction is given to a company under section 24, and

    (*b*) when the notice is given, conditions A to D of section 24 are satisfied in relation to the transaction.

(2) The company must compute (or recompute) for the purposes of corporation tax its income or chargeable gains, or its liability to corporation tax—

    (*a*) for the accounting period specified in the notice under section 24, and

    (*b*) for any subsequent accounting period,

in accordance with rules A and B.

(3) Rule A is that, in respect of the specified transaction, no amount is allowable as a deduction for the purposes of the Corporation Tax Acts to the extent that, in relation to the expense in question, an amount may be otherwise deducted or allowed in computing the income, profits or losses of any person for the purposes of any tax (including any foreign tax) other than—

    (*a*) petroleum revenue tax, or

    (*b*) the tax chargeable under section 501A(1) of ICTA (supplementary charge in respect of ring fence trades).

(4) The reference in subsection (3) to an amount otherwise deducted or allowed in computing the income, profits or losses of any person for the purposes there mentioned includes a reference to an amount that would be so deducted or allowed but for any rule that has the same effect as rule A.

(5) For the purposes of subsection (4) "rule" means—

    (*a*) a provision of the Tax Acts, or

    (*b*) a rule having effect under the tax law of any territory outside the United Kingdom.

(6) Rule B applies if—

    (*a*) a transaction, or a series of transactions, forming part of the scheme by reference to which conditions A to D are satisfied makes or imposes provision as a result of which one person ("the payer") makes a payment and another person ("the payee") receives, or becomes entitled to receive, a payment or payments,

    (*b*) in respect of the payment by the payer, an amount may be deducted or otherwise allowed to the payer, or to another person who is party to, or concerned in, the scheme, in computing any profits or losses for tax purposes, and

    (*c*) in respect of the payment or payments that the payee receives or is entitled to receive as a result of the transaction or series of transactions, or part of such payment or payments, the payee is not liable to tax or, if liable, his liability to tax is reduced as a result of provision made or imposed by the scheme.

(7) Without prejudice to the generality of subsection (6)(*c*), the payee's liability to tax in respect of the payment or payments that he receives or is entitled to receive as a result of the transaction or series of transactions shall be treated for the purposes of subsection (6)(*c*) as reduced as a result of provision made or imposed by the scheme if—

    (*a*) an amount arising from the transaction or series of transactions forming part of the scheme, or from another transaction or series of transactions forming part of the scheme, falls to be deducted or otherwise allowed to the payee in computing for tax purposes any profits or losses arising from the payment or payments or the entitlement to receive the payment or payments, or

    (*b*) an amount of relief arising from the transaction or series of transactions forming part of the scheme, or from another transaction or series of transactions forming part of the scheme, may be deducted from the amount of income or gains arising from the payment or payments or the entitlement to receive the payment or payments.

(8) The requirement in subsection (6)(*c*) is not satisfied if the payee is not liable to tax because he is not liable to tax on any income or gains received by him or for his benefit under the tax law of any territory.

(9) The requirement in subsection (6)(*c*) is not satisfied if, or to the extent that, the payee is not subject to tax because his liability to tax is subject to an exemption falling within subsection (10).

(10) An exemption falls within this subsection if—

    (*a*) it exempts a person from being liable to tax in respect of income or gains, without providing for that income or those gains to be treated as the income or gains of one or more other persons, and

    (*b*) it is conferred by a provision contained in or having the force of an Act or by a provision of the tax law of any territory outside the United Kingdom.

(11) Rule B is that the aggregate of the amounts allowable as a deduction for the purposes of the Corporation Tax Acts in computing any profits to the company arising from—

(*a*) the specified transaction, and

(*b*) any other transaction that forms part of the scheme and to which the company is party,

is to be reduced in accordance with subsections (12) and (13).

(12) If, in respect of the payment or payments that the payee receives or is entitled to receive, the payee is not liable to tax for the purposes of the requirement in subsection (6)(*c*), the aggregate is to be reduced to nil.

(13) If, in respect of the payment or payments, the payee is liable to tax as regards part or his liability to tax is reduced as described in subsection (6)(*c*), the aggregate is to be reduced to such proportion of the aggregate as is equal to the proportion of the payment or payments on which the payee is liable to tax; and for this purpose the amount by which the payee's liability is reduced is to be treated as an amount on which the payee is not liable to tax.

(14) The company may choose to incorporate in its company tax return for the specified accounting period such relevant adjustments as are necessary for counteracting those effects of the scheme that are referable to the purpose referred to in condition C.

(15) If, as a consequence of incorporating relevant adjustments in that company tax return, the company counteracts those effects of the scheme that are referable to the purpose referred to in condition C, the company is to be treated, so far as regards the scheme, as having complied with subsection (2).

(16) The following are relevant adjustments—

(*a*) treating all or part of a deduction allowable for corporation tax purposes as not being allowable;

(*b*) treating all or part of an amount that for corporation tax purposes may be set off against profits in an accounting period as not falling to be set off.

(17) In this section, references to tax purposes include a reference to the purposes of any foreign tax; and foreign tax has the meaning given by section 403D of ICTA.

(18) In this section, "company tax return" means the return required to be delivered pursuant to a notice under paragraph 3 of Schedule 18 to FA 1998, as read with paragraph 4 of that Schedule.

GENERAL NOTE

Where the new legislation applies, the company concerned must compute its corporation tax liability in accordance with Rule A and Rule B.

Rule A

Rule A denies a corporation tax deduction to the extent that a deduction or allowance for the same expense would be allowed for the purposes of more than one tax code. In this context, 'tax' means a tax on profits or gains, but not indirect taxes.

As regards 'same expense', HMRC's guidance notes indicate that this does not extend to cover 'separate legal arrangements with a shared objective. For example, rental payments under a sub-lease are not the same expense as payments under a head lease, even though the asset subject to the lease may be the same in both cases or sequential leasing is part of an overall provision of an asset.'

HMRC concede that if a similar rule in another country's tax code would also act to deny a deduction, the legislation will still apply to the deduction in the UK, and that this may well give rise to a double disallowance.

Rule B

Rule B applies in certain circumstances where a payment qualifies for a tax deduction and either the payee is not taxed on the receipt, or the tax charge is reduced. The rule disallows the deduction to the extent that the payee is not effectively taxed on the receipt.

HMRC's guidance notes indicate that the exempt receipt need not be in respect of the same payment as gave rise to the UK tax deduction. 'For example, a UK resident company A makes a tax deductible payment to a non-resident company B, which is taxed on the receipt. B makes a matching payment to company C, whereby B obtains a tax deduction but C is not taxed on the receipt. In this example A is the payer and

C is the payee for the purposes of Rule B.' However, the tax-deductible payment and the untaxed receipt must arise out of the same transaction or series of transactions.

Rule B applies if the tax reduction results from any of the following circumstances:

(1) the income or gain is exempt from tax otherwise than by reason of a general exemption from tax for the payee (eg by way of a participation exemption);

(2) the income or gain is exempt from tax because of an exemption from income or gains that takes the form of taxing a different person in respect of the income or gain; or

(3) the income or gain is matched by a deduction or relief for the payee that arises from transactions forming part of the scheme.

Rule B does not apply where:

(1) the payee is generally exempt from tax and the payee's income or gains are not taxed as the income or gains of any other person;

(2) the payee is liable to tax but is covered by a statutory exemption. For example, charities and pension funds are within the scope of taxation but are not liable to tax as they benefit from a statutory exemption under many tax codes; or

(3) the payee has relief available to set off against the income and the relief does not arise as part of the scheme. For example, an arrangement would not be caught by the legislation simply because loss relief unrelated to the transactions in question was available to set off against income in computing the recipient's taxable income or profits.

Disclaimer

A company may disclaim relief for part or all of an expense in order to avoid an adjustment under the above rules (s 25(14)).

26 Receipts cases

(1) If the Commissioners for Her Majesty's Revenue and Customs consider, on reasonable grounds, that conditions A to E are or may be satisfied in relation to a company resident in the United Kingdom, they may give the company a notice under this section.

(2) Condition A is that a scheme makes or imposes provision ("the actual provision") as between the company and another person ("the paying party") by means of a transaction or series of transactions.

(3) Condition B is that the actual provision includes the making by the paying party, by means of a transaction or series of transactions, of a payment that is a qualifying payment in relation to the company.

(4) Condition C is that, as regards the qualifying payment made by the paying party, there is an amount that—

(*a*) is available as a deduction for the purposes of the Tax Acts, or

(*b*) may be deducted or otherwise allowed in respect of the payment under the tax law of any territory outside the United Kingdom,

and does not fall to be disregarded as described in subsection (5).

(5) An amount is to be disregarded if or to the extent that it is, for tax purposes, set against any income arising to the paying party from the transaction or transactions forming part of the scheme.

(6) Condition C is not to be treated as satisfied if—

(*a*) the paying party is a dealer,

(*b*) in the ordinary course of his business, he incurs losses in respect of the transaction or transactions forming part of the scheme to which he is party, and

(*c*) the amount by reference to which condition C would, but for this subsection, be satisfied is an amount in respect of those losses.

(7) In subsection (6), "dealer" means a person who is a dealer in relation to a distribution within the meaning of section 95(2) of ICTA or who would, if he were resident in the United Kingdom, be such a dealer.

(8) Condition D is that at least part of the qualifying payment is not an amount to which subsection (9) or (10) applies.

(9) This subsection applies to an amount that is, for the purposes of the Corporation Tax Acts—

(*a*) income or gains arising to the company in the accounting period in which the qualifying payment was made in relation to the company, or (*b*) income arising to any other company resident in the United Kingdom in a corresponding accounting period.

(10) This subsection applies to an amount that is taken into account in determining the debits and credits to be brought into account by a company for the purposes of Chapter 2 of Part 4 of FA 1996 as respects a share in another company by virtue of section 91A or 91B of FA 1996 (shares treated as loan relationships).

(11) Condition E is that the company and the paying party expected on entering into the scheme that a benefit would arise as a result of condition D being satisfied (whether by reference to all or part of the qualifying payment).

(12) A notice under this section is a notice—

(*a*) informing the company of the Commissioners' view under subsection (1),

(*b*) specifying the qualifying payment by reference to which the Commissioners consider conditions B to E are or may be satisfied,

(*c*) specifying the accounting period of the company in which the payment is made, and

(*d*) informing the company that as a consequence section 27 has effect in relation to the payment.

(13) For the purposes of this section a payment is a qualifying payment in relation to a company if it constitutes a contribution to the capital of the company.

(14) For the purposes of this section the accounting period of a company ("company A") corresponds to the accounting period of another company ("company B") if at least one day of company A's accounting period falls within company B's accounting period.

GENERAL NOTE

The receipts rules apply where a scheme involving a hybrid entity or hybrid instrument involves a UK-resident company receiving a sum that is not wholly chargeable to UK tax. Where the legislation applies, the effect will be that the receipt becomes chargeable.

The receipts rules apply if all of the following conditions are met:

(1) a company has entered into a scheme under which it receives an amount on which it is not liable to UK tax;

(2) that amount may be deducted from or allowed against taxable income of the person making the payment;

(3) the mismatch in tax treatment was expected by the parties to the scheme; and

(4) the payment constitutes a contribution to the capital of the company.

If HMRC believe the above conditions are met they will issue a notice giving effect to the legislation. The company must then take account of the legislation in its self-assessment.

27 Rule as to qualifying payment

(1) The following provisions of this section apply in relation to a payment that is a qualifying payment in relation to a company if—

(*a*) a notice specifying that payment is given to the company under section 26, and

(*b*) when the notice is given, conditions A to E of section 26 are satisfied in relation to the company.

(2) The company must compute (or recompute) for the purposes of corporation tax for the accounting period specified in the notice its income or chargeable gains, or its liability to corporation tax, as if the relevant part of the qualifying payment were an amount of income chargeable under Case VI of Schedule D arising to the company in that period.

(3) The relevant part of the qualifying payment is the part by reference to which conditions C and D are satisfied; and, where conditions C and D are satisfied in relation to the whole of the qualifying payment, the relevant part is the whole of the qualifying payment.

(4) In this section "qualifying payment" has the same meaning as in section 26.

GENERAL NOTE

Where HMRC issue a notice under s 26, the company must treat the relevant part of the receipt as income arising under Schedule D Case VI.

28 Notices under sections 24 and 26

(1) Subsection (2) applies if the Commissioners for Her Majesty's Revenue and Customs give a notice to a company under section 24 or 26 before the company has made its company tax return for the accounting period specified in the notice.

(2) If the company makes its return for that period before the end of the period of 90 days beginning with the day on which the notice is given, it may—

(a) make a return that disregards the notice, and

(b) at any time after making the return and before the end of the period of 90 days, amend the return for the purpose of complying with the provision referred to in the notice.

(3) If a company has made a company tax return for an accounting period, the Commissioners may only give the company a notice under section 24 or 26 in relation to that period if a notice of enquiry has been given to the company in respect of its return for that period.

(4) After any enquiries into the return for that period have been completed, the Commissioners may only give the company a notice under section 24 or 26 if the requirements in subsections (5) and (7) are satisfied.

(5) The first requirement is that at the time the enquiries into the return were completed, the Commissioners could not have been reasonably expected, on the basis of information made available to them or to an officer of Revenue and Customs before that time, to have been aware that the circumstances were such that a notice under section 24 or 26 could have been given to the company in relation to that period.

(6) Paragraph 44(2) and (3) of Schedule 18 to FA 1998 (information made available) applies for the purposes of subsection (5) as it applies for the purposes of paragraph 44(1).

(7) The second requirement is that—

(a) the company was requested to produce or provide information during an enquiry into the return for that period, and

(b) if the company had duly complied with the request, the Commissioners could reasonably have been expected to give the company a notice under section 24 or 26 in relation to that period.

(8) If a company is given a notice under section 24 or 26 in relation to an accounting period after having made a company tax return for that period, the company may amend the return for the purpose of complying with the provision referred to in the notice at any time before the end of the period of 90 days beginning with the day on which the notice is given.

(9) If the notice under section 24 or 26 is given to the company after it has been given a notice of enquiry in respect of its return for the period, no closure notice may be given in relation to the company's tax return until—

(a) the end of the period of 90 days beginning with the day on which the notice under section 24 or 26 is given, or

(b) the earlier amendment of the company tax return for the purpose of complying with the provision referred to in the notice.

(10) If the notice under section 24 or 26 is given to the company after any enquiries into the return for the period are completed, no discovery assessment may be made as regards the income or chargeable gain to which the notice relates until—

(a) the end of the period of 90 days beginning with the day on which the notice under section 24 or 26 is given, or

(b) the earlier amendment of the company tax return for the purpose of complying with the provision referred to in the notice.

(11) Subsections (2)(b) and (8) do not prevent a company tax return for a period becoming incorrect if—

(a) a notice under section 24 or 26 is given to the company in relation to that period,

(b) the return is not amended in accordance with subsection (2)(b) or (8) for the purpose of complying with the provision referred to in the notice, and

(c) the return ought to have been so amended.

(12) In this section—

"closure notice" means a notice under paragraph 32 of Schedule 18 to FA 1998;

"company tax return" means the return required to be delivered pursuant to a notice under paragraph 3 of Schedule 18 to FA 1998, as read with paragraph 4 of that Schedule;

"discovery assessment" means an assessment under paragraph 41 of Schedule 18 to FA 1998;

"notice of enquiry" means a notice under paragraph 24 of Schedule 18 to FA 1998.

GENERAL NOTE

This section sets out the interaction between the provisions for issuing a notice and the procedures relating to the filing of returns and amended returns, and the enquiries procedure.

HMRC's guidance indicates that, where a notice is issued, the company must consider what effect the legislation has on its tax liability in the same way as it considers any other relevant tax legislation, and should base its self-assessment on its own view of its tax liabilities as calculated, taking the new legislation into account. However, if a return is not made in accordance with a notice, or is not amended following the issue of a notice, then it may be regarded as being incorrect (s 28(11)).

The guidance includes the following statement:

After a notice has been given, a return or an amended return is incorrect if it fails properly to take account of the legislation. As usual, penalties in respect of an incorrect return arise only if the return was incorrect as a result of the fraudulent or negligent conduct of the company. If a company believed that the legislation did not apply, or that its effect differed from that finally determined, and this view resulted from a reasonable and tenable view of the law, then there would be no possibility of a penalty.

29 Amendments relating to company tax returns

(1) In Schedule 18 to FA 1998 (company tax returns, assessments, etc), in paragraph 25(1) (scope of enquiry) after "relief)" insert "or a notice under section 24 or 26 of the Finance (No. 2) Act 2005 (avoidance involving tax arbitrage)".

(2) In paragraph 42 of that Schedule (restrictions on power to make discovery assessment etc), in sub-paragraph (2A), after "1988" insert "or section 24 or 26 of the Finance (No. 2) Act 2005".

GENERAL NOTE

There are consequential amendments to FA 1998 Sch 18 (corporation tax self-assessment).

30 Interpretation

(1) For the purposes of this Chapter—

(a) references to a scheme are references to any scheme, arrangements or understanding of any kind whatever, whether or not legally enforceable, involving a single transaction or two or more transactions;

(b) it shall be immaterial in determining whether any transactions have formed or will form part of a series of transactions or scheme that the parties to any of the transactions are different from the parties to another of the transactions; and

(c) the cases in which any two or more transactions are to be taken as forming part of a series of transactions or scheme shall include any case in which it would be reasonable to assume that one or more of them—

(i) would not have been entered into independently of the other or others, or

(ii) if entered into independently of the other or others, would not have taken the same form or been on the same terms.

(2) For the purposes of this Chapter, a scheme achieves a UK tax advantage for a person if in consequence of the scheme the person is in a position to obtain, or has obtained—

(a) a relief or increased relief from income tax or corporation tax,

(b) a repayment or increased repayment of income tax or corporation tax, or

(c) the avoidance or reduction of a charge to income tax or corporation tax.

(3) In subsection (2)(a) the reference to relief includes a reference to a tax credit.

(4) For the purposes of subsection (2)(c) avoidance or reduction may in particular be effected by—

(a) receipts accruing in such a way that the recipient does not pay or bear tax on them, or

(b) a deduction in computing profits or gains.

GENERAL NOTE

'Scheme' is defined to include any arrangements or understanding of any kind, whether or not legally enforceable.

'Tax advantage' means obtaining any relief or increased relief from income tax or corporation tax, or a repayment or increased repayment, or the avoidance or reduction of a charge.

31 Commencement

(1) The deduction cases provisions have effect in relation to accounting periods of a company beginning on or after 16th March 2005.

(2) Where an accounting period of a company begins before, and ends on or after 16th March 2005, it shall be assumed for the purposes of the deduction cases provisions (and subsection (1) of this section) that that accounting period ("the straddling period") consists of two separate accounting periods—

    (*a*) the first beginning with the straddling period and ending with 15th March 2005, and

    (*b*) the second beginning with 16th March 2005 and ending with the straddling period,

and the company's profits and losses shall be computed accordingly for tax purposes.

(3) The deduction cases provisions do not have effect so far as regards a transaction to which a company is party on 16th March 2005 and which on that date forms part of a scheme, if—

    (*a*) the company is not on 16th March 2005 connected with a person who is on that date also party to, or concerned in, the scheme, and

    (*b*) the scheme ceases to exist before 31st August 2005.

Section 839 of ICTA applies for the purposes of this subsection.

(4) The receipts cases provisions have effect in relation to any contribution to the capital of a company resident in the United Kingdom that is made on or after 16th March 2005.

(5) In this section—

"the deduction cases provisions" means—

    (*a*) sections 24 and 25 and Schedule 3, and

    (*b*) sections 28 to 30 so far as relating to the provisions in paragraph (*a*);

"the receipts cases provisions" means—

    (*a*) sections 26 and 27, and

    (*b*) sections 28 to 30 so far as relating to the provisions in paragraph (*a*).

GENERAL NOTE

The rules apply to accounting periods commencing on or after 16 March 2005. There are rules for periods straddling that date.

CHAPTER 5

CHARGEABLE GAINS

Residence, location of assets etc

32 Temporary non-residents

(1) Section 10A of TCGA 1992 is amended as follows.

(2) In subsection (3) (certain gains or losses to be excluded from being treated by virtue of subsection (2) as accruing to the taxpayer in year of return)—

    (*a*) in paragraph (*a*), for "he was neither resident nor ordinarily resident in the United Kingdom" substitute—

        "(i) he was neither resident nor ordinarily resident in the United Kingdom, or

        (ii) he was resident or ordinarily resident in the United Kingdom but was Treaty non-resident;";

    (*b*) in paragraph (*d*), after "152(1)(*b*)" insert ", 153(1)(*b*)".

(3) In subsection (8) (definitions) in the definition of "relevant disposal", after "United Kingdom" insert "and was not Treaty non-resident".

(4) For subsection (9) substitute—

"(9) For the purposes of this section an individual satisfies the residence requirements for a year of assessment—

(*a*) if, during any part of that year of assessment, he is resident in the United Kingdom and not Treaty non-resident, or

(*b*) if he is ordinarily resident in the United Kingdom during that year of assessment, unless he is Treaty non-resident during that year of assessment.

(9A) For the purposes of this section an individual is Treaty non-resident at any time if, at that time, he falls to be regarded as resident in a territory outside the United Kingdom for the purposes of double taxation relief arrangements having effect at that time.

(9B) Where this section applies in the case of any individual in circumstances in which one or more intervening years would, but for his being Treaty non-resident during some or all of that year or those years, not be an intervening year, this section shall have effect in the taxpayer's case—

(*a*) as if subsection (2)(*a*) above did not apply in the case of any amount treated by virtue of section 87 or 89(2) as an amount of chargeable gains accruing to the taxpayer in any such intervening year, and

(*b*) as if any such intervening year were not an intervening year for the purposes of subsections (2)(*b*) and (*c*) and (6) above.".

(5) After subsection (9B) (as inserted by subsection (4) above) insert—

"(9C) Nothing in any double taxation relief arrangements shall be read as preventing the taxpayer from being chargeable to capital gains tax in respect of any of the chargeable gains treated by virtue of subsection (2)(*a*) above as accruing to the taxpayer in the year of return (or as preventing a charge to that tax from arising as a result).".

(6) Omit subsection (10) (section to be without prejudice to right to claim relief under double taxation relief arrangements).

(7) The amendments in subsections (2)(*a*), (4), (5) and (6) have effect—

(*a*) in any case in which the year of departure is, or (on the assumption that the amendment in subsection (4) had always had effect) would be, the year 2005–06 or a subsequent year of assessment; and

(*b*) in any case in which—

(i) the year of departure is, or (on that assumption) would be, the year 2004–05, and

(ii) at a time in that year on or after 16th March 2005, the taxpayer was resident or ordinarily resident in the United Kingdom and was not Treaty non-resident (within the meaning given by section 10A(9A) of TCGA 1992, as inserted by subsection (4)).

(8) The amendment in subsection (2)(*b*) has effect in relation to relevant disposals made on or after 16th March 2005.

(9) The amendment in subsection (3) has effect for determining whether a disposal of an asset is a relevant disposal for the purposes of section 10A of TCGA 1992 in any case in which the person making the disposal acquired the asset on or after 16th March 2005.

GENERAL NOTE

This section amends TCGA 1992 s 10A.

Background

TCGA 1992 s 10A was enacted in 1998. It applies where an individual is non-resident for less than five complete tax years and treats gains and losses realised during the years of absence as accruing in the tax year in which the individual returns. There are exceptions, notably for assets acquired during the period of absence and for individuals who were not long-term UK residents prior to departure.

Hitherto s 10A has been subject to any applicable double tax treaty (s 10A(10)) and has not applied to individuals who, even though remaining UK resident under UK domestic law, become non-resident under the tie-breaker clause in an applicable double tax treaty. It is those two features which are addressed by the present section.

Operative Provisions

The first substantive provision is that an individual is now treated as non-resident for the purposes of s 10A if he is either non-resident as a matter of domestic law or if he is non-resident under the tie-breaker clause in a treaty (sub-s(4)). If, under either of these tests, he is non-resident throughout a tax year, that year is a year of non-residence for the purposes of 10A. If there are fewer than five such years then, subject to the various exceptions noted above, s 10A applies in the year of return. However this deferral of gains and losses to the year of return does not apply to gains from non-resident trusts accruing under either the settlor or the beneficiary charges (TCGA 1992 ss 86 and 87) or to gains apportioned from non-resident companies (see s 13 above). These gains are, as before, only deferred to the year of return if in the year in which they accrue the individual is non-resident solely as a matter of UK domestic law (new s 10A(9B), inserted by sub-s (4)).

The second substantive provision is that double tax treaties are now prevented from precluding a charge under s 10A (sub-s (5)). The former rule in s 10A(10) allowing treaties to prevail is repealed (sub-s (6)).

Commencement

The changes made by this section apply where the year of departure is 2005–06 or a subsequent year (sub-s (7)). They also apply if the year of departure was 2004–05, but only if the individual became non-resident by virtue of the tie-breaker clause in a treaty after 16 March 2005 (sub-s(7)).

Minor Amendments

Sub-s (2) makes it clear that an asset is not outside s 10A if its acquisition cost is reduced by a partial roll-over claim (TCGA 1992 s 153) as well as by a complete roll-over claim (see s 152). It also makes it clear that an asset is protected from the s 10A charge if (subject to the exceptions specified in s 10A(3)) if it is acquired at a time of non-residence under a treaty as well as at a time of non-residence under domestic law.

33 Trustees both resident and non-resident in a year of assessment
(1) After section 83 of TCGA 1992 insert—

"83A Trustees both resident and non-resident in a year of assessment
(1) This section applies if a chargeable gain accrues to the trustees of a settlement on the disposal by them of an asset in a year of assessment and the trustees—
    (a) are within the charge to capital gains tax in that year of assessment, but
    (b) are non-UK resident at the time of the disposal.

(2) Where this section applies, nothing in any double taxation relief arrangements shall be read as preventing the trustees from being chargeable to capital gains tax (or as preventing a charge to tax arising, whether or not on the trustees) by virtue of the accrual of that gain.

(3) For the purposes of this section the trustees of a settlement are within the charge to capital gains tax in a year of assessment—
    (a) if, during any part of that year of assessment, they are resident in the United Kingdom and not Treaty non-resident, or
    (b) if they are ordinarily resident in the United Kingdom during that year of assessment, unless they are Treaty non-resident during that year of assessment.

(4) For the purposes of this section the trustees of a settlement are non-UK resident at a particular time if, at that time,—
    (a) they are neither resident nor ordinarily resident in the United Kingdom, or
    (b) they are resident or ordinarily resident in the United Kingdom but are Treaty non-resident.

(5) For the purposes of this section the trustees of a settlement are Treaty non-resident at any time if, at that time, they fall to be regarded as resident in a territory outside the United Kingdom for the purposes of double taxation relief arrangements having effect at that time.".

(2) The amendment made by this section has effect in relation to disposals made on or after 16th March 2005.

GENERAL NOTE

This section disapplies any exemption from UK CGT otherwise conferred on trustees by a double tax treaty in certain limited circumstances. It does so by inserting a new s 83A into TCGA 1992.

To understand s 83A it is necessary to recall three basic CGT rules. The first is that the trustees of a settlement are treated as a single continuing body of persons (TCGA 1992 s 69). In other words they are a single taxable entity regardless of who the actual trustees are from time to time. The second is that that entity, like any other non-corporate person, is subject to CGT on gains realised during a tax year if it is resident in the UK during any part of the year (TCGA 1992 s 2). The third is that CGT is subject to applicable double tax treaties. As a general rule a taxable entity which is resident in the treaty territory under the residency rules in the treaty is not subject to CGT save as respects certain UK situs assets.

Section 83A deals with the position when trustees realise a gain at a time when they are either non-resident under UK domestic law or, although resident under UK domestic law, non-resident by virtue of the tie breaker clause in an applicable treaty. It prevents the treaty from applying to the gain if at any time in the tax year in which the gain is realised the trustees are "within charge to capital gains tax". By within charge to capital gains tax is meant resident in the UK under UK domestic law and not (if the treaty is then applicable) non-resident under the tie breaker clause in the treaty.

Section 83A blocks CGT avoidance schemes involving changes of trustee residence part way during the tax year. Many such schemes involved Mauritius, although the UK/Mauritius treaty was recently amended to prevent Mauritius being used in this way.

Commencement

This section applies to disposals on or after 16 March 2005 (sub-s (2)).

34 Location of assets etc

Schedule 4 (which makes provision in relation to the situation of assets for the purposes of TCGA 1992 and which makes minor amendments in that Act in relation to non-resident companies with United Kingdom permanent establishments) has effect.

GENERAL NOTE

This section introduces Sch 4.

Miscellaneous

35 Exercise of options etc

Schedule 5 (which makes provision, for the purposes of the taxation of chargeable gains, in relation to options) has effect.

GENERAL NOTE

This section introduces Sch 5. These provisions are intended to counter a 'defect' in the legislation regarding options, which could enable chargeable gains to be avoided, or capital losses to be created without incurring a corresponding commercial loss. The rules apply mainly to options exercised from 2 December 2004.

36 Notional transfers within a group

(1) Section 171A of TCGA 1992 (notional transfers within a group) is amended as follows.

(2) After subsection (3) insert—

"(3ZA) In a case where B—

(*a*) is not resident in the United Kingdom, but

(*b*) is carrying on a trade in the United Kingdom through a permanent establishment there, the asset or part deemed to be transferred to B by A is to be treated for the purposes of subsections (2)(*c*) and (3) above as having been acquired by B for use by or for the purposes of the permanent establishment; but that shall not be taken to affect the question whether or not the asset or part is situated in the United Kingdom at any time.".

(3) The amendment made by this section has effect in relation to disposals made on or after 16th March 2005.

GENERAL NOTE

The scope of TCGA 1992 s 171A (Notional transfers within a group) is extended, to allow group companies to elect for the disposal of an asset to be treated as made by a non-UK resident group member carrying on a trade in the UK through a permanent establishment, rather than by the company that owned the asset. A new sub-s 3ZA is inserted in TCGA 1992 s 171A to this effect, in relation to disposals made from 16 March 2005. This rule potentially provides the non-UK resident company with the opportunity to utilise capital losses against a gain on the disposal of an asset, or to offset a loss on the disposal of an asset against capital gains made by the non-UK resident company in the current or future accounting periods.

CHAPTER 6

MISCELLANEOUS

Accounting practice and related matters

37 Accounting practice and related matters

Schedule 6 (accounting practice and related matters) has effect.

GENERAL NOTE

This section introduces Sch 6, which contains provisions on accounting practice and other matters principally related to the adoption of International Accounting Standards. Individual companies are permitted, but not required, to adopt IAS for accounting periods beginning on or after 1 January 2005. Accounts prepared under IAS will be accepted as complying with Generally Accepted Accounting Practice, and therefore as a valid basis for computation of profit for corporation tax. FA 2004 ss 50–52 and FA 2005 ss 80–84 contain the general rules and address special cases.

Schedule 6 refines or repeals and replaces parts of the existing legislation, addresses concerns relating to convertibles, derivatives and hedging, and gives the Treasury powers to make regulations relating to derivatives or fair value accounting which may take effect from 1 January 2005.

Financial avoidance etc

38 Charges on income for the purposes of corporation tax

(1) Section 338A of ICTA (meaning of "charges on income" for the purposes of corporation tax) is amended as follows.

(2) In subsection (2) (what are charges on income) paragraph (*a*) (annuities or other annual payments that meet the conditions in section 338B) shall cease to have effect.

(3) In section 125(1) of ICTA (annual payments for non-taxable consideration) for "income tax," substitute "income tax and".

(4) In section 434A(2)(*a*) of ICTA (loss resulting to insurance company from computation in accordance with Case I of Schedule D: reduction by specified amounts) omit sub-paragraph (i) (which relates to charges on income).

(5) The side-note to section 494 of ICTA (charges on income) becomes "Loan relationships etc.".

(6) The amendment made by subsection (4) has effect for accounting periods beginning on or after 1st April 2004.

(7) The other amendments made by this section have effect in relation to payments made on or after the commencement date in respect of annuities or other annual payments.

(8) Where—

(*a*) an accounting period of a company begins before, and ends on or after, the commencement date,

(*b*) a payment in respect of an annuity or other annual payment is made by the company in that period but before the commencement date, and

(*c*) the payment is deductible as a charge on income for the purposes of corporation tax,

subsection (9) applies.

(9) In any such case, so much of any amount as represents that payment—

(*a*) is not deductible under section 75 of ICTA (expenses of management), and

(*b*) is not to be brought into account under section 76 of that Act (expenses of insurance companies) as expenses payable,

for that or any subsequent accounting period.

(10) Subsection (12) applies in any case where—

(*a*) a payment in respect of an annuity or other annual payment is made by a company on or after the commencement date, and

(*b*) the condition in subsection (11) is satisfied.

(11) The condition is that the payment represents an amount which (apart from subsection (12))—

(*a*) would not be deductible under section 75 of ICTA, or

(*b*) would not fall to be brought into account under section 76 of that Act,

by reason only of section 337A(1)(*b*) of that Act (company's income from any source to be computed without any deduction in respect of charges on income) as it applies by virtue of section 338A(2)(*a*) of that Act.

(12) In any such case, the amount represented by the payment—

(*a*) is deductible under section 75 of ICTA, or

(*b*) falls to be brought into account under section 76 of that Act as expenses payable,

for the accounting period in which the payment is made.

(13) In this section "the commencement date" means 16th March 2005.

GENERAL NOTE

This section removes annuities and other annual payments from the scope of "charges on income" for the purposes of corporation tax (TA 1988 s 388A). Any such payments incurred for a business purpose will fall to be deducted as expenses of management. Charitable payments continue to be treated as charges on income.

Annuities and annual payments are removed from TA 1988 s 338A(2)(a) and therefore no longer count as charges on income in any case where they are not deductible in computing the profits of a trade. The only types of payment that remain deductible as charges on income are charitable donations (under gift aid) and gifts of shares to charity within TA 1988 s 587B. Section 338A(4) (insurance companies – exceptions from treating annuities as charges on income) is also repealed as unnecessary (Sch 11 Pt 2(7)).

Subsection (3) amends TA 1988 s 125. That section denies relief for annuities and other annual payments not made for a taxable consideration. The amendment, taken with the repeals, has the effect that, for corporation tax purposes, TA 1988 s 125 has effect only where the question is whether an annual payment is deductible in computing income such as the profits of a trade or the profits of a company with investment business.

Where an accounting period of a company straddles Budget Day (16 March 2005), and a payment is made before Budget Day which is deductible as a charge on income, special commencement rules apply. Because charges are deductible when paid and management expenses and expenses payable under TA 1988 s 76 on the basis of accounting recognition, sub-s (9) provides that no deduction is to be given under s 75 or 76 for any amount already relieved as a charge on income.

Conversely, where a payment of an annuity or annual payment is made on or after Budget Day (16 march 2005) and the payment would have been deducted under TA 1988 s 75 or 76, the amount may be deducted under s 75 or 76 for the accounting period in which the payment is made. This rule will apply to payments made after they are accrued in a company's accounts.

BACKGROUND NOTE

FA 1996 and subsequent Finance Acts removed many of the charges on income in TA 1988 s 338 (as it then stood) that could be set off against profits for the purposes of corporation tax, including annual interest. Charges that remained are:

– annuities and other annual payments (not paid by trading companies);

– qualifying donations within TA 1988 s 339; and

– amounts falling with TA 1988 s 587B (gifts of assets to charity).

Certain disclosures under FA 2004 Part 7 (the disclosure rules) have shown that annual payments are being used in schemes to create an artificial deduction which is not matched by any taxable income.

The Government is acting in advance of any decision on corporation tax reform. At this stage, however, the concept of charges on income is being retained to deal with qualifying donations to charity and payments under TA 1988 s 587B, pending the outcome of the consultation on the Pre-Budget Report (2 December 2004) Technical Note on corporation tax reform.

39 Avoidance involving financial arrangements

Schedule 7 (which makes provision in relation to tax avoidance involving financial arrangements) has effect.

GENERAL NOTE

This section introduces Sch 7.

Financing of companies etc

40 Transfer pricing and loan relationships

Schedule 8 (which amends Schedule 28AA to ICTA and Schedule 9 to FA 1996) has effect.

GENERAL NOTE

This section introduces Sch 8.

Intangible fixed assets

41 Intangible fixed assets

(1) Schedule 29 to FA 2002 (gains and losses of a company from intangible fixed assets) is amended as set out in subsections (2) to (4).

(2) In paragraph 92 (transfer between company and related party treated as being at market value)—

(*a*) in sub-paragraph (1), for "the following two exceptions" substitute "the following four exceptions";

(*b*) after sub-paragraph (4) insert—

"(4A) The third exception is where—

(*a*) the asset is transferred from the company at less than its market value, or to the company at more than its market value,

(*b*) the related party—

(i) is not a company, or

(ii) is a company in relation to which the asset is not a chargeable intangible asset immediately after the transfer to it or (as the case may be) immediately before the transfer from it,

and

(*c*) by virtue of any provision of—

(i) section 209 of the Taxes Act 1988 (meaning of "distribution"), or

(ii) Part 3 of the Income Tax (Earnings and Pensions) Act 2003 (employment income: earnings and benefits etc treated as earnings), the transfer gives rise (or would give rise but for sub-paragraph (1)) to an amount to be taken into account in computing any person's income, profits or losses for tax purposes.

(4B) Where the third exception applies, sub-paragraph (1) does not apply, in relation to the computation mentioned in sub-paragraph (4A)(*c*), for the purposes of any such provision as is mentioned there.

(4C) The fourth exception is where—

 (*a*) the asset is transferred to the company, and
 (*b*) on a claim for relief under section 165 of the Taxation of Chargeable Gains Act 1992 (relief for gifts of business assets) in respect of the transfer, a reduction is made under subsection (4)(*a*) of that section.

(4D) Where the fourth exception applies—

 (*a*) the transfer is treated for the purposes of this Schedule as being at market value less the amount of the reduction;
 (*b*) all such adjustments as may be required, by way of assessment, amendment of returns or otherwise, may be made (notwithstanding any time limit on the making of an assessment or the amendment of a return).".

(3) In paragraph 95 (meaning of "related party") for Case Three substitute—

"Case Three

C is a close company and P is, or is an associate of—

 (*a*) a participator in C, or
 (*b*) a participator in a company that has control of, or holds a major interest in, C.".

(4) In paragraph 132 (roll-over relief: transitory interaction with relief on replacement of business asset), in sub-paragraph (5) (disapplication for certain corporation tax purposes of Classes 4 to 7 in section 155 of TCGA 1992)—

 (*a*) for "4 to 7" substitute "4 to 7A";
 (*b*) for "(goodwill and various types of quota)" substitute "(goodwill and certain other intangible assets)".

(5) In section 86(2) of FA 1993 (roll-over relief: power to amend section 155 of TCGA 1992 by order) for the words after "may make such consequential amendments" substitute "of—

 (*a*) Schedule 7AB to the Taxation of Chargeable Gains Act 1992, or
 (*b*) paragraph 132 of Schedule 29 to the Finance Act 2002,

as appear to the Treasury to be appropriate.".

(6) The amendments made by subsection (2) have effect in relation to any transfer of an asset made on or after 16th March 2005.

(7) The amendment made by subsection (3) has effect, for the purposes of paragraph 92 of Schedule 29 to FA 2002 as it applies otherwise than for determining the debits or credits to be brought into account under that Schedule, in relation to any transfer of an asset made on or after 16th March 2005.

(8) That amendment has effect, for all other purposes of that Schedule, in relation to the debits or credits to be brought into account for accounting periods beginning on or after 16th March 2005 (and, in relation to the debits or credits to be brought into account for any such period, shall be deemed always to have had effect).

(9) An accounting period beginning before, and ending on or after, that date is treated for the purposes of subsection (8) as if so much of that period as falls before that date, and so much of that period as falls on or after that date, were separate accounting periods.

(10) The amendments made by subsection (4) have effect in relation to any such acquisition as is referred to in paragraph 132(5) of Schedule 29 to FA 2002 made on or after 22nd March 2005.

GENERAL NOTE

This section amends the legislation dealing with companies' intangible fixed assets as set out in FA 2002 Sch 29.

Two new exceptions

It inserts two further exceptions to the rule in FA 2002 Sch 29 para 92.

Paragraph 92 provides that transfers between related parties are treated as taking place at market value. This is an exception to the general rule that tax is based on the expense of creating the intangible fixed assets. The previous exemptions related to transfer pricing and any other rule under Sch 29 treating a transfer as tax neutral.

The first new exemption applies when a transfer occurs that shifts the value out of the company, the other party is not within the intangible fixed assets charging regime and the transfer is chargeable to tax as a distribution or as employment income, in which case the market value rule does not apply for the purposes of calculating either of those tax charges.

The second new exemption applies if the parties are related and the transferee claims capital gains tax holdover relief. In these circumstances, for the purposes of the intangible fixed assets regime, the transfer is deemed to take place at an amount equal to the market value less than the amount held over. The provision permits any required adjustments to returns, which appears extremely broad. However, the intention is that an amount equal to the held-over gain is eventually taxed on the company under Sch 29.

For the purposes of the intangible fixed assets regime, FA 2002 Sch 29 para 95 sets out the circumstances in which a person "P" is related to the relevant company (C) by reference to three cases. Subsection (3) substitutes a new case three for the existing case three in para 95. Case three referred to a participator in C or an associate of such a participator. The new case three extends the definition also to include those who participate in, or are associated with, a company that controls the relevant company.

TA 1988 s 417 defines "associate" and "participator" (FA 2002 Sch 29 para 100(1) excludes a loan creditor form the definition of participator, for these purposes).

TA 1988 ss 414–415 define "close company".

These amendments come into effect for transfers made on or after Budget day (16 March 2005). So, for example, parties that become related by virtue of the amendment may lose their entitlement to credits and debits in relation to any transfer before 16 March 2005. The new section provides a mechanism to identify credits and debits to be accounted for as a result of this amendment which is to deem the end of the accounting period and the commencement of a new accounting period.

Rollover relief

TCGA 1992 ss 152–153 provide for rollover relief for capital gains tax purposes. TCGA 1992 s 155 defines the classes of assets qualifying for rollover relief. FA 2002 Sch 2 para 132 limits the availability of the rollover relief in respect of assets within the intangible assets regime. This new section adds to that list the entitlement to payment under the single payment scheme for farmers (for details of the Single Payment Scheme, see Tolley's Practical Tax, 29 July 2005, Vol 26 No 16). Council Regulation (EC) No 1782/2003 introduced that scheme. The Finance Act 1993, Section 86(2), (Single Payment Scheme) Order, SI 2005/409 added the payments to the list in s 155, with effect from 22 March 2005.

This addition of the new category of assets comes into force with effect from 22 March 2005.

The section also provides for further categories of excluded assets to be added to s155 and Sch 7AB and consequential changes to be made to Sch 29.

Insurance companies etc

42 Insurance companies etc

Schedule 9 (which makes provision about insurance companies etc) has effect.

GENERAL NOTE

Section 42 introduces Sch 9 which makes a number of changes to the regime for taxing life insurance companies. Schedule 9 introduces two significant measures designed to counter tax planning; the first on a transfer of insurance business from one company to another, the second by way of prescriptive rules for determining which accounts in an insurer's regulatory return are recognised for tax purposes. The Schedule also introduces a regulation making power allowing amendment of the apportionment rules and makes a number of minor changes to existing legislation, some of which deal with alterations to the regulatory regime by the FSA and others which tidy up inconsistencies and uncertainties stemming from recent changes.

International matters

43 Implementation of the amended Parent/Subsidiary Directive

(1) Section 801 of ICTA (dividends paid between related companies: relief for UK and third country taxes) is amended as follows.

(2) After subsection (5) (meaning of one company being related to another) insert—

"(5A) For the purposes of subsections (2) and (3) above (including any determination of the extent to which underlying tax paid by the third, fourth or subsequent company in question would be taken into account under this Part if the conditions specified for the purpose in subsection (2) above were satisfied) a company is also related to another company if that other company—

(a) controls directly or indirectly, or

(b) is a subsidiary of a company which controls directly or indirectly,

not less than 10% of the ordinary share capital of the first-mentioned company.".

(3) The amendment made by this section has effect where the dividend mentioned in section 799(1) of ICTA is paid on or after 1st January 2005.

GENERAL NOTE

There is a consequential amendment to the 10% holding test for entitlement to underlying tax relief on foreign company dividends (TA 1988 s 801). The test can now be met if the recipient company holds at least 10% of the ordinary share capital of the paying company. This is an alternative to the '10% of the voting power' test.

44 Territories with a lower level of taxation: reduction of amount of local tax

(1) Section 750 of ICTA (controlled foreign companies: territories with a lower level of taxation) is amended as follows.

(2) In subsection (1), after "if" insert ", after giving effect to subsections (1A) and (1B) below,".

(3) After subsection (1) insert—

"(1A) If in the case of that accounting period there is any income, or any income and any expenditure, of the company—

(a) which is brought into account in determining the profits of the company in respect of which tax is paid under the law of that territory, but

(b) which does not also fall to be brought into account in determining the chargeable profits of the company,

the local tax shall be treated for the purposes of this Chapter as reduced to what it would have been had that income and any such expenditure not been so brought into account.

(1B) If—

(a) under the law of that territory any tax ("the company's tax") falls to be paid by the company in respect of profits of the company arising in that accounting period,

(b) under that law, any repayment of tax, or any payment in respect of a credit for tax, is made to a person other than the company, and

(c) that payment or repayment is directly or indirectly in respect of the company's tax,

the local tax shall be treated for the purposes of this Chapter as reduced (or further reduced) by the amount of that payment or repayment.".

(4) The amendments made by this section have effect in relation to accounting periods of companies resident outside the United Kingdom beginning on or after 2nd December 2004.

(5) Where an accounting period of a company resident outside the United Kingdom—

(a) would, without amendment, have ended on or after 2nd December 2004, but

(b) is amended on or after that date so as to end before that date,

an accounting period of the company shall be deemed for the purposes of Chapter 4 of Part 17 of ICTA to have ended with 1st December 2004.

(6) In this section "accounting period" has the same meaning as in Chapter 4 of Part 17 of ICTA (see section 751).

GENERAL NOTE

This section tightens up the rules on controlled foreign companies (CFCs) rules in two ways:

(1) In determining whether a CFC is subject to a lower level of taxation, if any income that is subject to foreign tax is not included in the CFC's chargeable profits, the foreign tax is left out of account.

(2) Where foreign tax paid by one company is repaid to an associated person, that tax is left out of account.

Miscellaneous

45 Lloyd's underwriters: assessment and collection of tax

(1) Omit section 173 of, and Schedule 19 to, FA 1993 (Lloyd's underwriters: assessment and collection of tax).

(2) In section 182 of that Act (regulations) in subsection (1)(*a*) (power of Commissioners for Her Majesty's Revenue and Customs to make regulations providing for assessment and collection of tax charged in accordance with section 171 of FA 1993, so far as not provided for by Schedule 19 to that Act) omit "(so far as not provided for by Schedule 19 to this Act)".

(3) In that section, at the end insert—

"(6) Any power to make regulations conferred by this section includes power to make—

(*a*) different provision for different cases or different purposes, and

(*b*) incidental, supplemental or transitional provision and savings.".

(4) Omit section 221 of FA 1994 (Lloyd's underwriters: corporations etc: assessment and collection of tax).

(5) Renumber section 229 of that Act (regulations) as subsection (1) of that section.

(6) In subsection (1) of that section (as amended by subsection (5) above), in paragraph (*a*) (power of Commissioners for Her Majesty's Revenue and Customs to make regulations providing for assessment and collection of tax charged in accordance with section 219 of FA 1994, so far as not provided for by Schedule 19 to FA 1993 as applied by section 221 of FA 1994) omit "(so far as not provided for by Schedule 19 to the 1993 Act as applied by section 221 above)".

(7) In that section, at the end insert—

"(2) Any power to make regulations conferred by this section includes power to make—

(*a*) different provision for different cases or different purposes, and

(*b*) incidental, supplemental or transitional provision and savings.".

(8) For the purpose of enabling the making of any regulations under—

(*a*) section 182(1)(*a*) of FA 1993 (as amended by subsection (2)), or

(*b*) section 229(1)(*a*) of FA 1994 (as amended by subsection (6)),

subsections (1) to (7) come into force on the day on which this Act is passed.

(9) Subject to that, those subsections come into force in accordance with provision made by the Treasury by order.

(10) Section 828(3) of ICTA shall not apply in relation to an order under subsection (9).

(11) The Commissioners for Her Majesty's Revenue and Customs may by regulations make such amendments, repeals or revocations in any enactment (including an enactment amended by this section) as appear to them to be appropriate in consequence of any one or more of the following—

(*a*) any amendment made by this section;

(*b*) the exercise by them of the power in section 182(1)(*a*) of FA 1993 (as amended by subsection (2));

(*c*) the exercise by them of the power in section 229(1)(*a*) of FA 1994 (as amended by subsection (6)).

(12) Any power conferred by this section to make an order or regulations includes power to make—

(*a*) different provision for different cases or different purposes, and (*b*) incidental, supplemental or transitional provision and savings.

(13) In this section—

"enactment" includes an enactment comprised in subordinate legislation;

"subordinate legislation" has the same meaning as in the Interpretation Act 1978 (c. 30) (see section 21 of that Act).

GENERAL NOTE

This measure amends the regulation-making powers in relation to Lloyd's underwriters, primarily in order to permit the repeal of Finance Act 1993 s 173, Sch 19 and replace them with regulations made by statutory instrument. This allows for greater flexibility when amending and modernising the current procedures by, for example, allowing for electronic filing of syndicate returns and by applying self-assessment principles to the determination of syndicate profits. (Lloyd's managing agents are required to make returns to HM Revenue and Customs of syndicate profits and losses, computed for tax purposes.) This measure will apply to regulations made on or after 20 July 2005.

46 Energy Act 2004 and Health Protection Agency Act 2004

(1) This section provides for certain enactments to cease to have effect which relate to—

(*a*) the United Kingdom Atomic Energy Authority ("UKAEA"),

(*b*) the National Radiological Protection Board ("NRPB"), or

(*c*) pension schemes run by UKAEA.

(2) In ICTA the following provisions shall cease to have effect—

(*a*) section 349B(3)(*g*) (no deduction of tax from certain payments to UKAEA);

(*b*) section 349B(3)(*h*) (no deduction of tax from certain payments to NRPB);

(*c*) section 512(1) and (3) (certain exemptions from income tax and corporation tax for UKAEA and NRPB);

(*d*) section 512(2) (treatment of certain income of pension schemes run by UKAEA).

(3) In section 271(7) of TCGA 1992 (miscellaneous exemptions from tax in respect of chargeable gains)—

(*a*) for "Memorial Fund, the" substitute "Memorial Fund and the";

(*b*) omit ", the United Kingdom Atomic Energy Authority";

(*c*) omit "and the National Radiological Protection Board";

(*d*) omit from "; and for the purposes" to the end of the subsection (treatment of gains accruing to pension schemes run by UKAEA).

(4) In subsection (2)—

(*a*) paragraph (*a*) has effect in relation to payments made on or after 1st April 2005;

(*b*) paragraph (*b*) has effect in relation to payments made after 1st April 2005;

(*c*) paragraph (*c*), so far as relating to UKAEA, has effect on and after 1st April 2005;

(*d*) paragraph (*c*), so far as relating to NRPB, has effect after 1st April 2005;

(*e*) paragraph (*d*) has effect in relation to income arising on or after 1st April 2005.

(5) In subsection (3)—

(*a*) paragraphs (*a*) and (*c*) have effect in relation to gains accruing after 1st April 2005;

(*b*) paragraphs (*b*) and (*d*) have effect in relation to gains accruing on or after 1st April 2005.

(6) The repeal of subsection (3)(*g*) of section 349B of ICTA does not affect the application of any other provision of that section in relation to UKAEA.

(7) Nothing in this section affects—

(*a*) any accounting period of UKAEA ending before 1st April 2005, or

(*b*) any accounting period of NRPB ending on or before 1st April 2005.

GENERAL NOTE

The Energy Act 2004 changes the management of public sector civil nuclear liabilities. As a consequence the role of the United Kingdom Atomic Energy Authority (UKAEA) in relation to nuclear decommissioning has changed significantly. The Health Protection Agency Act 2004 created a new Health Protection Agency, taking over the functions of the National Radiological Protection Board (NRPB), which in turn has ceased to exist.

As a consequence of changes made in the Energy Act 2004 and the Health Protection Agency Act 2004, exemptions and redundant provisions relating to the UKAEA and NRPB are removed. In particular the removal of the exemptions for the UKAEA reflects its changed role following the creation of the Nuclear Decommissioning Authority.

In the case of UKAEA, these changes apply for payments made or gains accrued on or after 1 April 2005. For the NRPB the changes apply after 1 April 2005. These minor differences reflect the fact that the UKAEA will continue but the NRPB will cease to exist (sub-ss (4) and (5)). None of these changes affects any accounting period of the UKAEA ending before 1 April 2005 or any accounting period of the NRPB ending on or before 1 April 2005.

TA 1988 s 349B(3)(g) and (h), which provide exemption from deduction of income tax from certain property and investment income of the UKAEA and the NRPB cease to apply. Similarly, TA 1988 s 512(1) and (3) (certain exemptions from income tax and corporation tax for UKAEA and NRPB no longer apply; nor does TA 1988 s 512(2) (treatment of certain income of pension schemes run by the UKAEA (for payments made on or after 1 April 2005)). In practice this has no effect because the schemes remain subject to the normal rules for pension schemes.

The removal of TA 1988 s 349B(3)(g) does not effect the application of TA 1988 s 349B generally in relation to payments made to the UKAEA, which are treated like payments to other companies when payers decide if they need to deduct tax.

The equivalent exemptions from tax on chargeable gains, given by TCGA 1992 s 271(1), are also withdrawn.

PART 3

STAMP TAXES

Stamp duty land tax

47 E-conveyancing

(1) In section 9(1) of the Public Finance and Accountability (Scotland) Act 2000 (asp 1) (Keeper of the Registers of Scotland: financial arrangements) after "Sums" insert "(other than payments of stamp duty land tax)".

(2) In section 79(1) of FA 2003 (registration of land transactions) after "in relation to the transaction" insert "or such information about compliance as the Commissioners for Her Majesty's Revenue and Customs may specify in regulations."

(3) In section 119(1) of FA 2003 (land transactions: effective date) for "the date of completion" substitute—

"(*a*) the date of completion, or
(*b*) such alternative date as the Commissioners for Her Majesty's Revenue and Customs may prescribe by regulations."

(4) After paragraph 7(1) of Schedule 10 to FA 2003 (land transaction returns: correction of errors) insert—

"(1A) The power under sub-paragraph (1) may, in such circumstances as the Commissioners for Her Majesty's Revenue and Customs may specify in regulations, be exercised—

(*a*) in relation to England and Wales, by the Chief Land Registrar;
(*b*) in relation to Scotland, by the Keeper of the Registers of Scotland;
(*c*) in relation to Northern Ireland, by the Registrar of Titles or the registrar of deeds;
(*d*) in any case, by such other persons with functions relating to the registration of land as the regulations may specify."

(5) The Commissioners for Her Majesty's Revenue and Customs—

(*a*) may make regulations conferring administrative functions on a land registrar in connection with stamp duty land tax, and
(*b*) may make payments to land registrars in respect of the exercise of those functions.

(6) In subsection (5) "land registrar" means—

(*a*) in relation to England and Wales, the Chief Land Registrar,
(*b*) in relation to Scotland, the Keeper of the Registers of Scotland,
(*c*) in relation to Northern Ireland, the Registrar of Titles or the registrar of deeds, and

(*d*) in any case, such other persons with functions relating to the registration of land as regulations under subsection (5) may specify.

(7) Regulations under subsection (5)—

(*a*) shall be made by statutory instrument, and

(*b*) shall be subject to annulment in pursuance of a resolution of the House of Commons.

GENERAL NOTE

Section 47 is an enabling section connected with electronic conveyancing and its impact on SDLT. E-conveyancing envisages title transfer being effected electronically. Accordingly s 47 introduces regulation making powers (including the power for HMRC to make payments to land registrars (as defined in sub-s (6)); in Scotland enables such amounts received by the Keeper of Registers as are referable to SDLT – as opposed to fees – to be handed over to HMRC; confers a power on land registrars to correct errors, where permitted by regulations; enables a different date of completion to be prescribed, relevant to FA 2003 s 119; and facilitates the provision of information in a form other than a certificate from HMRC.

48 Disclosure of information contained in land transaction returns

(1) After section 78 of FA 2003 insert—

"78A Disclosure of information contained in land transaction returns

(1) Relevant information contained in land transaction returns delivered under section 76 (whether before or after the commencement of this section) is to be available for use—

(*a*) by listing officers appointed under section 20 of the Local Government Finance Act 1992, for the purpose of facilitating the compilation and maintenance by them of valuation lists in accordance with Chapter 2 of Part 1 of that Act,

(*b*) as evidence in an appeal by virtue of section 24(6) of that Act to a valuation tribunal established under Schedule 11 to the Local Government Finance Act 1988,

(*c*) by the Commissioner of Valuation for Northern Ireland, for the purpose of maintaining a valuation list prepared, and from time to time altered, by him in accordance with Part 3 of the Rates (Northern Ireland) Order 1977, and

(*d*) by such other persons or for such other purposes as the Treasury may by regulations prescribe.

(2) In this section, "relevant information" means any information of the kind mentioned in paragraph 1(4) of Schedule 10 (information corresponding to particulars required under previous legislation).

(3) The Treasury may by regulations amend the definition of relevant information in subsection (2)."

(2) In section 245 of FA 1994 (production of documents: supplementary) for subsection (2) substitute—

"(2) The information contained in any document produced to the Commissioners under section 244(2) above shall be available for use by the Commissioner of Valuation for Northern Ireland."

(3) For the heading to Part 6 of FA 1994 substitute "Stamp duty".

(4) Regulation 3 of the Stamp Duty Land Tax (Consequential Amendment of Enactments) Regulations 2005 (S. I. 2005/82) is hereby revoked.

(5) Subsections (1) to (4) come into force on such day as the Treasury may by order appoint.

(6) Section 114(3) of FA 2003 (negative resolution procedure) does not apply to an order made under subsection (5).

GENERAL NOTE

Section 48 authorises 'relevant information' on SDLT Land Transaction Returns to be made available to the Valuation Office Agency (England and Wales) and the Northern Ireland equivalent, and to such other persons (unspecified) as are authorised by HMRC, for valuation purposes.

'Relevant information' currently defined in FA 2003 Sch 10 para 1(4) may be redefined if the Treasury pass the necessary regulations.

49 Miscellaneous amendments
Schedule 10 (which makes miscellaneous amendments of Part 4 of FA 2003) has effect.

GENERAL NOTE

Section 49 introduces Sch 10 which contains the anti-avoidance provisions, in broadly similar form, to those dropped from the Finance (No 1) Bill because of the General Election.

Stamp duty and stamp duty reserve tax

50 Power to extend exceptions relating to recognised exchanges
(1) The Treasury may by regulations extend the application of the provisions mentioned in subsection (2) to any market (specified by name or by description) which—

(*a*) is not a recognised exchange, but

(*b*) is a multilateral trading facility (or, assuming compliance with the provisions of Title II of the Directive (authorisation and operating conditions), would be such a facility).

(2) The provisions referred to in subsection (1) are—

(*a*) sections 80A and 80C of FA 1986 (stamp duty: exceptions for sales to intermediaries and for repurchases and stock lending), and

(*b*) sections 88A and 89AA of that Act (stamp duty reserve tax: exceptions for intermediaries and for repurchases and stock lending).

(3) In this section—

"the Directive" means Directive 2004/39/EC of the European Parliament and of the Council of 21 April 2004 on markets in financial instruments;

"multilateral trading facility" has the same meaning as in the Directive (see Article 4(15));

"recognised exchange" means any of the following—

(*a*) an EEA exchange,

(*b*) a recognised foreign exchange,

(*c*) a recognised foreign options exchange,

within the meaning of the provisions mentioned in subsection (2).

(4) Regulations under this section may provide for the application of the provisions mentioned in subsection (2) subject to any adaptations appearing to the Treasury to be necessary or expedient.

(5) In subsection (1)(*b*) the words "(or, assuming compliance with the provisions of Title II of the Directive (authorisation and operating conditions), would be such a facility)" shall cease to have effect on such day as the Treasury may by order appoint.

(6) Section 117 of FA 2002 (power to extend the exceptions in subsection (2) to any market prescribed by order under section 118(3) of the Financial Services and Markets Act 2000) shall cease to have effect on such day as the Treasury may by order appoint.

(7) The power to make regulations or an order under this section is exercisable by statutory instrument.

(8) A statutory instrument containing—

(*a*) regulations under this section, or

(*b*) an order under subsection (5),

shall be subject to annulment in pursuance of a resolution of the House of Commons.

Prospective amendments—Words in sub-s (1)(*b*) to be repealed by F(No 2)A 2005 s 50(5) with effect from a day to be appointed.

GENERAL NOTE

Section 50 is a relieving provision. Currently the stamp duty and SDRT legislation permits certain reliefs, e g on stock lending, certain dealings with intermediaries, and repo transactions to members of EEA (European Economic Area) exchanges, recognised foreign exchanges or to exchanges prescribed under the FSMA 2000 s 118(3). The EU Markets in Financial Instruments Directive (MiFID) introduces the concept of a Multilateral Trading Facility (MTF). Section 50 authorises the extension of these reliefs to members of an MTF or to members of any market that, if it complied with Title II of MiFID, would be an MTF. Section 50(6) removes the power to extend the reliefs to exchanges prescribed under FSMA 2000 s 118(3) from a day to be appointed.

PART 4
EUROPEAN COMPANY STATUTE

51 Chargeable gains
(1) After section 140D of TCGA 1992 (transfer of non-UK trade) insert—

"Formation of SE by merger
140E Merger leaving assets within UK tax charge
(1) This section applies where—
    (*a*) an SE is formed by the merger of two or more companies in accordance with Articles 2(1) and 17(2)(*a*) or (*b*) of Council Regulation (EC) 2157/2001 on the Statute for a European Company (Societas Europaea),
    (*b*) each merging company is resident in a member State,
    (*c*) the merging companies are not all resident in the same State, and
    (*d*) section 139 does not apply to any qualifying transferred assets.

(2) Where this section applies, qualifying transferred assets shall be treated for the purposes of corporation tax on chargeable gains as if acquired by the SE for a consideration resulting in neither gain nor loss for the transferor.

(3) For the purposes of subsections (1) and (2) an asset is a qualifying transferred asset if—
    (*a*) it is transferred to the SE as part of the process of the merger forming it, and
    (*b*) subsections (4) and (5) are satisfied in respect of it.

(4) This subsection is satisfied in respect of a transferred asset if—
    (*a*) the transferor is resident in the United Kingdom at the time of the transfer, or
    (*b*) any gain that would have accrued to the transferor, had it disposed of the asset immediately before the time of the transfer, would have been a chargeable gain forming part of the transferor's chargeable profits in accordance with section 10B.

(5) This subsection is satisfied in respect of a transferred asset if—
    (*a*) the transferee SE is resident in the United Kingdom on formation, or
    (*b*) any gain that would accrue to the transferee SE were it to dispose of the asset immediately after the transfer would be a chargeable gain forming part of the SE's chargeable profits in accordance with section 10B.

(6) For the purposes of this section a company is resident in a member State if—
    (*a*) it is within a charge to tax under the law of the State as being resident for that purpose, and
    (*b*) it is not regarded, for the purposes of any double taxation relief arrangements to which the State is a party, as resident in a territory not within a member State.

(7) This section does not apply to the formation of an SE by merger if—
    (*a*) it is not effected for bona fide commercial reasons, or
    (*b*) it forms part of a scheme or arrangements of which the main purpose, or one of the main purposes, is avoiding liability to corporation tax, capital gains tax or income tax;
and section 138 (clearance in advance) shall apply to this subsection as it applies to section 137 (with any necessary modifications).

140F Merger not leaving assets within UK tax charge
(1) This section applies where—
    (*a*) an SE is formed by the merger of two or more companies in accordance with Articles 2(1) and 17(2)(*a*) or (*b*) of Council Regulation (EC) 2157/2001 on the Statute for a European Company (Societas Europaea),
    (*b*) each merging company is resident in a member State,
    (*c*) the merging companies are not all resident in the same State,
    (*d*) in the course of the merger a company resident in the United Kingdom ("company A") transfers to a company resident in another member State ("company B") all assets and liabilities relating to a business which company A carried on in a member State other than the United Kingdom through a permanent establishment, and

(*e*) the aggregate of the chargeable gains accruing to company A on the transfer exceeds the aggregate of any allowable losses so accruing.

(2) Where this section applies, for the purposes of this Act—

(*a*) the allowable losses accruing to company A on the transfer shall be set off against the chargeable gains so accruing, and

(*b*) the transfer shall be treated as giving rise to a single chargeable gain equal to the aggregate of those gains after deducting the aggregate of those losses.

(3) Where this section applies, section 815A of the Taxes Act shall also apply.

(4) Subsections (6) and (7) of section 140E apply for the purposes of this section as they apply for the purposes of that section.

140G Treatment of securities issued on merger

(1) This section applies where—

(*a*) an SE is formed by the merger of two or more companies in accordance with Articles 2(1) and 17(2)(*a*) or (*b*) of Council Regulation (EC) 2157/2001 on the Statute for a European Company (Societas Europaea),

(*b*) each merging company is resident in a member State,

(*c*) the merging companies are not all resident in the same State, and

(*d*) the merger does not constitute or form part of a scheme of reconstruction within the meaning of section 136.

(2) Where this section applies, the merger shall be treated for the purposes of section 136 as if it were a scheme of reconstruction.

(3) Where section 136 applies by virtue of subsection (2) above section 136(6) (and section 137) shall not apply.

(4) Subsections (6) and (7) of section 140E apply for the purposes of this section as they apply for the purposes of that section."

(2) Subsection (1) shall have effect in relation to the formation of an SE which occurs on or after 1st April 2005.

GENERAL NOTE

Sections 51–65 contain legislation to accommodate in the UK tax legislation the Societas Europaea (SE), a new European company. These measures are necessary to ensure that a UK company's decision to merge with a company in another member state to form an SE is not affected by tax considerations. The new rules are intended to enable UK businesses to take advantage of this new corporate vehicle if they wish. Section 51 inserts new ss 140E–G in TCGA 1992 concerning the formation of an SE through the merger of companies where not all the merging companies are resident in the same member state. These provisions apply to SEs formed from 1 April 2005.

New s 140E applies if an SE is formed by the merger of companies not all of which are resident in the same member state, where s 139 (Reconstruction involving transfer of business) does not apply. The effect of s 140E is that qualifying transferred assets are treated for the purposes of corporation tax on chargeable gains as being made on a 'no gain, no loss' basis. A 'qualifying transferred asset' is an asset transferred to the SE as part of the merger, subject to the following conditions. Firstly, the transferor must be UK resident at the time of transfer, or be carrying on a trade in the UK through a permanent establishment in the UK, such that gains on asset disposals immediately before the transfer would form part of profits chargeable to corporation tax. Secondly, the SE must be UK resident on formation, or carry on a trade in the UK through a permanent establishment in the UK such that gains on asset disposals immediately before the transfer would form part of profits chargeable to corporation tax. The application of s 140E is subject to a 'bona fide commercial' test, and does not apply if the formation of the SE by merger forms part of a scheme or arrangement to avoid corporation tax, capital gains tax or income tax. The advance clearance procedure in TCGA 1992 s 138 applies for these purposes.

New s 140F applies (as for s 140E) if an SE is formed by the merger of companies not all of which are resident in the same member state. However, further conditions must be satisfied. Firstly, a UK resident company transfers to a company resident in another member state all assets and liabilities relating to a business which the UK company carried on through a permanent establishment in a member state other than the UK. Secondly, the UK company chargeable gains on the transfer exceed any allowable losses. If s 140F applies, the UK company losses may be set off against chargeable gains, and the transfer is treated as giving rise to a single chargeable net gain. The double tax relief provisions in TA 1988, s 815A apply, as does the bona fide commercial test and clearance procedure in s 140E (see above).

New s 140G applies if an SE is formed by the merger of companies not all of which are resident in the same member state, and if the merger is not a scheme of reconstruction within TCGA 1992 s 136. If s 140G applies, the merger is treated as if s 136 does apply. The anti-avoidance condition in s 137(1) is disapplied in favour of a similar condition and clearance procedure in s 140E (see above). These provisions are relevant for SE formations from 1 April 2005.

52 Intangible fixed assets

(1) After paragraph 85 of Schedule 29 to FA 2002 (intangible fixed assets: gains and losses: transfer of trade) insert—

"Formation of SE by merger

85A (1) This paragraph applies where—

(*a*) an SE is formed by the merger of two or more companies in accordance with Articles 2(1) and 17(2)(*a*) or (*b*) of Council Regulation (EC) 2157/2001 on the Statute for a European Company (Societas Europaea),

(*b*) each merging company is resident in a member State,

(*c*) the merging companies are not all resident in the same State, and

(*d*) paragraph 84 above does not apply to any qualifying transferred assets.

(2) Where this paragraph applies a transfer of qualifying transferred assets is treated for the purposes of this Schedule as tax-neutral (see paragraph 140).

(3) For the purposes of sub-paragraphs (1) and (2) an asset is a qualifying transferred asset if—

(*a*) it is transferred as part of the process of the merger,

(*b*) it is a chargeable intangible asset in relation to the transferor immediately before the transfer, and

(*c*) it is a chargeable intangible asset in relation to the transferee immediately after the transfer.

(4) Sub-paragraph (2) shall apply in relation to the formation of an SE by merger only if—

(*a*) it is effected for bona fide commercial reasons, and

(*b*) it does not form part of a scheme or arrangements of which the main purpose, or one of the main purposes, is avoiding liability to corporation tax, capital gains tax or income tax.

(5) Paragraph 84(6) (and therefore paragraph 88) shall apply, with any necessary modifications, in relation to sub-paragraph (4) above as in relation to paragraph 84(5).

(6) For the purposes of this paragraph a company is resident in a member State if—

(*a*) it is within a charge to tax under the law of the State as being resident for that purpose, and

(*b*) it is not regarded for the purposes of any double taxation relief arrangements to which the State is a party, as resident in a territory not within a member State."

(2) Subsection (1) shall have effect in relation to the formation of an SE which occurs on or after 1st April 2005.

GENERAL NOTE

A new s 85A is inserted into the intangible fixed assets provisions in FA 2002 Sch 29. It applies if a Societas Europaea (SE) is formed by the merger of companies not all of which are resident in the same member state, and if FA 2002 Sch 29 para 84 (company reconstruction involving transfer of business) does not apply to any 'qualifying transferred assets' (as defined in sub-para 3). If s 85A applies, the transfer of those assets is treated as tax neutral for the purposes of the intangible fixed asset regime, subject to the merger satisfying a bona fide commercial test (sub-para 4). An advance clearance procedure is available (FA 2002 Sch 29 para 88). These provisions apply to SE formations from 1 April 2005.

53 Intangible fixed assets: permanent establishment in another member State

(1) After paragraph 87 of Schedule 29 to FA 2002 (intangible fixed assets: gains and losses: transfer of non-UK trade) insert—

> *"Formation of SE by merger: transfer of non-UK trade*
>
> **87A** (1) This paragraph applies where—
>
> (*a*) an SE is formed by the merger of two or more companies in accordance with Articles 2(1) and 17(2)(*a*) or (*b*) of Council Regulation (EC) 2157/2001 on the Statute for a European Company (Societas Europaea),
>
> (*b*) each merging company is resident in a member State,
>
> (*c*) the merging companies are not all resident in the same State,
>
> (*d*) in the course of the merger a company resident in the United Kingdom ("the transferor") transfers to a company resident in another member State ("the transferee") the whole or part of a trade that, immediately before the transfer, the transferor carried on in a member State other than the United Kingdom through a permanent establishment,
>
> (*e*) the transfer includes the whole of the assets of the transferor used for the purposes of the trade or part,
>
> (*f*) the transfer includes intangible fixed assets—
>
>> (i) that are chargeable intangible assets in relation to the transferor immediately before the transfer, and
>>
>> (ii) in the case of one or more of which the proceeds of realisation exceed the cost recognised for tax purposes, and
>
> (*g*) no claim is made under paragraph 86 above in relation to those assets.
>
> (2) Where tax would, but for the Mergers Directive, have been chargeable in the member State in which the permanent establishment is located, Part 18 of the Taxes Act 1988 (double taxation relief), including any arrangements having effect by virtue of section 788 (double taxation agreements), shall have effect as if the amount of tax that would, but for the Mergers Directive, have been charged in respect of the transfer of the chargeable intangible assets, had actually been charged.
>
> (3) In this paragraph "the Mergers Directive" has the same meaning as in paragraph 87.
>
> (4) For the purposes of this paragraph a company is resident in a member State if—
>
>> (*a*) it is within a charge to tax under the law of the State as being resident for that purpose, and
>>
>> (*b*) it is not regarded, for the purposes of any double taxation relief arrangements to which the State is a party, as resident in a territory not within a member State.
>
> (5) This paragraph does not apply to the formation of an SE by merger if—
>
>> (*a*) it is not effected for bona fide commercial reasons, or
>>
>> (*b*) it forms part of a scheme or arrangements of which the main purpose, or one of the main purposes, is avoiding liability to corporation tax, capital gains tax or income tax.
>
> (6) Sub-paragraph (5) shall not affect the operation of this paragraph in any case where, before the transfer, Her Majesty's Revenue and Customs have, on the application of the transferor, notified the transferor that they are satisfied that the merger will be effected for bona fide commercial reasons and will not form part of any such scheme or arrangements as are mentioned in sub-paragraph (5)(*b*).
>
> (7) An application under sub-paragraph (6) must be made in accordance with paragraph 88."

(2) Subsection (1) shall have effect in relation to the formation of an SE which occurs on or after 1st April 2005.

GENERAL NOTE

New para 87A inserted into the intangible fixed assets provisions in FA 2002 Sch 29 applies if a Societas Europaea (SE) is formed by the merger of companies not all of which are resident in the same member state. Further conditions apply. Firstly, in the course of the merger, a UK resident company must transfer all or part of a trade carried on through a permanent establishment outside the UK to a company in another member state. Secondly, all the trade assets must be transferred. Thirdly, the transfer includes chargeable intangible fixed assets in the transferor's hands, the realisation proceeds from (some or all) of which exceed the tax cost. Fourthly, no claim is made under FA 2002 Sch 29 para 86 (postponement of charge on transfer of assets to non-resident company). If para 87A applies, provision is made for double tax relief where tax would, but for the mergers directive, have been chargeable in the member state in which the permanent establishment is located, as if the amount of tax otherwise chargeable had actually been charged. Paragraph 87A is subject to a bona fide commercial test (sub-para 5). An advance clearance procedure is available for these purposes, in accordance with FA 2002 Sch 29 para 88. These provisions apply to SE formations from 1 April 2005.

54 Loan relationships

(1) After paragraph 12A of Schedule 9 to FA 1996 (loan relationships: gains and losses: continuity of treatment for groups) insert—

"Formation of SE by merger

12B (1) This paragraph applies where—

(*a*) an SE is formed by the merger of two or more companies in accordance with Articles 2(1) and 17(2)(*a*) or (*b*) of Council Regulation (EC) 2157/2001 on the Statute for a European Company (Societas Europaea),

(*b*) each merging company is resident in a member State,

(*c*) the merging companies are not all resident in the same State, and

(*d*) either—

(i) immediately after formation the SE is resident in the United Kingdom and within the charge to corporation tax in accordance with section 6 of the Taxes Act, or

(ii) immediately after formation the SE is not resident in the United Kingdom but is within the charge to corporation tax in accordance with section 11 of the Taxes Act 1988.

(2) Where this paragraph applies, the transfer in the course of the merger of an asset or liability which represents a loan relationship shall be disregarded except—

(*a*) for the purpose of determining the debits or credits to be brought into account in respect of exchange gains or losses and identifying the company which is to bring them into account, and

(*b*) for the purpose of identifying the company in whose case a debit or credit which does not relate to the transfer is to be brought into account.

(3) Where this paragraph applies, the transferor and the transferee companies of an asset or liability which represents a loan relationship shall be deemed, except for the purposes specified in sub-paragraph (2)(*a*) and (*b*), to be the same company.

(4) Paragraph 12(2A) shall have effect (with any necessary modifications) in relation to this paragraph as in relation to paragraph 12.

(5) Sub-paragraphs (2) and (3) shall apply in relation to the formation of an SE by merger only if—

(*a*) it is effected for bona fide commercial reasons, and

(*b*) it does not form part of a scheme or arrangements of which the main purpose, or one of the main purposes, is avoiding liability to corporation tax, capital gains tax or income tax.

(6) But sub-paragraph (5) shall not have the effect of preventing sub-paragraphs (2) and (3) from applying if before the merger Her Majesty's Revenue and Customs have on the application of the merging companies notified them that Her Majesty's Revenue and Customs are satisfied that sub-paragraph (5) will not have that effect.

(7) For the purposes of this paragraph a company is resident in a member State if—

(*a*) it is within a charge to tax under the law of the State as being resident for that purpose, and

(*b*) it is not regarded for the purposes of any double taxation relief arrangements to which the State is a party, as resident in a territory not within a member State."

(2) Subsection (1) shall have effect in relation to the formation of an SE which occurs on or after 1st April 2005.

GENERAL NOTE

A new para 12B is inserted into FA 1996 Sch 9, dealing with the transfer in a merger of assets or liabilities that represent a loan relationship. It applies if a Societas Europaea (SE) is formed by the merger of companies not all of which are resident in the same member state. A further condition is that immediately after formation the SE is within the charge to corporation tax, either through being resident in the UK or by carrying on a trade in the UK through a permanent establishment. If para 12B applies, the transfer of a loan relationship in a merger is disregarded, subject to two exceptions, ie for determining debits and credits for exchange gain and loss purposes and identifying the company to bring them into account, and for identifying which company is to account for debits or credits not relating to the transfer (eg interest). The loan relationship transferor and transferee are deemed to be the same companies, subject to the above two exceptions. If the transferor company uses fair value accounting for the loan relationship, the transfer is not disregarded. Both the transferor and transferee companies must apply a fair value basis (sub-para 4). Paragraph 12B is subject to a bona fide commercial test (sub-para 5), but this anti-avoidance provision is not applied if HM Revenue & Customs notify the merging companies before the merger that they are satisfied that sub-para 5 will not have effect. These rules apply to SE formations from 1 April 2005.

55 Derivative contracts

(1) After paragraph 30A of Schedule 26 to FA 2002 (derivative contracts: profits: groups) insert—

"Formation of SE by merger

30B (1) This paragraph applies where—

(*a*) an SE is formed by the merger of two or more companies in accordance with Articles 2(1) and 17(2)(*a*) or (*b*) of Council Regulation (EC) 2157/2001 on the Statute for a European Company (Societas Europaea),

(*b*) each merging company is resident in a member State,

(*c*) the merging companies are not all resident in the same State, and

(*d*) either—

(i) immediately after formation the SE is resident in the United Kingdom and within the charge to corporation tax in accordance with section 6 of the Taxes Act, or

(ii) immediately after formation the SE is not resident in the United Kingdom but is within the charge to corporation tax in accordance with section 11 of the Taxes Act 1988.

(2) Where this paragraph applies, the transfer in the course of the merger of rights or liabilities under a derivative contract shall be disregarded except—

(*a*) for the purpose of determining the debits or credits to be brought into account in respect of exchange gains or losses and identifying the company which is to bring them into account, and

(*b*) for the purpose of identifying the company in whose case a debit or credit which does not relate to the transfer is to be brought into account.

(3) Where this paragraph applies, the transferor and the transferee companies of a right or liability under a derivative contract shall be deemed, except for the purposes specified in sub-paragraph (2)(*a*) and (*b*), to be the same company.

(4) Paragraph 30 shall apply, with any necessary modifications, in relation to this paragraph as in relation to paragraph 28.

(5) Sub-paragraphs (2) and (3) shall apply in relation to a merger only if—

(*a*) it is effected for bona fide commercial reasons, and

(*b*) it does not form part of a scheme or arrangements of which the main purpose, or one of the main purposes, is avoiding liability to corporation tax, capital gains tax or income tax.

(6) But sub-paragraph (5) shall not have the effect of preventing sub-paragraphs (2) and (3) from applying if before the merger Her Majesty's Revenue and Customs have on the application of the merging companies notified them that Her Majesty's Revenue and Customs are satisfied that sub-paragraph (5) will not have that effect.

(7) For the purposes of this paragraph a company is resident in a member State if—

(*a*) it is within a charge to tax under the law of the State as being resident for that purpose, and

(*b*) it is not regarded for the purposes of any double taxation relief arrangements to which the State is a party, as resident in a territory not within a member State."

(2) Subsection (1) shall have effect in relation to the formation of an SE which occurs on or after 1st April 2005.

GENERAL NOTE

A new para 30B is inserted into FA 2002 Sch 26, dealing with the transfer in a merger of rights or liabilities under a derivative contract in relation to the formation of a Societas Europaea (SE) by merger. It applies if the same conditions are satisfied as for new FA 1996 Sch 9 para 12B to apply (see s 54 above). If para 30B applies, the transfer of rights or liabilities under a derivative contract in a merger is disregarded, subject to two exceptions, ie firstly for determining debits and credits for exchange gain and loss purposes and identifying the company to bring them into account, and secondly for identifying which company is to account for debits or credits not relating to the transfer (eg periodic payments under a swap). The derivative contract transferor and transferee companies are deemed to be the same companies, subject to the above two exceptions. If the transferor company uses fair value accounting, a fair value accounting basis applies in respect of the derivative contract (sub-para 4). Paragraph 30B is subject to a bona fide commercial test (sub-para 5), but this anti-avoidance provision is not applied if HM Revenue & Customs notify the merging companies before the merger that they are satisfied that sub-para 5 will not have effect. These provisions apply to SE formations from 1 April 2005.

56 Capital allowances

(1) After section 561 of CAA 2001 (transfer of UK trade to company in another member State) insert—

"**561A Transfer during formation of SE by merger**

(1) This section applies to the transfer of a qualifying asset as part of the process of a merger to which section 140E of TCGA 1992 (formation of SE by merger) applies (or would apply but for section 140E(1)(*d*)).

(2) Where this section applies to a transfer—

(*a*) the transfer does not give rise to any allowance or charge under this Act,

(*b*) anything done to or by the transferor in relation to assets transferred is to be treated after the transfer as having been done to or by the transferee (with any necessary apportionment of expenditure being made in a reasonable manner), and

(*c*) section 343 of ICTA (company reconstruction without change of ownership) shall not apply.

(3) For the purposes of subsection (1) an asset is a "qualifying asset" if—

(*a*) it is transferred to the SE as part of the merger forming it, and

(*b*) subsections (4) and (5) are satisfied in respect of it.

(4) This subsection is satisfied in respect of an asset if—

(*a*) the transferor is resident in the United Kingdom at the time of the transfer, or

(*b*) the asset is an asset of a permanent establishment in the United Kingdom of the transferor.

(5) This subsection is satisfied in respect of an asset if—

(*a*) the transferee SE is resident in the United Kingdom on formation, or

(*b*) the asset is an asset of a permanent establishment in the United Kingdom of the transferee SE on its formation."

(2) Subsection (1) shall have effect in relation to a transfer made on or after 1st April 2005.

GENERAL NOTE

New s 561A inserted into CAA 2001 deals with the transfer in a merger of assets in respect of which capital allowances can be claimed. It applies where the circumstances in TCGA 1992 s 140E apply (see s 51 above), ie if a Societas Europaea (SE) is formed by the merger of companies not all of which are resident in the same member state, where s 139 (Reconstruction involving transfer of business) does not apply. The new section also applies to mergers to form an SE falling within s 139. If s 561A does apply, the transfer of a qualifying asset does not give rise to an allowance or charge under CAA 2001. An asset is a 'qualifying asset' if it is transferred to the SE in the merger. In addition, the transferor and transferee SE must be UK resident, or the asset must be an asset of their permanent UK establishment. The transferee broadly 'stands in the shoes' of the transferor in relation to the assets, and the company reconstructions without change of ownership rules (TA 1988, s 343) do not apply. This section applies to transfers during the formation of an SE by merger from 1 April 2005.

57 Stamp duty reserve tax

(1) At the end of section 99(4) of FA 1986 (stamp duty reserve tax: interpretation: chargeable securities) add—

", or

(*d*) they are issued or raised by an SE (whether or not in the course of its formation in accordance with Article 2 of Council Regulation (EC) 2157/2001 on the Statute for a European Company (Societas Europaea)) and, at the time when it falls to be determined whether the securities are chargeable securities, the SE has its registered office in the United Kingdom.

(4A) "Chargeable securities" does not include securities falling within paragraph (*a*), (*b*) or (*c*) of subsection (3) above if—

(*a*) they are securities issued or raised by an SE (whether or not in the course of its formation in accordance with Article 2 of Council Regulation (EC) 2157/2001 on the Statute for a European Company (Societas Europaea)), and

(*b*) at the time when it falls to be determined whether the securities are chargeable securities, the SE has its registered office outside the United Kingdom;".

(2) Subsection (1) shall have effect for the purposes of determining, in relation to anything occurring on or after 1st April 2005, whether securities (whenever issued or raised) are chargeable securities for the purposes of Part IV of FA 1986.

GENERAL NOTE

Sections 57 and 58 make appropriate changes to the stamp duty and SDRT legislation to facilitate the use of the European Companies or SEs (Societas Europaea).

Section 57 amends the definition of chargeable securities in FA 1986 s 99 to provide that securities issued or raised by an SE which at the relevant time has its registered office in the UK are chargeable securities and to make it clear that such securities are not chargeable securities if at the relevant time its registered office is in another member state.

58 Bearer instruments: stamp duty and stamp duty reserve tax

(1) In section 90(3C)(*a*) of FA 1986 (stamp duty reserve tax: bearer instruments) after "United Kingdom" insert "(other than an SE which has its registered office outside the United Kingdom following a transfer in accordance with Article 8 of Council Regulation (EC) 2157/2001 on the Statute for a European Company (Societas Europaea))".

(2) In section 90(3E)(*a*) of FA 1986 (stamp duty reserve tax: bearer instruments) after "United Kingdom" insert "(other than an SE which has its registered office outside the United Kingdom following a transfer in accordance with Article 8 of Council Regulation (EC) 2157/2001 on the Statute for a European Company (Societas Europaea))".

(3) In paragraph 11 of Schedule 15 to FA 1999 (bearer instruments) for the definition of "UK company" substitute—

""UK company" means—

(*a*) a company that is formed or established in the United Kingdom (other than an SE which has its registered office outside the United Kingdom following a transfer in accordance with Article 8 of Council Regulation (EC) 2157/2001 on the Statute for a European Company (Societas Europaea)), or

(*b*) an SE which has its registered office in the United Kingdom following a transfer in accordance with Article 8 of that Regulation; ".

(4) This section shall have effect for the purposes of determining whether or not stamp duty or stamp duty reserve tax is chargeable in respect of anything done on or after 1st April 2005.

GENERAL NOTE

Section 58 amends the SDLT legislation which provides that agreements to transfer certain bearer instruments are liable to SDRT notwithstanding that transfer of the resulting instruments are exempt stamp duty. The amendment to FA 1986 s 90(3C) and s 90(3E) respectively permit an agreement relating to bearer instruments of an SE incorporated in the UK but at the relevant time having its registered office outside the UK not to be liable to SDLT.

The amendment to FA 1999 Sch 15, para 11 (definition of UK company for bearer instrument duty) causes the relevant charging provisions to bearer instrument duty only to apply to companies incorporated in the UK (as now), to SEs incorporated in the UK and still having a UK registered office, and to SEs incorporated outside the UK which have a registered office in the UK.

59 Consequential amendments

(1) In section 815A(1) of ICTA (transfer of a non-UK trade) after "section 140C" insert "or 140F".

(2) In section 35(3)(*d*)(i) of TCGA 1992 (re-basing to 1982, &c.) after "140A," insert "140E,".

(3) In section 140A of TCGA 1992 (transfer of UK trade)—

    (*a*) in subsection (1)(*b*) for "securities" substitute "shares or debentures", and
    (*b*) in subsection (7) omit the definition of "securities".

(4) In section 140C of TCGA 1992 (transfer of non-UK trade)—

    (*a*) in subsection (1)(*c*) for "securities" substitute "shares or debentures", and
    (*b*) in subsection (9) omit the definition of "securities".

(5) In paragraph 88(1) and (5) of Schedule 29 to FA 2002 (intangible fixed assets: gains and losses: transferred assets: application for clearance) after "85(5)," insert "85A(5), 87A(6),".

(6) In paragraph 127 of that Schedule (acquired assets to be treated as existing assets) after sub-paragraph (1)(*b*)(ii) insert—

    ", or

      (iii) section 140E of that Act (transfer on formation of SE by merger),".

(7) Subsections (3) and (4) shall have effect in relation to an issue effected on or after 1st April 2005.

GENERAL NOTE

A number of minor amendments are made in consequence of the new provisions on the formation of a Societas Europaea (SE) by merger in the preceding sections.

60 Residence

(1) After section 66 of FA 1988 (company residence) insert—

"66A Residence of SE

(1) This section applies to an SE which transfers its registered office to the United Kingdom (in accordance with Article 8 of Council Regulation (EC) 2157/2001 on the Statute for a European Company (Societas Europaea)).

(2) Upon registration in the United Kingdom the SE shall be regarded for the purposes of the Taxes Acts as resident in the United Kingdom; and accordingly, if a different place of residence is given by any rule of law, that place shall not be taken into account for those purposes.

(3) The SE shall not cease to be regarded as resident in the United Kingdom by reason only of the subsequent transfer from the United Kingdom of its registered office.

(4) In this section "the Taxes Acts" has the same meaning as in the Taxes Management Act 1970."

(2) In section 249(3) of FA 1994 (certain companies to be treated as non-resident) after "resident there)" insert ", by virtue of section 66A of that Act (residence of SE)".

(3) Subsection (1) shall have effect in relation to the transfer of a registered office which occurs on or after 1st April 2005.

GENERAL NOTE

A new s 66A is inserted into FA 1988, which applies to a Societas Europaea (SE) that transfers its registered office to the UK. The effect is that an SE is treated as UK resident for tax purposes, and remains so even if it subsequently transfers its registered office outside the UK. The 'tie breaker' test of company residence in FA

1994 s 249 is extended to include SEs treated as UK resident by virtue of this section, which applies to transfers of registered offices from 1 April 2005.

61 Continuity for transitional purposes

(1) If at any time a company ceases to be resident in the United Kingdom in the course of the formation of an SE by merger (whether or not the company continues to exist after the formation of the SE) the provision specified in subsection (3) shall apply after that time, but in relation to liabilities accruing and matters arising before that time—

(*a*) as if the company were still resident in the United Kingdom, and

(*b*) where the company has ceased to exist, as if the SE were the company.

(2) If at any time an SE transfers its registered office from the United Kingdom and ceases to be resident in the United Kingdom, the provision specified in subsection (3) shall apply after that time, but in relation to liabilities accruing and matters arising before that time, as if the SE were still resident in the United Kingdom.

(3) The provision mentioned in subsections (1) and (2) is Schedule 18 to FA 1998 (tax returns, assessments, &c.).

GENERAL NOTE

If a company ceases to be UK resident following the formation of a Societas Europaea (SE) by merger, the corporation tax self-assessment provisions of FA 1998 Sch 18 continue to apply in relation to returns, liabilities etc before that time as if the company was still UK resident or, if the company has ceased to exist, as if the SE were the company. The same applies if an SE transfers its registered office from the UK and ceases to be UK resident.

62 Groups

(1) After section 170(10) of TCGA 1992 (groups: merger, &c.) insert—

"(10A) Where the principal company of a group (Group 1)—

(*a*) becomes an SE by reason of being the acquiring company in the formation of an SE by merger by acquisition (in accordance with Articles 2(1), 17(2)(*a*) and 29(1) of Council Regulation (EC) 2157/2001 on the Statute for a European Company (Societas Europaea)),

(*b*) becomes a subsidiary of a holding SE (formed in accordance with Article 2(2) of that Regulation), or

(*c*) is transformed into an SE (in accordance with Article 2(4) of that Regulation),

Group 1 and any group of which the SE is a member on formation shall be regarded as the same; and the question whether or not a company has ceased to be a member of a group shall be determined accordingly."

(2) Subsection (1) shall have effect in relation to the formation of an SE (including its formation by transformation) which occurs on or after 1st April 2005.

GENERAL NOTE

A new sub-s (10A) is inserted into TCGA 1992 s 170. If the principal company of a group becomes a Societas Europaea (SE) (ie as the acquiring company in the formation of an SE by merger by acquisition, or by becoming a subsidiary of an SE, or by transformation into an SE), then that group plus any group of which the SE is a member on formation is regarded as the same for the purposes of the group provisions in TCGA 1992 ss 170–181. This applies to SE formations and transformations from 1 April 2005.

63 Groups: intangible fixed assets

(1) After paragraph 51 of Schedule 29 to the FA 2002 (groups: continuity) insert—

"**51A** For the purposes of this Schedule where the principal company of a group (Group 1)—

(*a*) becomes an SE by reason of being the acquiring company in the formation of an SE by merger by acquisition (in accordance with Articles 2(1), 17(2)(*a*) and 29(1) of Council Regulation (EC) 2157/2001 on the Statute for a European Company (Societas Europaea)),

(*b*) becomes a subsidiary of a holding SE (formed in accordance with Article 2(2) of that Regulation), or

(*c*) is transformed into an SE (in accordance with Article 2(4) of that Regulation),

Group 1 and any group of which the SE is a member on formation shall be regarded as the same; and the question whether or not a company has ceased to be a member of a group shall be determined accordingly."

(2) Subsection (1) shall have effect in relation to the formation of an SE (including its formation by transformation) which occurs on or after 1st April 2005.

GENERAL NOTE

A new para 51A is inserted into FA 2002 Sch 29. If the principal company of a group becomes a Societas Europaea (SE) (ie as the acquiring company in the formation of an SE by merger by acquisition, or by becoming a subsidiary of an SE, or by transformation into an SE), then that group plus any group of which the SE is a member on formation is regarded as the same for the purposes of the intangible fixed assets group provisions, in relation to SE formations and transformations from 1 April 2005.

64 Held-over gains

(1) In section 116(11) of TCGA 1992 (shares: reorganisation, &c.) after "140A," insert "140E,".

(2) After section 140(6A) of that Act (postponement of charge on transfer of assets to foreign company) insert—

"(6B) If, as part of the process of a merger forming an SE in circumstances in which section 140E applies, securities are transferred to the SE by a transferor company—

(*a*) the transfer to the SE shall be disregarded for the purposes of subsection (4), and

(*b*) the SE shall be treated as if it were the transferor company in relation to—

(i) any subsequent disposal of the securities, and

(ii) any subsequent disposal by the transferee company of assets to which subsection (5) applies."

(3) After section 154(2) of that Act (held over gains: depreciating assets) insert—

"(2A) If, as part of the process of a merger forming an SE in circumstances in which section 140E applies, asset No 2 or shares in a company which holds asset No 2 are transferred to the SE, the transfer to the SE shall be disregarded for the purposes of subsection (2), and—

(*a*) if the SE holds asset No 2, it shall be treated for the purposes of subsection (2), in relation to asset No 2, as if it were the claimant, or

(*b*) if the SE holds shares in the company which holds asset No 2, section 175 shall apply in relation to the group of which the SE is a member as if it were the same group as any group of which the claimant was a member before the formation of the SE.

(2B) If, as part of the process of a merger forming an SE in circumstances in which section 140E applies, the SE becomes a member (whether or not as the principal company) of a group of which the claimant is also a member, for the purposes of subsection (2) section 175 shall apply in relation to the trade carried on by the claimant as if the group of which the SE is a member were the same group as the group of which the claimant was a member before the formation of the SE."

(4) After section 179(1A) of that Act (company ceasing to be member of group) insert—

"(1B) Where, as part of the process of a merger to form an SE in circumstances in which section 140E applies, a company which is a member of a group ("Group 1") ceases to exist and in consequence of that cessation—

(*a*) assets are transferred to the SE, or

(*b*) shares in one or more companies which were also members of the group are transferred to the SE,

a company which has ceased to exist, or the shares in which have been transferred to the SE, shall not be treated for the purposes of this section as having left Group 1.

(1C) If subsection (1B) applies in relation to a company then for the purposes of this section—

(*a*) the SE and a company which has ceased to exist in consequence of the merger to form the SE shall be treated as the same entity, and

(*b*) if the SE is a member of a group ("Group 2") following its formation (whether or not as the principal company of the group) a company which was a member of Group 1 and became a member of Group 2 in consequence of the formation of the SE shall be treated, for the purposes of this section, as if Group 1 and Group 2 were the same."

(5) This section shall have effect in relation to the formation of an SE in accordance with Article 2 of Council Regulation (EC) 2157/2001 on the Statute for a European Company (Societas Europaea) which occurs on or after 1st April 2005.

GENERAL NOTE

A number of amendments to TCGA 1992 provide for continuity of group membership upon the formation of a Societas Europaea (SE), in relation to SE formations from 1 April 2005. The scope of TCGA 1992 s 116(11) (reorganisations, conversions and reconstructions) is extended in the case of disposals falling within s 140E (see s 51 above). In addition, a new sub-s (6A) is inserted into TCGA 1992 s 140, which applies to mergers forming an SE within s 140E, and provides that the transfer of securities to the SE is disregarded for the purposes of s 140(4) (under which deferred gains are brought into charge on a disposal of securities). It also provides that the SE is treated as the transferor company, firstly on any subsequent disposal of the securities, and secondly on a disposal by the transferee company of assets to which s 140(5) applies (ie the six-year rule for bringing deferred gains back into charge on relevant asset disposals).

New sub-ss (2A) and (2B) are inserted into TCGA 1992 s 154 (the 'depreciating assets' provisions), both in respect of mergers forming an SE within s 140E from 1 April 2005. The transfer to an SE of the replacement asset ('Asset No 2') or shares in a company holding that asset are disregarded for the purposes of s 154(2) (which determines the earliest time at which the held-over gain on the original asset accrues), and an SE holding asset No 2 is treated as the claimant for those purposes. If the SE holds shares in the company holding asset No 2, s 175 (Replacement of business assets by group members) applies as if SE's group is the same as any group of which the claimant was a member before the SE's formation (sub-s (2A)). In a merger forming an SE within s 140E, if the SE becomes a member of a group of which the claimant is also a member, s 175 applies to the trade carried on by the claimant as if the SE's group is the same as the claimant's group before the SE's formation (sub-s (2B)).

New sub-ss (1B) and (1C) are inserted into TCGA 1992 s 179 (the de-grouping charge rules). In a merger forming an SE within s 140E, if a member of a group (Group 1) ceases to exist and assets or group member shares are transferred to the SE, the company which has ceased to exist or the group member shares transferred are not treated as having left Group 1 (sub-s (1B)). If sub-s (1B) applies, the SE and the company that has ceased to exist are treated as the same company, and if the SE is a member of a group (Group 2) following its formation, a company that was a member of Group 1 and became a member of Group 2 due to the SE's formation will be treated as if both groups were the same (sub-s (1C)).

65 Restrictions on set-off of pre-entry losses

(1) Schedule 7A to TCGA 1992 (restrictions on set-off of pre-entry losses) shall be amended as follows.

(2) After paragraph 1(3A)(*a*) insert—

"(aa) in a case in which (whether or not paragraph (*a*)(i) also applies)—

(i) the company is an SE resident in the United Kingdom, and

(ii) the asset was transferred to the SE as part of the process of its formation by the merger by acquisition of two or more companies in accordance with Articles 2(1) and 17(2)(*a*) or (*b*) of Council Regulation (EC) 2157/2001 on the Statute for a European Company (Societas Europaea),

are references to the asset becoming a chargeable asset in relation to the SE or, if at the time of the formation of the SE the asset was a chargeable asset in relation to a company which ceased to exist as part of the process of the formation of the SE, to the asset becoming a chargeable asset in relation to that company;".

(3) In the definition of "chargeable asset" in paragraph 1(3A) after "section 10B" insert "(or, if the company is an SE, by reason of the asset having been transferred to the SE on its formation)".

(4) In paragraph 1(6)(*a*) after "subsection (10)" insert "or (10A)".

(5) In paragraph 9(6) after "subsection (10)" insert "or (10A)".

(6) This section shall have effect in relation to the formation of an SE which occurs on or after 1st April 2005.

GENERAL NOTE

The rules restricting the set-off of pre-entry capital losses (TCGA 1992 Sch 7A) are amended in relation to Societas Europaea (SE) formations from 1 April 2005. A new para 1(3A)(aa) is inserted into Sch 7A, which adds a further 'relevant event' for calculating losses on pre-entry assets. It applies to a UK resident SE if the asset in question was transferred to the SE as part of its formation by merger by acquisition of two or more companies. The relevant event in that case is the asset becoming a chargeable asset in relation to the SE, or the asset becoming a chargeable asset in relation to a company that ceased to exist as part of the SE formation process.

PART 5

MISCELLANEOUS MATTERS

66 Vehicle excise duty: late renewal supplements

(1) VERA 1994 is amended as follows.

(2) Section 7A (supplement payable on late renewal of vehicle licence) is amended as follows.

(3) In subsection (1) (cases in which regulations may provide for supplement to be payable), for the words from "in prescribed cases" to the end substitute "where—

(*a*) a vehicle has ceased to be appropriately covered,

(*b*) the vehicle is not, before the end of the relevant prescribed period, appropriately covered as mentioned in paragraph (*a*) or (*b*) of subsection (1A) below with effect from the time immediately after it so ceased or appropriately covered as mentioned in paragraph (*d*) of that subsection, and

(*c*) the circumstances are not such as may be prescribed."

(4) After that subsection insert—

"(1A) For the purposes of this section and section 7B a vehicle is appropriately covered if (and only if)—

(*a*) a vehicle licence or trade licence is in force for or in respect of the vehicle,

(*b*) the vehicle is an exempt vehicle in respect of which regulations under this Act require a nil licence to be in force and a nil licence is in force in respect of it,

(*c*) the vehicle is an exempt vehicle that is not one in respect of which regulations under this Act require a nil licence to be in force, or

(*d*) the vehicle is neither kept nor used on a public road and the declarations and particulars required to be delivered by regulations under section 22(1D) have been delivered in relation to it in accordance with the regulations within the immediately preceding period of 12 months.

(1B) Where a vehicle for or in respect of which a vehicle licence is in force is transferred by the holder of the vehicle licence to another person, the vehicle licence is to be treated for the purposes of subsection (1A) as no longer in force unless it is delivered to the other person with the vehicle.

(1C) Where—

(*a*) an application is made for a vehicle licence for any period, and

(*b*) a temporary licence is issued pursuant to the application, subsection (1B) does not apply to the licence applied for if, on a transfer of the vehicle during the currency of the temporary licence, the temporary licence is delivered with the vehicle to the transferee.

(1D) In subsection (1)(*b*) "the relevant prescribed period" means such period beginning with the date on which the vehicle ceased to be appropriately covered as is prescribed."

(5) In subsection (2)(*c*) (amount of supplement variable according to length of period between expiry of licence and payment of supplement or renewal of licence), for sub-paragraphs (i) and (ii) substitute—

> "(i) the time of a notification (in accordance with regulations under section 7B(1)) to, or in relation to, a person by whom it is payable, and
> (ii) the time at which it is paid."

(6) In subsection (3)(*b*) (supplement not to cease to be payable by reason of taking out of vehicle licence), for "a vehicle licence being taken out for the vehicle" substitute "the vehicle being again appropriately covered".

(7) Omit subsection (4)(*a*) (definition of "expiry of a vehicle licence").

(8) In the heading, for "late renewal of vehicle licence" substitute "vehicle ceasing to be appropriately covered".

(9) Section 7B (late-renewal supplements: further provisions) is amended as follows.

(10) In subsection (1) (notification of person in whose name vehicle is registered)—

> (*a*) for "on non-renewal of a vehicle licence for" substitute "in relation to", and
> (*b*) for "failure to renew a vehicle licence" substitute "the vehicle ceasing to be appropriately covered".

(11) In the heading, for "Late-renewal" substitute "Section 7A".

GENERAL NOTE

Continuous registration was introduced to assist with reducing vehicle excise duty (VED) evasion, to improve the accuracy of the Driver and Vehicle Licensing Agency (DVLA) vehicle record database, and to reduce vehicle crime. Each keeper of a registered vehicle must contact the DVLA at least once a year to ensure the vehicle record is updated. This can be done by means of a licence (or nil licence) renewal, or by a statutory off-road notice (SORN). Where a SORN is given, this applies if the vehicle was licensed, or nil licensed, after 30 January 1998 if registered in Great Britain or after 29 November 2002 if registered in Northern Ireland.

The purpose of continuous registration is undermined if vehicle keepers do not contact the DVLA on an annual basis. If DVLA records are inaccurate, it is difficult to tackle VED, MOT and insurance evasion. The obligation to pay VED, at least on an annual basis, is a means of ensuring that up to date insurance and MOT documentation are available for the vehicle concerned.

The amendments made to the Vehicle Excise Registration Act 1994 s 7A (supplement payable on late renewal of vehicle licence) extend the circumstances where a late renewal supplement may arise (sub-ss (1) and (2)). This supplement is the initial means of ensuring the operation of continuous registration. A penalty is due if a vehicle remains unlicensed and lacks a requisite nil licence or SORN declaration.

Road Vehicles (Registration and Licensing) (Amendment) (No 3) Regulations, SI 2003/2981 Regulations (made under VERA 1994 s 7A(1)) provide for a supplement to be due where a vehicle has ceased to be 'appropriately covered' and circumstances do not meet the criteria laid down in the regulations. There is, in effect, a period of grace, so that the supplement is not payable if, before the end of a 'relevant prescribed period', the vehicle is appropriately covered from immediately after it so ceased or a SORN has been given (sub-s (3)). A relevant prescribed period is a period beginning when the vehicle 'ceased to be appropriately covered as prescribed' (VERA 1994 s 7A(1D) as inserted by sub-s (4)).

Except in prescribed circumstances, this allows regulations to be made requiring that a supplement is due where a vehicle has ceased to be appropriately covered (as defined in sub-s (4) and such cover is not maintained or reinstated during a prescribed grace period.

If a vehicle for which a vehicle licence is in force is transferred by the holder of the vehicle licence to another person, the vehicle licence is treated as no longer in force. Where, however, the licence is delivered to the other person along with the vehicle, the licence is deemed to be still in force and affording appropriate cover (VERA 1994 s 7A(1B), as inserted by sub-s (4)).

This does not apply where an application is made, and a temporary licence is issued, when – on a transfer of the vehicle during its currency – the temporary licence is delivered with the vehicle to the transferee (VERA 1994 s 7A(1C) as amended by sub-s (4)).

Under VERA 1994 s 7A(2)(c), as amended by sub-s (5), the supplement:

(a) is payable by such person as may be prescribed, or jointly and severally by such persons,

(b) falls due at such time as may be prescribed, and

(c) may be of an amount that varies according to the length of the period between:

(i) the time of a notification to, or in relation to, a person from whom it is due (under regulations made under VERA 1994, and

(ii) the time at which it is paid.

This allows a period of grace to be prescribed, and allows the amount of the supplement payable to be varied according to the time between notification that it is due and when it is paid.

Under VERA 1994 s 7A(3)(b), as amended by sub-s (6), a supplement that has become payable:

(a) is in addition to any VED charged for the vehicle concerned,

(b) does not cease to be payable because appropriate cover for the vehicle has been reinstated, and

(c) may, without prejudice to VERA 1994 ss 6 or 7B(2) and (3) or any other provision of VERA 1994, be recovered as a debt due to the Crown.

Under VERA 1994 s 7A(4)(a), omitting redundant definitions, as amended by sub-s (7), here:

(a) 'prescribed' means prescribed by, or determined in accordance with, regulations, and

(b) 'regulations' means regulations made by the Secretary of State with the consent of the Treasury.

None of the following regulations can be made unless a draft thereof has been laid before, and approved by a resolution of, each House of Parliament (VERA 1994 s 7A(5)). This applies to regulations that:

(a) provide for a supplement in a case where one would not otherwise fall due,

(b) increase the amount of a supplement,

(c) provide for a supplement to be payable earlier than it would otherwise be payable, or

(d) provide for a supplement to be payable by a person by whom the supplement would not otherwise be payable.

(VERA 1994 s 7A(6)).

Regulations may provide for notification that a supplement may, or has, become payable upon a vehicle ceasing to be appropriately covered, and when, following the vehicle ceasing to be appropriately covered, the registered keeper may be guilty of an offence under VERA 1994 s 31A (offence by registered keeper where vehicle unlicensed) (VERA 1994 s 7B(1), as amended by sub-s (10)).

67 Reorganisation of water and sewerage services in Northern Ireland

(1) In this section "relevant transfer" means a transfer of property, rights or liabilities where—

(*a*) the transfer is of property, rights or liabilities which—

(i) are specified or described in or determined in accordance with a scheme, and

(ii) consist of or include relevant property, rights or liabilities,

(*b*) the transfer is from a Northern Ireland department or persons which include a Northern Ireland department to a company or companies specified in the scheme ("transferee company"), and

(*c*) the transfer is effected by or under an enactment which—

(i) is made after the coming into force of this section, and

(ii) relates to the provision of water or sewerage services in Northern Ireland.

(2) In this section "relevant property, rights or liabilities" means property, rights or liabilities connected with the provision of any water or sewerage services.

(3) The Treasury may by regulations make provision for or in connection with varying the way in which a relevant tax or duty would, apart from the regulations, have effect in relation to, or in connection with, any of the following—

(*a*) anything done for the purpose of, or under or in consequence of, a relevant transfer of relevant property, rights or liabilities from a Northern Ireland department to a transferee company;

(*b*) any relevant property, rights or liabilities which are the subject of a relevant transfer from a Northern Ireland department to a transferee company;

(*c*) any relevant property, rights or liabilities of a transferee company.

(4) The provision that may be made by the regulations includes provision for or in connection with any of the following—

(*a*) a tax provision not to apply or to apply with modifications in prescribed cases or circumstances;

(*b*) anything done to have or not to have a specified consequence for the purposes of a tax provision in prescribed cases or circumstances;

(*c*) any relevant property, rights or liabilities which are the subject of a relevant transfer from a Northern Ireland department to a transferee company to be treated in a specified way for the purposes of a tax provision in prescribed cases or circumstances;

(*d*) the withdrawal of relief (whether or not granted by virtue of the regulations), and the charging of tax, in prescribed cases or circumstances;

(*e*) requiring or enabling the Secretary of State, with the consent of the Treasury, to determine or to specify the method to be used for determining anything (including amounts or values, or times or periods of time) which needs to be determined for the purposes of any tax provision (whether or not modified by the regulations) as it applies in relation to, or in connection with,—

(i) anything done for the purpose of, or under or in consequence of, a relevant transfer of relevant property, rights or liabilities from a Northern Ireland department to a transferee company, or

(ii) any relevant property, rights or liabilities which are the subject of a relevant transfer from a Northern Ireland department to a transferee company.

(5) A provision of regulations made by virtue only of subsection (3)(*c*) ("a subsection (3)(*c*) provision") (whether or not also by virtue of subsection (4)) shall not have effect for an accounting period of a transferee company unless the company is wholly owned by the Crown during the whole of that accounting period.

(6) Regulations under this section may provide that, for the purposes of a subsection (3)(*c*) provision, an accounting period of a transferee company shall be taken to have ended on the company ceasing to be wholly owned by the Crown.

(7) For the purposes of this section, a company shall be regarded as wholly owned by the Crown at any time when each of the issued shares in the company is held by, or by a nominee of,—

(*a*) the Treasury,

(*b*) the Secretary of State,

(*c*) a Northern Ireland department, or

(*d*) another company which is wholly owned by the Crown.

(8) In this section—

"enactment" includes a provision comprised in—

(*a*) Northern Ireland legislation, or

(*b*) an instrument made under an enactment;

"prescribed" means prescribed by or determined in accordance with regulations under this section;

"relevant tax or duty" means income tax, corporation tax, capital gains tax, stamp duty or stamp duty reserve tax;

"tax provision" means a provision of an enactment about a relevant tax or duty.

(9) Any power to make regulations under this section is exercisable by statutory instrument.

(10) A statutory instrument containing regulations under this section shall be subject to annulment in pursuance of a resolution of the House of Commons.

(11) Any power to make regulations under this section includes power—

(*a*) to make different provision for different cases or circumstances;

(*b*) to make incidental, supplemental, consequential or transitional provision or savings.

GENERAL NOTE

At the time of writing, the Treasury are planning to make regulations that will deal with the consequences of setting up a new company to operate the Water Service in Northern Ireland (NI). Currently, the Northern Ireland Water Service, an Executive Agency of the Department for Regional Development, provides water and sewerage services in NI. The functions, property and liabilities of the Water Service are due to be transferred in 2006 to a new company that will be owned by the Department for Regional Development.

In order to ensure that the tax treatment of the new company is fair and reasonable, a number of tax provisions are needed to set appropriate values, for tax purposes, of the assets and liabilities transferred to a transferee company and to deal with other consequences of the reorganisation.

68 EU Mutual Assistance Directive: notifications

(1) This section applies where, in accordance with Article 8a of the Mutual Assistance Directive, the competent authority of another member State ("the applicant authority") requests the Commissioners for Her Majesty's Revenue and Customs to notify an instrument to the person to whom the instrument is addressed.

(2) The Commissioners must take the necessary measures to notify the instrument to that person.

(3) The notification shall be given in accordance with the law applicable to notification of similar instruments in the part of the United Kingdom in which it is given.

(4) The Commissioners must—

(*a*) inform the applicant authority immediately of their response to the request, and

(*b*) confirm to the applicant authority, as soon as is reasonably practicable, the date on which the instrument was notified to the person concerned.

(5) The Commissioners may request additional information from the applicant authority for the purpose of giving the notification.

(6) In this section "the Mutual Assistance Directive" means Council Directive 77/799/EEC as amended (in particular by Council Directive 2004/56/EC).

(7) In this section references to the Commissioners for Her Majesty's Revenue and Customs include, in relation to any time before 18th April 2005,—

(*a*) the Commissioners of Customs and Excise;

(*b*) the Commissioners of Inland Revenue.

(8) In this section "instrument" means any instrument or decision which—

(*a*) emanates from the administrative authorities of the member State in which the applicant authority is situated, and

(*b*) concerns the application in that member State of legislation on taxes covered by the Mutual Assistance Directive.

(9) This section has effect in relation to requests received by the Commissioners for Her Majesty's Revenue and Customs on or after 1st January 2005.

GENERAL NOTE

The UK tax authorities are empowered to deliver documents on behalf of another EU member state to a UK resident taxpayer in relation to a tax liability of his in that other member state. The ability of member states to assist each other in this way is a requirement of the Directive on mutual assistance in tax matters, following its amendment in April 2004.

Directive 2004/56/EC was adopted by the Council of Ministers of the European Union on 21 April 2004. It makes a number of amendments to the existing Mutual Assistance Directive (MAD), which dates from 1977 (Directive 77/799/EEC) (sub-s (6)). The MAD as amended must be transposed by EU member states into their domestic law.

The purpose of the MAD is to allow co-operation between member states so as to combat international tax evasion and avoidance. The competent authorities of the member states may exchange any information and provide certain other forms of assistance to enable them to make a correct assessment of the taxes covered by the Directive. Currently, taxes on income, capital and insurance premiums are covered; separate EC regulations provide for very similar forms of mutual assistance in relation to VAT and excises.

The amendments to the MAD adopted by the Council in April 2004 include a new Article 8a, which requires the competent authorities of the member states (when requested by another member state) to notify persons living in their territory of instruments and decisions affecting those persons emanating from the other member state. This is something the Commissioners for HM Revenue and Customs (HMRC) are already required to do in relation to cross-border recovery of tax debts.

It can be seen that the starting point of this procedure is a request from another member state, made under the relevant Article of the MAD, to notify a UK resident about instruments and decisions concerning the application of the tax laws of the requesting state.

HMRC must take the necessary measures to act on the request to notify the instrument to that person, and must use the same method to notify the taxpayer as UK domestic law allows for similar documents in the part of the UK in which it is given.

HMRC must immediately acknowledge, to the applicant authority, receipt of the request and inform them of their response to the request. They must also confirm to the applicant authority, as soon as is reasonably practicable, the date on which the instrument was notified to the person concerned). They may request additional information from the applicant authority before acting on the request.

Most elements of the MAD have already been transposed into UK law. In particular, in FA 1990 s 125 and FA 2003 s 197. The UK tax authorities are enabled to act in relation to requests they receive on or after 1 January 2005 (the date by which all member states are required to have transposed the amended Directive).

69 Abolition of statutory adjudicator for National Savings and Investments

(1) After the coming into force of this section, no further disputes shall be referred to a person appointed under section 84 of the Friendly Societies Act 1992 (c. 40) (adjudicator for disputes under the National Savings Bank Act 1971 and the National Debt Act 1972).

(2) This section comes into force on 1st September 2005.

GENERAL NOTE

The office of Statutory Adjudicator for National Savings and Investments (NS&I) is abolished with effect from 1 September 2005.

NS&I currently have a separate adjudicator, appointed under the Friendly Societies Act 1992, to arbitrate in a customer dispute. In contrast, customer complaints against financial services organisations regulated by the Financial Services Authority (FSA) are arbitrated by the Financial Ombudsman Service (FOS). This amendment brings NS&I more closely into line with the rest of the savings industry.

Following abolition of the Statutory Adjudicator for NS&I on 1 September 2005, NS&I will transfer to the 'voluntary jurisdiction' of the FOS who will arbitrate in cases where customers have unresolved complaints against NS&I in the same way as for an FSA regulated firm. The jurisdiction is 'voluntary' but NS&I consider this a binding commitment. A public statement to this effect will be added to the agency's framework document.

The change is taking effect from 1 September to ensure that both FOS and NS&I have the necessary time to put all internal procedures in place. The transfer is being implemented in such a way as to ensure that NS & I customers have continuous right of recourse to an arbitrator.

PART 6

SUPPLEMENTARY PROVISIONS

70 Repeals

(1) The enactments mentioned in Schedule 11 (which include provisions that are spent or of no practical utility) are repealed to the extent specified.

(2) The repeals specified in that Schedule have effect subject to the commencement provisions and savings contained or referred to in the notes set out in that Schedule.

71 Interpretation

In this Act—

"CAA 2001" means the Capital Allowances Act 2001 (c. 2);
"FA", followed by a year, means the Finance Act of that year;
"ICTA" means the Income and Corporation Taxes Act 1988 (c. 1);
"ITEPA 2003" means the Income Tax (Earnings and Pensions) Act 2003 (c. 1);
"ITTOIA 2005" means the Income Tax (Trading and Other Income) Act 2005 (c. 5);
"TCGA 1992" means the Taxation of Chargeable Gains Act 1992 (c. 12);

"VATA 1994" means the Value Added Tax Act 1994 (c. 23);
"VERA 1994" means the Vehicle Excise and Registration Act 1994 (c. 22).

72 Short title

This Act may be cited as the Finance (No. 2) Act 2005.

SCHEDULES

SCHEDULE 1
DISCLOSURE OF VALUE ADDED TAX AVOIDANCE SCHEMES
Section 6

Introduction

1 Schedule 11A to VATA 1994 (disclosure of avoidance schemes) is amended in accordance with this Schedule.

GENERAL NOTE

This Schedule amends the provisions relating to the disclosure of VAT avoidance schemes. It substitutes a new VATA 1994 Sch 11A para 2, inserts a new para 2A, and amends paras 1, 6, 7, 11, 12.

Interpretative provisions

2 In paragraph 1 (interpretation), after the definition of "designated scheme" insert—
" "non-deductible tax", in relation to a taxable person, has the meaning given by paragraph 2A;".

GENERAL NOTE

This paragraph inserts a new definition in VATA 1994 Sch 11A para 1. For the meaning of 'non-deductible tax', see para 4 below.

3 For paragraph 2 substitute—
"**2**— (1) For the purposes of this Schedule, a taxable person obtains a tax advantage if—
  (*a*) in any prescribed accounting period, the amount by which the output tax accounted for by him exceeds the input tax deducted by him is less than it would otherwise be,
  (*b*) he obtains a VAT credit when he would not otherwise do so, or obtains a larger VAT credit or obtains a VAT credit earlier than would otherwise be the case,
  (*c*) in a case where he recovers input tax as a recipient of a supply before the supplier accounts for the output tax, the period between the time when the input tax is recovered and the time when the output tax is accounted for is greater than would otherwise be the case, or
  (*d*) in any prescribed accounting period, the amount of his non-deductible tax is less than it would otherwise be.
(2) For the purposes of this Schedule, a person who is not a taxable person obtains a tax advantage if his non-refundable tax is less than it would otherwise be.
(3) In sub-paragraph (2), "non-refundable tax", in relation to a person who is not a taxable person, means—
  (*a*) VAT on the supply to him of any goods or services,
  (*b*) VAT on the acquisition by him from another member State of any goods, and
  (*c*) VAT paid or payable by him on the importation of any goods from a place outside the member States,
but excluding (in each case) any VAT in respect of which he is entitled to a refund from the Commissioners by virtue of any provision of this Act."

GENERAL NOTE

This paragraph substitutes a new VATA 1994 Sch 11A para 2.
The new Sch 11A para 2(1) sets out the four circumstances in which a taxable person obtains a tax advantage. Heads (a), (b) and (c) replicate the circumstances currently set out in Sch 11A para 2(1) and (2). Head (d) provides that a taxable

person obtains a tax advantage if the amount of his non-deductible tax for a prescribed accounting period is less than it would otherwise be. For 'non-deductible tax', see para 4 below.

The new Sch 11A para 2(2), (3) provide that a person who is not a taxable person obtains a tax advantage if his non-refundable tax is less than it would otherwise be. The VAT incurred by him on purchases, acquisitions and importations of goods or services is 'non-refundable tax' for this purpose if he is not entitled to a refund in respect of it. For circumstances where a non-taxable person may be entitled to a refund of VAT, see in particular VATA 1994 ss 33 (local authorities and other bodies), 33A (museums and galleries), 35 (persons constructing buildings) and 40 (new means of transport). Only the last-mentioned relief is specifically confined to non-taxable persons.

4 After paragraph 2 insert—

"Meaning of "non-deductible tax"

2A— (1) In this Schedule "non-deductible tax", in relation to a taxable person, means—

(*a*) input tax for which he is not entitled to credit under section 25, and

(*b*) any VAT incurred by him which is not input tax and in respect of which he is not entitled to a refund from the Commissioners by virtue of any provision of this Act.

(2) For the purposes of sub-paragraph (1)(*b*), the VAT "incurred" by a taxable person is—

(*a*) VAT on the supply to him of any goods or services,

(*b*) VAT on the acquisition by him from another member State of any goods, and

(*c*) VAT paid or payable by him on the importation of any goods from a place outside the member States."

GENERAL NOTE

This paragraph inserts a new VATA 1994 Sch 11A para 2A. This defines 'non-deductible tax'. The VAT incurred by a taxable person on purchases, acquisitions and importations of goods or services is 'non-deductible tax' if he is not entitled to a credit or refund in respect of it.

For input tax credit, see VATA 1994 s 26(1). For input tax excluded from credit, see VATA 1994 s 25(7); VAT (Tour Operators) Order 1987, SI 1987/1806, art 12 (goods and services for re-supply by a tour operator as a designated travel service); VAT (Input Tax) Order 1992, SI 1992/3222, arts 4 (works of art, antiques, collectors' items and second-hand goods), 5 (business entertainment), 6 (goods incorporated in a building or its site) and 7 (motor cars).

For refunds in respect of non-business activities, see in particular VATA 1994 ss 33 (local authorities and other bodies), 33A (museums and galleries) and 35 (persons constructing buildings).

Duty to notify Commissioners

5— (1) Paragraph 6 (duty to notify Commissioners) is amended as follows.

(2) In sub-paragraph (1)—

(*a*) omit the word "or" at the end of paragraph (*a*), and

(*b*) after paragraph (*b*) insert ", or

(*c*) the amount of his non-deductible tax in respect of any prescribed accounting period is less than it would be but for such a scheme."

(3) After sub-paragraph (2) insert—

"(2A) Sub-paragraph (2) does not apply to a taxable person in relation to any scheme if he has on a previous occasion—

(*a*) notified the Commissioners under that sub-paragraph in relation to the scheme, or

(*b*) provided the Commissioners with prescribed information under sub-paragraph (3) (as it applied before the scheme became a designated scheme) in relation to the scheme."

(4) For sub-paragraph (5) substitute—

"(5) Sub-paragraph (3) also does not apply where the scheme is one in respect of which the taxable person has on a previous occasion provided the Commissioners with prescribed information under that sub-paragraph."

GENERAL NOTE

This paragraph amends VATA 1994 Sch 11A para 6, which deals with the duty to notify a 'notifiable scheme' (as defined in Sch 11A para 5). It makes three changes to the duty to notify imposed on taxable persons.

First, a new Sch 11A para 6(1)(c), in conjunction with Sch 11A para 6(2), (3) (which are unchanged), provides that a taxable person has a duty to notify if, as a result of a notifiable scheme to which he is a party, the amount of his non-deductible tax for a prescribed accounting period is less than it would otherwise be. The new Sch 11A para 2(1)(d) (inserted by para 3 above) provides that he obtains a tax advantage in these circumstances. For 'non-deductible tax', see para 4 above.

Secondly, a new Sch 11A para 6(2A)(a) and substituted para 6(5) replicate the effect of the current para 6(5). A taxable person is not required to notify the reference number of a designated scheme or provide the prescribed information regarding a 'hallmarked scheme' if he has already done so on a previous occasion.

Thirdly, a new Sch 11A para 6(2A)(b) deals with the situation where a taxable person has provided the prescribed information regarding a 'hallmarked scheme' and, by virtue to an amendment to VAT (Disclosure of Avoidance Schemes) (Designations) Order 2004, SI 2004/1933, Sch 1, a scheme of that description subsequently becomes a designated scheme. The taxable person is not required to notify the reference number of the designated scheme in these circumstances.

A non-taxable person may obtain a tax advantage under the new Sch 11A para 2(2) (as inserted by para 3 above), so that the means adopted to reduce his non-refundable tax may amount to a designated scheme (see Sch 11A para 3(1)(a)) or 'hallmarked scheme' (see Sch 11A para 5(1)(b), (3)), and therefore a notifiable scheme (see Sch 11A para 5(1)). However, the duty to notify is confined to taxable persons (see Sch 11A para 6(1), (2), (3)). It appears to follow that non-taxable persons do not have a duty to notify, although they are at liberty to do so in relation to a 'hallmarked scheme' if they so wish (see Sch 11A para 9(1)).

6 In paragraph 7 (exemptions from duty to notify) in the definition of "relevant period" in sub-paragraph (9) for "6(1)(*a*) or (*b*)" substitute "6(1)(*a*), (*b*) or (*c*)".

GENERAL NOTE

This paragraph amends Sch 11A para 7(9) in consequence of the new Sch 11A para 6(1)(c) inserted by para 5 above.

Amount of penalty

7— (1) Paragraph 11 (amount of penalty) is amended as follows.

(2) In sub-paragraph (3)—

(*a*) omit the word "and" at the end of paragraph (*a*), and
(*b*) after paragraph (*b*) insert ", and
    (*c*) to the extent that—
      (i) the case falls within paragraph 6(1)(*c*), and
      (ii) the excess of the notional non-deductible tax of the taxable person for the relevant periods over his non-deductible tax for those periods is not represented by a corresponding amount which by virtue of paragraph (*a*) or (*b*) is part of the VAT saving,
the amount of the excess."

(3) In sub-paragraph (4), after "(3)(*a*)" insert "and (*c*)".

(4) After sub-paragraph (4) insert—

"(5) In sub-paragraph (3)(*c*), "notional non-deductible tax", in relation to a taxable person, means the amount that would, but for the scheme, have been the amount of his non-deductible tax."

GENERAL NOTE

In principle, a person is liable to a penalty if he fails to notify the reference number of a designated scheme in accordance with Sch 11A para 6(2). The prescribed penalty is 15% of the VAT saving. The VAT saving now comprises three elements, each of which is related to a specific factual situation. The elements set out in Sch 11A para 11(3)(a) and (b) relate to the factual situations in Sch 11A para 6(1)(a) and (b) respectively. This paragraph inserts a new Sch 11A para 11(3)(c) and (5), which set out a third element relating to the factual situation in Sch 11A para 6(1)(c) (as inserted by para 5 above). The paragraph also makes a consequential amendment to Sch 11A para 11(4).

New VATA 1994 Sch 11A para 11(3)(c) and (5)

The factual situation is that a taxable person's 'non-deductible tax' for any prescribed accounting period has been reduced as a consequence of being a party to the scheme. The new VATA 1994 Sch 11A para 11(3)(c) provides that the element of the VAT saving attributable to this situation is the amount by which 'notional non-deductible tax' for the 'relevant periods' exceeds 'non-deductible tax' for those periods.

'Notional non-deductible tax' is the amount that would, but for the scheme, have been the amount of taxable person's non-deductible tax (new Sch 11A para 11(5)). For 'non-deductible tax', see Sch 11A para 2A (as inserted by para 4 above). For 'relevant periods', see Sch 11A para 11(4), which is unchanged.

All or part of the excess calculated under new Sch 11A para 11(3)(c) may also form part of the VAT saving calculated under Sch 11A para 11(3)(a) or (b). Where this is so, new VATA 1994 Sch 11A para 11(3)(c) provides that the excess is reduced accordingly.

Penalty assessments

8 In paragraph 12 (penalty assessments) for sub-paragraph (3) substitute—

"(3) In a case where—

(*a*) the penalty falls to be calculated by reference to the VAT saving as determined under paragraph 11(3), and

(*b*) the notional tax cannot readily be attributed to any one or more prescribed accounting periods,

the notional tax shall be treated for the purposes of this Schedule as attributable to such period or periods as the Commissioners may determine to the best of their judgment and notify to the person liable for the penalty.

(3A) In sub-paragraph (3) "the notional tax" means—

(*a*) the VAT that would, but for the scheme, have been shown in returns as payable by or to the taxable person, or

(*b*) any amount that would, but for the scheme, have been the amount of the non-deductible tax of the taxable person."

GENERAL NOTE

In principle, a person is liable to a penalty if he fails to notify the reference number of a designated scheme in accordance with Sch 11A para 6(2). The prescribed penalty is 15% of the VAT saving, which is calculated in accordance with Sch 11A para 11(3) (as amended by para 7 above).

The VAT saving in Sch 11A para 11(3)(a) is calculated by reference to the amount of VAT that would, but for the scheme, have been shown as being payable to or by the taxable person in his returns for the relevant prescribed accounting periods. Similarly, the VAT saving in new Sch 11A para 11(3)(c) is calculated by reference to the amount that would, but for the scheme, have been the amount of his non-deductible tax for those periods. For 'non-deductible tax', see Sch 11A para 2A (as inserted by para 4 above).

The VAT or non-deductible tax may not be readily attributable to specific prescribed accounting periods. Where this is so, the VAT or non-deductible tax is attributed to such period(s) as the Commissioners may determine. The determination must be made to the best of the Commissioners' judgment. The amount attributed to each period must be notified to the person liable to the penalty.

SCHEDULE 2
EMPLOYEE SECURITIES: ANTI-AVOIDANCE
Section 12

GENERAL NOTE

The rules relating to employee share acquisitions were completely rewritten in FA 2003 Sch 22 in an attempt to put a stop to the use of arrangements involving shares and securities as a way of avoiding income tax and NIC on what were, in commercial terms, payments of remuneration. At the time that these new rules were introduced various Inland Revenue spokesmen expressed confidence that Sch 22 had closed all of the perceived loopholes and that avoidance involving shares and securities would be a thing of the past. This has proved to be very wide of the mark. Schedule 22 has itself been shown to be full of new loopholes, and various attempts have been made over the last two years to plug some of the gaps. The new regime for the disclosure of tax-avoidance schemes has, however, demonstrated that Sch 22 was still capable of being exploited, and therefore in the 2004 Pre-Budget Report the government announced a further series of measures aimed at putting an end, once and for all, to the use of contrived arrangements involving shares to pay disguised remuneration.

Schedule 2 therefore contains a number of detailed technical amendments to Sch 22 but also, more importantly, introduces a number of more general anti-avoidance tests. The Government's aspiration of two years ago that it would be able to draft watertight legislation to prevent avoidance using shares and securities has now been shown to be unrealistic and it has been forced to introduce general anti-avoidance principles into significant parts of the regime. The cynic might argue that the real effect of Sch 22 has been to make life far more complex for ordinary commercial transactions involving shares while making very little difference to the market for artificial tax-avoidance schemes.

The most significant development in this area was however the Paymaster General's statement, on 2 December, that if any future abuses of the employee share scheme rules were identified the government would introduce further blocking measures, which would be retrospective to 2 December. In the written ministerial statement, the Paymaster General, *inter alia*, stated the following (HoC 2 December 2004: Column 46WS).

I am therefore giving notice of our intention to deal with any arrangements that emerge in future designed to frustrate our intention that employers and employees should pay the proper amount of tax and NICs on the rewards of employment. Where we become aware of arrangements which attempt to frustrate this intention we will introduce legislation to close them down, where necessary from today.

Such a clear announcement of the intention to introduce retrospective legislation is unprecedented in modern times. It does seem to have had the desired effect. Anecdotal evidence is that far fewer schemes involving employee shares have been launched onto the market since the date of the Paymaster's statement.

Introductory

1 ITEPA 2003 is amended as follows.

GENERAL NOTE

This introduces the Schedule.

Rights under certain insurance contracts to be securities

2— (1) Section 420 (income and exemptions relating to securities: meaning of "securities" etc.) is amended as follows.

(2) In subsection (1), after paragraph (*a*) insert—

"(aa) rights under contracts of insurance other than excluded contracts of insurance,".

(3) In paragraph (*b*) of that subsection, insert at the end "(other than contracts of insurance)".

(4) In paragraph (*g*) of that subsection, insert at the end "(other than contracts of insurance)".

(5) After that subsection insert—

"(1A) For the purposes of subsection (1)(aa) a contract of insurance is an excluded contract of insurance if it is—

(*a*) a contract for an annuity which is (or will be) pension income (see Part 9),

(*b*) a contract of long-term insurance, other than an annuity contract, which does not have a surrender value and is not capable of acquiring one (whether on conversion or in any other circumstances), or

(*c*) a contract of general insurance other than one which falls, in accordance with generally accepted accounting practice, to be accounted for as a financial asset or liability.

(1B) In this section—

"contract of insurance",
"contract of long-term insurance", and
"contract of general insurance",

have the same meaning as in the Financial Services and Markets Act 2000 (Regulated Activities) Order 2001."

(6) In subsection (5)—

(*a*) at the end of paragraph (*c*) insert "and", and

(*b*) omit paragraph (*d*) (exclusion of insurance contracts).

(7) In Part 2 of Schedule 1 (index of defined expressions), insert at the appropriate place—

"generally accepted accounting practice | Section 832(1) of ICTA"

(8) This paragraph has effect on and after 2nd December 2004 and applies in relation to rights under contracts of insurance acquired before that date, as well as those acquired on or after that date; and—

(*a*) for the purposes of the application of Chapter 3B of Part 7 of ITEPA 2003 (securities with artificially enhanced market value) by reason of this paragraph in relation to rights under contracts of insurance acquired before that date, section 446O of that Act (meaning of "relevant period") has effect as if they were acquired on that date, and

(*b*) for the purposes of section 420(1A)(*c*) of ITEPA 2003, section 50 of FA 2004 (meaning of "generally accepted accounting practice") has effect on and after that date, in spite of subsection (6) of that section.

GENERAL NOTE

One of the fundamental features of the Sch 22 regime is the broad definition of securities. However the disclosure regime has demonstrated that the original definition was not sufficient to catch all potential abuses. The draftsman has therefore extended the definition of a security to include rights under insurance contracts other than excluded contracts.

For this purpose a contract of insurance and related terms have the same meaning as in the Financial Services and Markets Act 2000 (Regulated Activities) Order 2001.

Excluded contracts are defined in para 2(5). These are annuity contracts, long-term insurance contracts which do not have a surrender value, or general insurance contracts which are not treated, under GAAP, as a financial asset or liability.

Paragraph 2 takes effect from 2 December 2004 but applies regardless of when the rights under the contract were acquired.

In the case of charges under ITEPA 2003 s 446L – artificial increases in the value of securities – any artificial increases in the value of an insurance contract are ignored if they took place before 2 December 2004.

Restricted securities

3 Chapter 2 of Part 7 (restricted securities) is amended as follows.

GENERAL NOTE

This introduces the amendments to the definition of a restricted security.

4— (1) Section 424 (employment-related securities which are not restricted securities or restricted interest in securities) is renumbered as subsection (1) of that section.

(2) In that subsection—

(*a*) at the end of paragraph (*a*) insert "or", and

(*b*) omit paragraph (*c*) (employment-related securities which are, or are an interest in, redeemable securities) and the word "or" before it.

(3) After that subsection insert—

"(2) Subsection (1) does not apply if the main purpose (or one of the main purposes) of the arrangements under which the right or opportunity to acquire the employment-related securities is made available is the avoidance of tax or national insurance contributions."

(4) This paragraph has effect on and after 2nd December 2004 and applies in relation to employment-related securities acquired before that date, as well as those acquired on or after that date; and section 422 of ITEPA 2003 (application of Chapter 2 of Part 7) applies to employment-related securities in relation to which this paragraph has effect and which were acquired before that date with the omission of the words "at the time of the acquisition".

GENERAL NOTE

Under the original legislation a redeemable security is not within the employment-related securities regime (unless the security is restricted for some other reason). This original definition has opened up avoidance opportunities. Paragraph 4 therefore brings redeemable securities within the definition of employment-related securities.

At present certain securities remain outside the scope of the restricted securities regime. For example, securities which are forfeitable on cessation of employment for misconduct are not within Chapter 2 (restricted securities). This exemption will no longer be available where the purpose (or one of the main purposes) of the arrangements under which the right or opportunity to acquire the employment-related securities is made available is the avoidance of tax or National Insurance contributions.

This new rule applies from 2 December 2004, regardless of the date on which the securities were acquired.

5— (1) In section 428 (amount of charge under section 426), after subsection (9) insert—

"(10) But subsection (9) does not apply if something which affects the employment-related securities has been done (at or before the time of the chargeable event) as part of a scheme or arrangement the main purpose (or one of the main purposes) of which is the avoidance of tax or national insurance contributions."

(2) This paragraph has effect where something such as is mentioned in section 428(10) of ITEPA 2003 has been done on or after 2nd December 2004.

GENERAL NOTE

Under s 428 there is a chargeable event where a restricted security is sold. If the security is sold for less than market value the tax charge which would normally arise is reduced pro-rata to the undervalue. This relief is now subject to the same avoidance test as in para 4 above. The anti-avoidance test applies to disposals on or after 2 December 2004.

6— (1) In section 429 (exception from charge under section 426 for certain company shares), for subsection (1A) substitute—

"(1A) This subsection is satisfied unless something which affects the employment-related securities has been done (at or before the time when section 426 would apply) as part of a scheme or arrangement the main purpose (or one of the main purposes) of which is the avoidance of tax or national insurance contributions."

(2) This paragraph has effect where something such as is mentioned in section 429(1A) of ITEPA 2003 has been done on or after 2nd December 2004.

GENERAL NOTE

Certain shares are removed from the scope of the restricted securities charge under s 429. These include, for example, shares in employee-controlled companies. Again, these shares will be brought within the scope of Chapter 2 where they were acquired for tax-avoidance reasons. The anti-avoidance rule applies for "things done" on or after 2 December 2004.

7— (1) After section 431A insert—

"431B Securities acquired for purpose of avoidance

Where employment-related securities are restricted securities or a restricted interest in securities, the employer and the employee are to be treated as making an election under section 431(1) in relation to the employment-related securities if the main purpose (or one of the main purposes) of the arrangements under which the right or opportunity to acquire the employment-related securities is made available is the avoidance of tax or national insurance contributions."

(2) This paragraph has effect in relation to employment-related securities acquired on or after 2nd December 2004.

GENERAL NOTE

This imposes a mandatory s 431(1) election on acquisition where the shares were acquired under tax-avoidance arrangements. The effect of this is that there will be an automatic up-front market value tax charge on the unrestricted market value of the securities. This mandatory s 431 election applies where the securities are acquired on or after 2 December 2004.

Convertible securities

8 Chapter 3 of Part 7 (convertible securities) is amended as follows.

GENERAL NOTE

This introduces the section.

9— (1) In section 436(*a*) (meaning of "convertible securities"), for "immediate or conditional entitlement" substitute "entitlement (whether immediate or deferred and whether conditional or unconditional)".

(2) Section 437 (adjustment of acquisition charge) is renumbered as subsection (1) of that section.

(3) After that subsection insert—

"(2) Subsection (1) does not apply if the main purpose (or one of the main purposes) of the arrangements under which the right or opportunity to acquire the employment-related securities is made available is the avoidance of tax or national insurance contributions unless the market value of the employment-related securities determined under subsection (1) would be greater than that determined under subsection (3).

(3) Where subsection (1) does not apply by virtue of subsection (2) the market value of the employment-related securities is to be determined—

(*a*) where the securities which are (or an interest in which is) the employment-related securities fall within paragraph (*a*) of section 436 and the entitlement to convert is not both immediate and unconditional, as if it were,

(*b*) where they fall within paragraph (*b*) of that section, as if the circumstances are such that an entitlement to convert to arises immediately, and

(*c*) where they fall within paragraph (*c*) of that section, as if provision were made for their immediate conversion;

and in each case is to be determined as if they were immediately and fully convertible.

(4) In subsection (3) "immediately and fully convertible" means convertible immediately after the acquisition of the employment-related securities so as to obtain the maximum gain that would be possible on a conversion at that time (assuming, where the securities into which the securities may be converted were not in existence at that

time and it is appropriate to do so, that they were) without giving any consideration for the conversion or incurring any expenses in connection with it."

(4) This paragraph has effect in relation to acquisitions on or after 2nd December 2004.

GENERAL NOTE

This corrects a drafting error in the original convertible securities regime. Under the original wording a security was caught when there was an "immediate or conditional" entitlement to conversion. Thus a deferred unconditional entitlement to convert was not caught. The new drafting makes it clear that all entitlements, whether immediate or deferred, conditional or unconditional, will now be caught.

In normal circumstances the tax liability on the acquisition of convertible securities is calculated without reference to the right to convert. However, where the convertible securities are acquired as part of tax-avoidance arrangements the right to convert is taken into account in valuing the securities. This rule does not apply if the market value of the securities, taking into account the right to convert, is less that the value ignoring the right to convert. Such cases will be unusual.

Where this market value rule is disapplied there is an alternative mechanism for determining market value. In such cases market value is to be determined as if the right to convert was both immediate and unconditional. In other words it is not possible to discount the value because of a contingency. In cases where the securities into which the original securities are to be converted do not exist at the time that the tax charge arises it is to be assumed that the new securities did in fact exist.

The new rules for convertible securities apply to acquisitions on or after 2 December 2004.

10— (1) In section 440 (amount of charge under section 438), after subsection (3) insert—

"(3A) If (because of subsection (2) of section 437) subsection (1) of that section did not apply in relation to the employment-related securities, the taxable amount is to be reduced by the amount by which—

(*a*) the market value of the employment-related securities for the purposes specified in that subsection, exceeded

(*b*) what it would have been had that subsection applied,

(less the aggregate of any amount by which the taxable amount on any previous chargeable event relating to the employment-related securities has been reduced under this subsection)."

(2) This paragraph has effect on and after 2nd December 2004.

GENERAL NOTE

The rules in para 9 present the possibility of double taxation. The conversion of securities will normally create a tax charge at the point of conversion, based on the uplift in market value at that point. If the shares have been valued up front taking account of the conversion rights then the charge arising on the conversion could result in the employee being taxed on a value greater than that which he ultimately received. Paragraph 10 therefore allows any excess value charged on acquisition to be set against the charge arising on conversion. This new rule also has effect from 2 December 2004.

11— (1) In section 443 (exception from charge under section 438 for certain company shares), for subsection (1A) substitute—

"(1A) This subsection is satisfied unless something which affects the employment-related securities has been done (at or before the time when section 438 would apply) as part of a scheme or arrangement the main purpose (or one of the main purposes) of which is the avoidance of tax or national insurance contributions."

(2) This paragraph has effect where something such as is mentioned in section 443(1A) of ITEPA 2003 has been done on or after 2nd December 2004.

GENERAL NOTE

This is a parallel measure to para 6. The exceptions to the normal charges under the convertible securities regime for employee-controlled companies and the like are not available where there is a "thing done" in respect of the securities which is part of tax-avoidance arrangements. This rule applies for things done on or after 2 December 2004.

Securities acquired for less than market value

12 Chapter 3C of Part 7 (securities acquired for less than market value) is amended as follows.

GENERAL NOTE

This introduces the section.

13— (1) In section 446R (exception from Chapter for certain company shares), for subsection (1A) substitute—

"(1A) This subsection is satisfied unless something which affects the employment-related securities has been done (at or before the time of the acquisition) as part of a scheme or arrangement the main purpose (or one of the main purposes) of which is the avoidance of tax or national insurance contributions."

(2) This paragraph has effect where something such as is mentioned in section 446R(1A) of ITEPA 2003 has been done on or after 2nd December 2004.

GENERAL NOTE

This is a parallel measure to paras 6 and 11. It disapplies the normal exemptions for acquisition of shares in employee-controlled companies etc where something has been done which affects the value of the securities (whether before or at the time of the acquisition) as part of tax-avoidance arrangements. This rules applies for things done on or after 2 December 2004.

14— (1) In section 446U(1) (discharge of notional loan), insert at the end "or

(c) something which affects the employment-related securities is done as part of a scheme or arrangement the main purpose (or one of the main purposes) of which is the avoidance of tax or national insurance contributions."

(2) This paragraph has effect where something such as is mentioned in section 443U(1)(c) of ITEPA 2003 has been done on or after 2nd December 2004.

GENERAL NOTE

In certain circumstances the acquisition of securities at undervalue, or not fully paid up, will give rise to a notional loan. That notional loan is normally discharged when there is a disposal of the securities or the securities become fully paid up and the discharge of the notional loan gives rise to an income tax liability. From 2 December 2004 there will also be a discharge of the notional loan (and hence a tax liability) where something which affects the securities is done as part of tax-avoidance **arrangements.**

15— (1) After section 446U insert—

"446UA Pre-acquisition avoidance cases

(1) Sections 446S to 446U do not apply if the main purpose (or one of the main purposes) of the arrangements under which the right or opportunity to acquire the employment-related securities is made available is the avoidance of tax or national insurance contributions.

(2) But instead an amount equal to what would (apart from this section) be the amount of the notional loan initially outstanding by virtue of sections 446S and 446T counts as employment income of the employee for the tax year in which the acquisition takes place."

(2) This paragraph has effect in relation to acquisitions on or after 2nd December 2004.

GENERAL NOTE

Paragraph 14 applies where the tax-avoidance arrangements come into place after the securities have been acquired. Where the right to acquire the securities was itself part of tax-avoidance arrangements para 15 disapplies the normal notional loan rule. Instead, an amount equal to what would normally have been the notional loan is treated as employment income in the year in which the acquisition takes place.

16— (1) Section 698 (PAYE: special charges on employment-related securities) is amended as follows.

(2) In subsection (1), after paragraph (*e*) insert—

"(ea) section 446UA (securities or interest acquired for less than market value: charge in avoidance cases),".

(3) In subsection (6), after paragraph (*d*) insert—

"(da) in relation to an amount counting as employment income under section 446UA, the date of the acquisition of the securities or interest in securities in question,".

(4) This paragraph has effect on and after the day on which this Act is passed.

GENERAL NOTE

The PAYE rules are amended to ensure that any charge under para 15 is subject to PAYE. Note that, although the substantive income tax charge arises in respect of acquisitions on or after 2 December, the PAYE amendment only takes place from 20 July 2005.

Post-acquisition benefits from securities

17 Chapter 4 of Part 7 (post-acquisition benefits from securities) is amended as follows.

GENERAL NOTE

This introduces the section.

18— (1) Section 447 (charge on other chargeable benefits from securities) is amended as follows.

(2) In subsection (1), for "by virtue of the ownership of employment-related securities by that person or another associated person" substitute "in connection with employment-related securities".

(3) For subsection (4) substitute—

"(4) If the benefit is otherwise chargeable to income tax this section does not apply unless something has been done which affects the employment-related securities as part of a scheme or arrangement the main purpose (or one of the main purposes) of which is the avoidance of tax or national insurance contributions."

(4) Sub-paragraph (2) has effect on and after 2nd December 2004 and sub-paragraph (3) has effect where something such as is mentioned in section 447(4) of ITEPA 2003 has been done on or after that date.

GENERAL NOTE

This is a drafting amendment. The original phrase "by virtue of the ownership of employment-related securities" gave rise to some doubts over whether or not it covered benefits which did not arise from the ownership of securities. The revised wording "in connection with employment-related securities" makes it clear that the section is not confined to benefits which arise from the ownership of securities.

In the normal course of events something which could be a post-acquisition benefit from a security but which is itself chargeable to tax in its own right will not also be taxed as a post-acquisition benefit. This exemption is removed in avoidance cases for things done on or after 2 December 2004.

This amendment caused considerable concern among advisors because it led to fears that it could give rise to double taxation in privately-owned companies. It could be argued that if an individual incorporated her business because it enabled profits to be extracted at a lower tax rate that was a tax-avoidance purpose. The shares in the newly-incorporated company would be employment-related securities and a dividend paid on those shares could be a post-acquisition benefit which was received in connection with those securities. This would mean that the dividend would be taxed twice: once under the normal rules and again as a post-acquisition benefit.

After representations were made on this issue the Paymaster General made the following statement in the select committee debate. (Standing Committee B 21 June 2005)

There has been some discussion about the scope of the proposal on employment-related securities in clause 12 and Schedule 2, about which I spoke briefly to the hon. Member for Runnymede and Weybridge (Mr. Hammond). These arrangements are devised to deal with the minority of cases where there are complex, contrived arrangements to avoid paying income tax and national insurance on employment rewards. The Government have made clear their intention to close that activity down permanently.

There has been some debate about whether small businesses are caught by the provisions, so I am grateful to have the opportunity to offer small businesses some reassurance.

A change being made to chapter 4 of the Income Tax (Earnings and Pensions) Act 2003 will remove, where avoidance is involved, the provision that automatically exempts benefits received in connection with securities from a full income tax and national insurance charge, if income tax has been paid elsewhere. I am aware, from representations made directly to me and my Department, that professionals have expressed concern about the possible scope of the change. I want to make it clear that this change does not bring all benefits derived from securities into a tax and national insurance charge. A reference to benefits in the context of the Schedule means the employment reward—the passing of value to an employee in return for the employee's labour. Where investors are carrying out their normal investment trans-action, this charge will not affect them.

The purpose test introduced in section 447 of the 2003 Act has been carefully designed to target complex, contrived avoidance arrangements that are used mainly to disguise cash bonuses. If taxpayers use contrived arrangements to get round anti-avoidance legislation—to avoid paying the proper amount of tax and national insurance—they cannot expect to be excluded from the charge. However, it will be absolutely clear from what I say about the purpose test that this measure will not affect the taxation of those small businesses that do not use contrived schemes to disguise remuneration to avoid tax and national insurance.

There is no connection between the changes proposed in this clause and schedule to tackle contrived avoidance schemes and last December's discussion paper on the taxation of small business, which focuses on the strategic issues relating to the taxation and treatment of the legal forms used by small businesses. Taxation of small businesses is a live issue that is being considered as part of our ongoing discussions with small businesses and their advisers. The provisions before the Committee today are not intended to address those points. Any proposals coming out of the discussion paper and further consideration will be brought before the House in the normal way.

I am grateful to you, Sir Nicholas, for allowing me to spell that out. There has been some confusion, and many inquiries have been made about that point. I was asked to explain the purpose of clause 12 and schedule 2 at the beginning of the debate on them. Clause 12 and schedule 2 contain important and necessary measures, which I should address on a point-by-point basis in our discussions on the amendments to the schedule.

Mr. Philip Hammond *(Runnymede and Weybridge) (Con): The Paymaster General is being extremely helpful. Will she confirm that what she is saying is that, with the exception of companies that fall within the scope of Inland Revenue 32, there is no intention to limit the ability to take profits in dividends within a business and to impute remuneration that is of another kind where profits are being taken as dividends?*

Dawn Primarolo: I was trying to be as clear as possible. Unless a scheme falls within the category of schemes contrived specifically to avoid income tax and national insurance on employment remuneration for an employee, it is not within the scope of clause 12 or schedule 2. There are matters to be discussed, but that will take a long time. I know that this topic has caused a great deal of interest, and I thought it would be helpful to provide to the Committee at the beginning of our deliberations as clear an idea as possible of the precise, narrow and targeted aim of schedule 2 and clause 12, and thereby to put to rest concerns that have been generated in some quarters.

19— (1) In section 449 (exception from charge under section 447 for certain company shares), for subsection (1A) substitute—

"(1A) This subsection is satisfied unless something which affects the employment-related securities has been done as part of a scheme or arrangement the main purpose (or one of the main purposes) of which is the avoidance of tax or national insurance contributions."

(2) This paragraph has effect where something such as is mentioned in section 449(1A) of ITEPA 2003 has been done on or after 2nd December 2004.

GENERAL NOTE

This is a parallel measure to those in paras 6, 11 and 13. It disapplies similar exemptions to those mentioned in those paras where post-acquisition benefits from securities are received in avoidance cases. It applies for things done on or after 2 December 2004.

Corporation tax relief: minor and consequential amendments

20— (1) Schedule 23 to FA 2003 (corporation tax relief for employee shares) is amended as follows.

(2) In paragraph 7 (award of shares: income tax position of employee), after sub-paragraph (2) insert—

"(3) It must be the case that section 446UA of the Income Tax (Earnings and Pensions) Act 2003 does not operate in relation to the shares."

(3) In paragraph 21(8) (amount of relief in case of restricted shares: provision to be disregarded in determining amount of relief on a chargeable event under section 426), for "446E(3)" substitute "446E(6)".

(4) In paragraph 22C (amount of relief in case of convertible shares), after sub-paragraph (4) insert—

"(4A) Subsections (2) and (3) of section 437 of the Income Tax (Earnings and Pensions) Act 2003 are to be disregarded in determining the amounts mentioned in sub-paragraphs (3) and (4)."

(5) In paragraph 25(1) (exclusion of other deductions where relief available under Schedule 23), after "Schedule is" insert "(or, apart from paragraph 7(3), would be)".

(6) Sub-paragraphs (2), (4) and (5) have effect in relation to awards on or after the day on which this Act is passed.

(7) Sub-paragraph (3) is to be treated as having come into force on 7th May 2004.

GENERAL NOTE

These are consequential amendments to ensure that the corporation tax relief for employee share acquisitions is consistent with the amendments to the income tax provisions.

SCHEDULE 3
QUALIFYING SCHEME
Section 24

GENERAL NOTE

This Schedule sets out a definition of qualifying scheme. Basically a scheme is a qualifying scheme if it involves a hybrid entity or a hybrid instrument.

A hybrid entity is an entity that is regarded as a legal person under one tax jurisdiction, but a transparent entity under another jurisdiction (Sch 3 para 3). An example is a limited partnership. Under UK tax law, the partnership is not a separate legal entity, but, dealings by it are treated as dealings by the partners. Under some jurisdictions, however, it may be regarded as a separate legal entity.

There are four categories of hybrid instrument:

Instrument of alterable character. This is an instrument under which one or more of the parties may make an election that alters a characteristic of the instrument. For example it might affect the treatment of income or gains derived from the instrument as income or capital for tax purposes, or neither (para 5).

Shares subject to conversion to debt. These are shares that may be converted to debt on the occurrence of some event which, at the date of issue or the date that the conversion right is created, the issuing company can reasonably expect to occur (para 6).

Securities subject to conversion to shares. These are securities (eg debentures, loan notes, etc) that may be converted to shares on the occurrence of some event which, at the date of issue or the date that the conversion right is created, the issuing company can reasonably expect to occur (para 7).

Debt instruments treated as equity. These are debt instruments that are treated as equity in the issuing company in accordance with GAAP (para 8).

There are two other categories of qualifying scheme:

Shares not conferring a qualifying beneficial entitlement. This refers to schemes involving an issue of shares to a connected person, where the shares are not ordinary shares carrying the usual rights to profit distribution and entitlement to assets upon winding up (para 10).

Transfer of rights. This refers to schemes where the rights to income or gains arising from a security are split between two or more connected persons as a result of a transaction or series of transactions (para 11).

PART 1
INTRODUCTORY

1 For the purposes of section 24 a scheme is a qualifying scheme if it falls within any of the following Parts of this Schedule.

PART 2
SCHEMES INVOLVING HYBRID ENTITIES

2 A scheme falls within this Part if a party to a transaction forming part of the scheme is a hybrid entity.

3— (1) An entity is a hybrid entity if—

(*a*) under the tax law of any territory, the entity is regarded as being a person, and

(*b*) the entity's profits or gains are, for the purposes of a relevant tax imposed under the law of any territory, treated as the profits or gains of a person or persons other than that person.

(2) The requirement in sub-paragraph (1)(*b*) is not to be regarded as satisfied in relation to an entity by reason only of its profits or gains being subject to a rule similar to that in section 747(3) of ICTA (imputation of chargeable profits of controlled foreign company) and having effect under the tax law of any territory outside the United Kingdom.

(3) For the purposes of this paragraph, the following are relevant taxes—

(*a*) income tax;

(*b*) corporation tax;

(*c*) any tax of a similar character to income tax or corporation tax that is imposed by the law of a territory other than the United Kingdom.

PART 3
SCHEMES INVOLVING HYBRID EFFECT

Schemes involving hybrid effect

4 A scheme falls within this Part if it satisfies the requirements of paragraph 5, 6, 7 or 8.

Instruments of alterable character

5— (1) A scheme satisfies the requirements of this paragraph if one of the parties to the scheme is party to an instrument falling within sub-paragraph (2).

(2) An instrument falls within this sub-paragraph if, under the law of a particular territory, a relevant characteristic of the instrument may be altered on the election of any party to the instrument.

(3) For the purposes of this paragraph a characteristic of an instrument is a relevant characteristic if, under the law of a particular territory, altering it has the effect of determining whether, for the tax purposes of that territory—

(*a*) the instrument is taken into account as giving rise to income,
(*b*) the instrument is taken into account as giving rise to capital, or
(*c*) the instrument does not fall to be taken into account as giving rise either to income or to capital.

(4) An instrument is taken into account as giving rise to capital if any gain on the disposal of the instrument would, or would if the person making the disposal were resident in the United Kingdom, be a chargeable gain.

Shares subject to conversion

6— (1) A scheme satisfies the requirements of this paragraph if it includes—

(*a*) the issuing by a company of shares subject to conversion, or
(*b*) the amendment of rights attaching to shares issued by a company such that the shares become shares subject to conversion.

(2) For the purposes of sub-paragraph (1) a company's shares are shares subject to conversion if—

(*a*) the rights attached to the shares include provision by virtue of which a holder of such shares is entitled, on the occurrence of an event, to acquire by conversion or exchange securities in the company or another company, and
(*b*) the occurrence of the event is within the reasonable expectation of the company at the relevant time.

(3) For the purposes of sub-paragraph (2) the relevant time is—

(*a*) the time when the shares are issued, or
(*b*) if at the time when the shares are issued the occurrence of the event is not within the company's reasonable expectation and the rights attaching to the shares are later amended as described in sub-paragraph (1)(*b*), the time when the rights attaching to the shares are so amended.

(4) In this paragraph "security" has the same meaning as in Part 6 of ICTA.

Securities subject to conversion

7— (1) A scheme satisfies the requirements of this paragraph if it includes—

(*a*) the issuing by a company of securities subject to conversion, or
(*b*) the amendment of rights attaching to securities issued by a company such that the securities become securities subject to conversion.

(2) For the purposes of sub-paragraph (1) a company's securities are securities subject to conversion if—

(*a*) the rights attached to the securities include provision by virtue of which a holder of such securities is entitled, on the occurrence of an event, to acquire by conversion or exchange shares in the company or another company, and
(*b*) the occurrence of the event is within the reasonable expectation of the company at the relevant time.

(3) For the purposes of sub-paragraph (2) the relevant time is—

(*a*) the time when the securities are issued, or

(b) if at the time when the securities are issued the occurrence of the event is not within the company's reasonable expectation and the rights attaching to the securities are later amended as described in sub-paragraph (1)(b), the time when the rights attaching to the securities are so amended.

(4) In this paragraph "security" has the same meaning as in Part 6 of ICTA.

Debt instruments treated as equity

8— (1) A scheme satisfies the requirements of this paragraph if it includes a debt instrument issued by a company that is treated as equity in the company under generally accepted accounting practice.

(2) For the purposes of this paragraph, a debt instrument is an instrument issued by a company that represents a loan relationship of the company or, if the company were a company resident in the United Kingdom, would represent a loan relationship of the company.

PART 4

SCHEMES INVOLVING HYBRID EFFECT AND CONNECTED PERSONS

Schemes involving hybrid effect and connected persons

9 A scheme falls within this Part if it satisfies the requirements of paragraph 10 or 11.

Scheme including issue of shares not conferring a qualifying beneficial entitlement

10— (1) A scheme satisfies the requirements of this paragraph if it includes the issue by a company to a person connected with the company of shares other than shares falling within sub-paragraph (2).

(2) Shares issued by a company fall within this sub-paragraph if—

(a) on their issue, they are ordinary shares that are fully paid-up,

(b) at all times in the accounting period of the company in which the issue takes place, the shares confer a qualifying beneficial entitlement, and

(c) when the issue takes place, there is no arrangement or understanding under which the rights attaching to the shares may be amended.

(3) A share in a company confers a qualifying beneficial entitlement if it confers a beneficial entitlement to the relevant proportion of—

(a) any profits available for distribution to equity holders of the company, and

(b) any assets of the company available for distribution to its equity holders on a winding-up.

(4) For the purposes of sub-paragraph (3) the relevant proportion, in relation to a share, is the same as the proportion of the issued share capital represented by that share.

(5) Schedule 18 to ICTA (equity holders and profits or assets available for distribution) applies for the purposes of sub-paragraph (3) as it applies for the purposes of section 403C of ICTA.

Scheme including transfer of rights under a security

11— (1) A scheme satisfies the requirements of this paragraph if it includes a transaction or a series of transactions under which a person ("the transferor")—

(a) transfers rights to receive a payment under a relevant security to one or more other persons, or

(b) otherwise secures that one or more other persons are similarly benefited,

and sub-paragraphs (3) and (4) are satisfied.

(2) A person is similarly benefited for these purposes if he receives a payment which would, but for the transaction or series of transactions, have arisen to the transferor.

(3) This sub-paragraph is satisfied if—

(a) the transferor, and

(b) at least one of the persons to whom a transfer of rights is made or a similar benefit is secured,

are connected with each other.

(4) This sub-paragraph is satisfied if following the transfer of rights or the securing of the similar benefit—

(a) two or more persons either hold rights to receive a payment under the security or enjoy a similar benefit, and (*b*) the rights held and benefits enjoyed by such of those persons as are connected have, taken together, a value equal to or greater than the value of any other rights to receive a payment under the security and of any other similar benefits, taken together.

(5) In sub-paragraph (4)(*b*) references to the value of rights to receive a payment under a relevant security are references to the market value of those rights; and references to the value of similar benefits are to be construed accordingly.

(6) In this paragraph a relevant security is—

(*a*) a security (within the meaning of Part 6 of ICTA), or

(*b*) any agreement under which a person receives an annuity or other annual payment (whether it is payable annually or at shorter or longer intervals) for a term which is not contingent on the duration of a human life or lives.

Interpretation

12 Section 839 of ICTA has effect for the purposes of this Part.

SCHEDULE 4

CHARGEABLE GAINS: LOCATION OF ASSETS ETC

Section 34

GENERAL NOTE

This Schedule amends and extends the express rules applicable to CGT which deal with the situs of assets.

Background

Situs becomes relevant to CGT in two contexts. The first where a non-resident is trading in the UK through a branch or agency or a permanent establishment. Such persons are, in contrast to other non-residents, subject to CGT, but only as respects certain categories of UK situs asset (TCGA 1992 ss 10 and 10B). The second is non-domiciled but resident individuals, who are subject to CGT on foreign situs assets only to the extent of sums received in the UK (TCGA 1992 s 12).

Hitherto, TCGA 1992 has contained express rules as to the situs of limited categories of assets and otherwise left the matter to the common law. The present Schedule amends TCGA 1992 s 275, the section containing those rules and, in addition, provides new rules, in new ss 275A–275C. However, even with those changes, statute is not comprehensive, and where it is not in point, the common law continues to apply.

Shares and other interests in companies

The changes to s 275 are effected by para 4. The principal change is that shares in or debentures of a company incorporated in the UK are *ipso facto* UK situs (new s 275(1)(da)). Hitherto it had been thought to be possible to render shares in UK companies foreign situs by issuing warrants to bearer within Companies Act 1985 ss 188 and 355.

It is also provided that, for these purposes, the terms share or debenture include interests in companies with no share capital (s 275(2)).

Apart from these changes the original rule in s 275 remains, namely that the registered shares and securities of any non-governmental company are situate where the register is situate or, if there is more than one register, where the principal register is situate. However the term "securities" is now replaced by "debentures", presumably on the basis that the latter has a wider meaning than the former.

Intangible Assets

Para 5 inserts the new ss 275A and 275B. These apply to an asset if (a) it is intangible or incorporeal property and (b) TCGA 1992 does not otherwise make express provision dealing with its situs (ss 275A(1) and 275B(1)).

The basic rule is that any such asset is UK situs if it is subject to UK law (s 275A(3)). By subject to UK law is meant either that it is enforceable in the UK or that it is governed by or otherwise subject to UK law (s 275B(2)).

This rule is extended in the case of futures and options not subject to UK law (s 275(4)). These are deemed to be subject to UK law and so UK situs if the underlying subject matter is intangible and subject to UK law (s 275A(5)). The same result follows if the underlying subject matter is an asset which under any of the other express CGT situs rules is situate in the UK or is shares or debentures of a UK company which have not yet been issued (s 275A(7)).

Co-owners

Para 5 also inserts a new s 275C to TCGA 1992. This deals with the interests of co-owners, whether the interests are joint or as tenants in common. The rule is simply that the situs of the interest is the same as that of the underlying asset.

Other amendments

Paras 1 and 2 make drafting amendments consequential on the substantive changes described above. Paras 3, 7, 8 and 9 are tidying up amendments. The most significant is para 7, which confirms that losses accruing on the chargeable assets of the permanent establishment of a non-resident company are allowable.

Commencement

The changes to TCGA 1992 s 275, and the new ss 275A, 275B and 275C, have effect in determining the situs of any asset at any time on or after 16 March 2005 (para 10). This is so regardless of when the asset was acquired.

PART 1

LOCATION OF ASSETS

Exceptions from sections 713 and 714 of ICTA

1— (1) Section 715 of ICTA is amended as follows.

(2) In subsection (8) (place where securities are situated to be determined under section 275 of TCGA 1992) for "section 275" substitute "sections 275(1) and (2)(*b*) and 275C".

Foreign securities: delayed remittances

2— (1) Section 723 of ICTA is amended as follows.

(2) In subsection (8) (place where securities are situated to be determined under section 275 of TCGA 1992) for "section 275" substitute "sections 275(1) and (2)(*b*) and 275C".

Designated international organisations

3— (1) Section 265 of TCGA 1992 is amended as follows.

(2) In subsection (3) (securities issued by designated international organisations to be taken to be situated outside UK for the purposes of capital gains tax) for "capital gains tax" substitute "this Act".

Location of assets: general

4— (1) Section 275 of TCGA 1992 is amended as follows.

(2) Re-number that section as subsection (1) of that section.

(3) In that subsection, in paragraph (*d*) (location of shares or securities issued by municipal or governmental authority etc) for "securities" substitute "debentures".

(4) In that subsection, after that paragraph insert—

"(da) subject to paragraph (*d*) above, shares in or debentures of a company incorporated in any part of the United Kingdom are situated in the United Kingdom,".

(5) In that subsection, in paragraph (*e*) (location of registered shares or securities)—

(*a*) for "subject to paragraph (*d*)" substitute "subject to paragraphs (*d*) and (da)";
(*b*) for "securities" substitute "debentures".

(6) In that subsection, for paragraph (*h*) (location of patents, trade marks and registered designs) substitute—

"(*h*) patents, trade marks, registered designs and corresponding rights are situated where they are registered, and if registered in more than one register, where each register is situated, and licences or other rights in respect of any such rights are situated in the United Kingdom if they or any right derived from them are exercisable in the United Kingdom,".

(7) In that subsection, for paragraph (*j*) (location of copyright, design right and franchises) substitute—

"(*j*) copyright, design right, franchises and corresponding rights, and licences or other rights in respect of any such rights, are situated in the United Kingdom if they or any right derived from them are exercisable in the United Kingdom,".

(8) After that subsection insert—

"(2) In subsection (1) above—

(*a*) in paragraphs (*d*), (da) and (*e*), the references to shares or debentures, in relation to a company that has no share capital, include any interests in the company possessed by members of the company, and

(*b*) in paragraphs (*d*) and (*e*), the references to debentures, in relation to a person other than a company, include securities.

(3) In subsection (1) above, in each of paragraphs (*h*) and (*j*), "corresponding rights" means any rights under the law of a country or territory outside the United Kingdom that correspond or are similar to those within that paragraph.

(4) Subsection (1) above is subject to—

section 265(3) (securities issued by designated international organisations to be taken to be situated outside UK),

section 266 (securities issued by Inter-American Development Bank to be taken to be situated outside UK), and

section 275C (location of assets: interests of co-owners).".

Location of certain intangible assets

5 After section 275 of TCGA 1992 insert—

"275A Location of certain intangible assets

(1) This section applies for the purpose of determining whether the situation of an intangible asset ("asset A") is in the United Kingdom if the situation of asset A is not otherwise determined (see section 275B(1)).

(2) In this section "intangible asset" means—

(*a*) intangible or incorporeal property and includes a thing in action, or

(*b*) anything that under the law of a country or territory outside the United Kingdom corresponds or is similar to intangible or incorporeal property or a thing in action.

(3) If asset A is subject to UK law (see section 275B(2)) at the time it is created, it shall be taken for the purposes of this Act to be situated in the United Kingdom at all times.

(4) Subsections (5) to (9) below have effect if asset A—

(*a*) is a future or option (see section 275B(3)), and

(*b*) is not subject to UK law at the time it is created.

(5) If, as a result of the application of the rule in subsection (6) below in relation to asset A or any other asset or assets, asset A falls to be treated as being subject to UK law at the time it is created, it shall be taken for the purposes of this Act to be situated in the United Kingdom at all times.

(6) That rule is that where, in the case of any intangible asset,—

(*a*) the asset is a future or option,

(*b*) the underlying subject matter (see section 275B(4)) of the asset consists of or includes an asset which is an intangible asset, and

(*c*) either—

(i) that intangible asset is subject to UK law at the time it is created and, on the assumption that there were no rights or interests in or over that asset, the situation of that asset would not be otherwise determined, or

(ii) that intangible asset is treated by this subsection as being so subject at that time,

the intangible asset mentioned in paragraph (*a*) above is to be treated for the purposes of subsection (5) above and this subsection as being so subject at the time it is created.

(7) If—

(*a*) asset A is not taken to be situated in the United Kingdom by virtue of subsection (5) above, and (*b*) as a result of the application of the rule in subsection (8) below in relation to asset A or any other asset or assets, asset A falls to be treated as being situated in the United Kingdom at any time,

it shall be taken for the purposes of this Act to be situated in the United Kingdom at that time.

(8) That rule is that where, in the case of any intangible asset,—

(*a*) the asset is a future or option, and

(*b*) the underlying subject matter of the asset consists of or includes an asset—

(i) which is, by virtue of subsection (9) below or of any provision of this Act apart from this section, situated in the United Kingdom at any time, or

(ii) which is treated by this subsection as being so situated at any time,

the intangible asset mentioned in paragraph (*a*) above is to be treated for the purposes of subsection (7) above and this subsection as being so situated at that time.

(9) Where—

(*a*) the underlying subject matter of a future or option consists of or includes shares or debentures issued by a company incorporated in any part of the United Kingdom, but

(*b*) at the time the future or option is created, those shares or debentures have not been issued,

the underlying subject matter of the future or option, so far as consisting of or including those shares or debentures, is to be taken, for the purposes of subsection (8) above, to consist of or include an asset which is situated in the United Kingdom at all times.

275B Section 275A: supplementary provisions

(1) For the purposes of section 275A, the situation of an asset is not otherwise determined if, apart from that section, this Act does not make any provision for determining—

(*a*) the situation of the asset, or

(*b*) whether the situation of the asset is in the United Kingdom.

(2) For the purposes of section 275A, an intangible asset is subject to UK law at a particular time if any right or interest which comprises or forms part of the asset is, at that time,—

(*a*) governed by, or otherwise subject to, or

(*b*) enforceable under,

the law of any part of the United Kingdom.

(3) Sub-paragraphs (6) to (10) of paragraph 12 of Schedule 26 to the Finance Act 2002 (meaning of "future" and "option") apply for the purposes of section 275A as they apply for the purposes of Part 2 of that Schedule.

(4) For the purposes of section 275A—

(*a*) the underlying subject matter of a future is the property which, if the future were to run to delivery, would fall to be delivered at the date and price agreed when the contract is made, and

(*b*) the underlying subject matter of an option is the property which would fall to be delivered if the option were exercised.

(5) Section 275A is subject to section 275C (location of assets: interests of co-owners).

(6) This section is to be construed as one with section 275A.".

Location of assets: interests of co-owners

6 After section 275B of TCGA 1992 (as inserted by paragraph 5) insert—

"275C Location of assets: interests of co-owners

(1) This section applies for determining for the purposes of this Act—

(*a*) the situation of an interest (see subsection (4)) in an asset, or

(*b*) whether the situation of an interest in an asset is in the United Kingdom.

(2) The situation of the interest in the asset shall be taken to be the same as the situation of the asset, as determined in accordance with subsection (3) below.

(3) The situation of the asset for the purposes of subsection (2) above shall be determined on the assumption that the asset is wholly-owned by the person holding the interest in the asset.

(4) In this section "interest", in relation to an asset, means an interest as a co-owner of the asset (whether the asset is owned jointly or in common and whether or not the interests of the co-owners are equal).".

PART 2

MINOR AMENDMENTS: NON-RESIDENT COMPANY WITH UK PERMANENT ESTABLISHMENT

Computation of losses

7— (1) Section 16 of TCGA 1992 is amended as follows.

(2) In subsection (3) (loss accruing to person in year of assessment during which he is not resident or ordinarily resident in UK not to be allowable loss unless, under section 10, he would be chargeable to tax in respect of chargeable gain if the loss had been a gain) after "section 10" insert "or 10B".

Reallocation within group of gain or loss accruing under section 179

8— (1) Section 179A of TCGA 1992 is amended as follows.

(2) In subsection (12) (asset is "chargeable asset" if gain accruing to company on disposal of asset would be chargeable gain and would by virtue of section 10(3) form part of company's chargeable profits for corporation tax) for "section 10(3)" substitute "section 10B".

Exemptions for disposals by companies with substantial shareholding

9— (1) Schedule 7AC to TCGA 1992 is amended as follows.

(2) In paragraph 3(2)(c)(ii) (one of conditions for exemption that chargeable gain accruing to company on disposal would by virtue of section 10(3) form part of company's chargeable profits for corporation tax) for "section 10(3)" substitute "section 10B".

PART 3

COMMENCEMENT

Commencement

10— (1) The amendments made by Part 1 of this Schedule have effect for determining for the purposes of TCGA 1992—

 (*a*) the situation of any asset, or

 (*b*) whether the situation of any asset is in the United Kingdom,

at any time on or after 16th March 2005 (irrespective of when the asset was acquired by the person holding it).

(2) The amendment made by paragraph 7 has effect in relation to any loss accruing to a company in an accounting period ending on or after 16th March 2005.

(3) The amendment made by paragraph 8 has effect for determining for the purposes of section 179A of TCGA 1992 whether an asset is a "chargeable asset" in relation to a company at any time on or after 16th March 2005.

(4) The amendment made by paragraph 9 has effect in relation to disposals on or after 16th March 2005.

SCHEDULE 5

CHARGEABLE GAINS: OPTIONS

Section 35

GENERAL NOTE

This section introduces Sch 3, which amends TCGA 1992 s 144ZA and makes those provisions subject to a new s 144ZB. Section 144ZA was introduced in FA 2003 to counter the effect of the decision in *Mansworth v Jelley* [2003] STC 53. Three new sections are introduced in total (ss 144ZB, 144ZC and 144ZD), with effect for options exercised from 2 December 2004. HM Revenue & Customs' Explanatory Notes to the new provisions indicate that they are introduced to counter 'inappropriate results' where the exercise price of an option is non-commercial. The defects that the provisions are intended to block presumably include an effective form of holdover relief. An example included in the Explanatory Notes illustrates this point, which is therefore reproduced below.

EXAMPLE

C and D are connected persons. C grants to D an option that allows D to sell an asset worth £90,000 to C for £30,000 in two months' time. D pays nothing for the option which, at the time it is granted, has no value. D paid £30,000 for the asset three years ago. D exercises the option and sells the asset to C. The current rules provide that D's disposal proceeds are treated as the price prescribed by the option, £30,000. So D has disposal proceeds of £30,000, from which are deducted his acquisition cost of £30,000. This means that there is no chargeable gain. C's acquisition cost of the asset is treated as the price paid on exercise of the option, £30,000. But D has effectively given away an asset worth £90,000. If he had simply disposed of it to C without using an option he would have been liable to tax on a gain (ignoring incidental costs of disposal and any reliefs to which he was entitled) of £60,000 (the market value of the asset less his acquisition cost of £30,000).

The effect of the new rules on the above example is that each party to the transaction is treated as disposing of (or acquiring, as the case may be) the asset at its market value when the option is exercised. However, the current rules (in s 144ZA) will continue to apply in certain circumstances, as outlined below.

New s 144ZB generally applies if s 144ZA would otherwise apply, and if the relevant option is 'non-commercial' (as defined in s 144ZC). However, s 144ZB does not apply if the option is a securities option (as defined), or if s 144ZD applies (see below). Where s 144ZB is in point, it replaces s 144ZA and also certain provisions in s 144, which determine the consideration or cost of binding (put and call) options. If an option binds the grantor to buy (a 'put' option), for tax purposes the grantor's acquisition cost of the asset acquired is its market value when the option is exercised. The corresponding disposal consideration is also the asset's market value when the option is exercised. If an option binds the grantor to sell (a 'call' option), for tax purposes the consideration for the asset disposal is its market value when the option is exercised. The corresponding acquisition cost is also the asset's market value when the option is exercised. If all or part of the 'underlying subject matter' (ie the asset falling to be bought or sold) of the option is subject to a right or restriction enforceable by the person selling it or a connected person (as defined in s 286), the right or restriction is ignored when determining its market value.

New s 144ZC defines 'non-commercial' in terms of the exercise of an option, for the purposes of s 144ZB. The exercise of a put option is non-commercial if the exercise price is less than the open market price of the underlying asset bought. The exercise of a call option is non-commercial if the exercise price is greater then the open market price of the underlying asset sold. 'Exercise price' excludes any amount paid for the option itself. The 'open market price' of the underlying asset does not take account of any right or restriction enforceable by the seller or any connected person, and the valuation rules in ss 272(2) and 273(3) apply as appropriate.

New s 144ZD sets out five conditions (each of which must be satisfied) for s 144ZB not to apply (so that s 144ZA is not prevented from applying), broadly where the exercise of the option is non-commercial and the option is not a securities option. The first condition is that s 144ZB would otherwise apply. Secondly, the open market price of the option's underlying asset at exercise differs from its open market price when the option was granted. Thirdly, some or all of that difference results from 'arrange-ments' involving a 'relevant person' (as defined), or from a transaction involving such a person. Fourthly, the exercise of the option would not be non-commercial if the change in the open market price were to be disregarded. The fifth condition is that (apart from s 144ZD) as a result of the relevant arrangements a capital gains tax (or corporation tax on chargeable gains) advantage would (or may be expected to) be obtained by the grantor of the option or the person exercising it.

Certain amendments are also made to TCGA 1992 for matters relating to share options (paras 3–5). In particular, the reference in TCGA 1992 s 149A(1)(b) (which determines consideration for the grant of a share option) to a right obtained by reason of employment as a director or employee is replaced with a reference to a 'securities option' as defined in accordance with the provisions of ITEPA 2003. This amendment applies to options granted from 2 December 2004.

PART 1
APPLICATION OF MARKET VALUE RULE IN CASE OF EXERCISE
OF OPTION

Application of market value rule in case of exercise of option

1— (1) Section 144ZA of TCGA 1992 is amended as follows.

(2) In subsection (1) (cases in which the section applies) at the beginning insert "Subject to section 144ZB,".

(3) In subsection (4) (where market value rule is set aside by the section, amount or value to be taken into account is, subject to section 120, to be actual amount or value) for "(subject to section 120) the actual amount or value" substitute "(subject to section 119A) the exercise price".

(4) After that subsection insert—

"(4A) In subsection (4) above "exercise price", in relation to an option, means the amount or value of the consideration which, under the terms of the option, is—

(*a*) receivable (if the option binds the grantor to buy), or
(*b*) payable (if the option binds the grantor to sell),

as a result of the exercise of the option (and does not include the amount or value of any consideration for the acquisition of the option (whether directly from the grantor or not)).".

(5) For subsection (5) substitute—

"(5) Subsections (5) and (6) of section 144 shall apply for the purposes of this section and sections 144ZB to 144ZD as they apply for the purposes of that section.".

Application of market value rule in case of exercise of option: exception

2 After section 144ZA of TCGA 1992 insert—

"144ZB Exception to rule in section 144ZA

(1) This section applies where—

(*a*) section 144ZA would apply but for this section in relation to an option, and
(*b*) the exercise of the option is non-commercial (see section 144ZC).

(2) But this section does not apply if—

(*a*) the option is a securities option within the meaning of Chapter 5 of Part 7 of ITEPA 2003 (see section 420(8) of that Act) to which that Chapter applies or would, apart from section 474 of that Act, apply (see section 471 of that Act), or
(*b*) section 144ZD of this Act (value of underlying subject matter of option altered with a view to obtaining a tax advantage) applies in relation to the option.

(3) Where this section applies, neither section 144ZA nor the following provisions of section 144 shall apply in relation to the option—

(*a*) in subsection (2), the words from "and accordingly" to the end of that subsection, and
(*b*) in subsection (3), the words from "and accordingly" to the end of that subsection;

but subsection (4) or (5) below shall instead have effect (subject to subsection (6) below).

(4) If the option binds the grantor to buy—

(*a*) the cost of acquisition incurred by the grantor in buying in pursuance of his obligations under the option, and
(*b*) the consideration for the disposal of what is bought by the grantor,

shall be deemed for the purposes of tax in respect of chargeable gains to be the market value, at the time the option is exercised, of what is bought.

(5) If the option binds the grantor to sell—

(*a*) the consideration for the sale, and
(*b*) the cost to the person exercising the option of acquiring what is sold,

shall be deemed for the purposes of tax in respect of chargeable gains to be the market value, at the time the option is exercised, of what is sold.

(6) But if the whole or any part of the underlying subject matter of the option (see subsection (7)) is subject to any right or restriction which is enforceable by the person disposing of the underlying subject matter or a person connected with him—

(*a*) the market value of the underlying subject matter shall be determined for the purposes of subsection (4) or (5) above as if the right or restriction did not exist, and

(*b*) to the extent that subsection (6) or (7) of section 18 would apply apart from this paragraph, it shall be disregarded.

(7) In this section "underlying subject matter", in relation to an option, means—

(*a*) if the option binds the grantor to sell, what falls to be sold on exercise of the option;

(*b*) if the option binds the grantor to buy, what falls to be bought on exercise of the option.

144ZC Section 144ZB: non-commercial exercise of option

(1) For the purposes of section 144ZB, the exercise of an option which binds the grantor to buy is non-commercial if the exercise price for the option (see subsection (3)) is less than the open market price (see subsection (4)) of what is bought.

(2) For the purposes of section 144ZB, the exercise of an option which binds the grantor to sell is non-commercial if the exercise price for the option is greater than the open market price of what is sold.

(3) In this section "exercise price", in relation to an option, means the amount or value of the consideration which, under the terms of the option, is—

(*a*) receivable (if the option binds the grantor to buy), or

(*b*) payable (if the option binds the grantor to sell),

as a result of the exercise of the option (and does not include the amount or value of any consideration for the acquisition of the option (whether directly from the grantor or not)).

(4) In this section "open market price", in relation to the underlying subject matter of an option (see section 144ZB(7)), means the price which the underlying subject matter might reasonably be expected to fetch on a sale in the open market at the time the option is exercised; and subsections (5) to (7) below apply for the purposes of this subsection.

(5) If the whole or any part of the underlying subject matter of the option is subject to any right or restriction which is enforceable by—

(*a*) the person disposing of the underlying subject matter, or

(*b*) a person connected with him,

the open market price of the underlying subject matter shall be determined as if the right or restriction did not exist.

(6) Section 272(2) (no reduction in estimated market value on account of assumption that whole of assets are placed on market at one time) shall apply in estimating the open market price of the underlying subject matter of an option as it applies in estimating the market value of any assets.

(7) Where the underlying subject matter of an option comprises or includes assets to which section 273 applies (unquoted shares and securities), subsection (3) of that section (assumption that relevant information is available) shall apply in determining the open market price of those assets as it applies for the purposes of a determination falling within subsection (1) of that section.

(8) This section is to be construed as one with section 144ZB.

144ZD Section 144ZB: alteration of value to obtain tax advantage

(1) This section applies in relation to an option if each of the following conditions is satisfied (as to the effect of this section applying, see section 144ZB(2)(*b*)).

(2) Condition 1 is that section 144ZB would, apart from subsection (2)(*b*) of that section, apply in relation to the option.

(3) Condition 2 is that, at the time the option is exercised, the open market price (see section 144ZC(4)) of the underlying subject matter of the option (see section 144ZB(7)) differs from the open market price of the underlying subject matter of the option at the time the option was granted.

(4) Condition 3 is that some or all of that change in the open market price of the underlying subject matter of the option results to any extent, directly or indirectly, from arrangements (see subsection (8)) ("the relevant arrangements")—

(*a*) to which a relevant person is or has been a party, or

(*b*) which include one or more transactions to which a relevant person is or has been a party.

(5) In subsection (4) above "relevant person" means any of the following—

(*a*) the grantor of the option;

(*b*) any person who at any time holds the option;

(*c*) a person connected with one or more of the persons mentioned in paragraph (*a*) or (*b*) above.

(6) Condition 4 is that, if there were to be disregarded so much of that change in the open market price of the underlying subject matter of the option as results to any extent, directly or indirectly, from the relevant arrangements, the exercise of the option would not be non-commercial (see section 144ZC).

(7) Condition 5 is that (apart from this section) as a result, directly or indirectly, of the relevant arrangements—

(*a*) the grantor of the option, or

(*b*) the person exercising the option,

would obtain or might be expected to obtain an advantage (see subsection (9)) in relation to capital gains tax or corporation tax in respect of chargeable gains directly or indirectly in consequence of, or otherwise in connection with, the exercise of the option.

(8) In this section "arrangements" includes any agreement, understanding, scheme, transaction or series of transactions (whether or not legally enforceable).

(9) In this section "advantage", in relation to capital gains tax or corporation tax in respect of chargeable gains, means—

(*a*) relief or increased relief from, or repayment or increased repayment of, that tax, or the avoidance or reduction of a charge to that tax or an assessment to that tax or the avoidance of a possible assessment to that tax, or

(*b*) the deferral of any payment of that tax or the advancement of any repayment of that tax.

(10) This section is to be construed as one with sections 144ZB and 144ZC.".

PART 2

MISCELLANEOUS AMENDMENTS RELATING TO SHARE OPTIONS ETC

Shares acquired on same day: election for alternative treatment

3— (1) Section 105A of TCGA 1992 is amended as follows.

(2) In subsection (1) (cases in which subsection (2) applies) in paragraph (*b*) (some of the acquired shares to be approved-scheme shares) for sub-paragraphs (i) and (ii) substitute—

"(i) the exercise of a qualifying option within the meaning given by section 527(4) of ITEPA 2003 (enterprise management incentives) in circumstances where section 530 or 531 of that Act (exercise of option to acquire shares) applies, or

(ii) the exercise of an option to which Chapter 7 or 8 of Part 7 of that Act (approved share option schemes) applies in circumstances where section 519(1) or 524(1) of that Act applies.".

Employment-related securities options

4— (1) Section 149A of TCGA 1992 is amended as follows.

(2) In subsection (1) (cases in which the section applies) for paragraph (*b*) (option to consist of right to acquire shares in body corporate and to be obtained by individual by reason of his office or employment) substitute—

"(*b*) the option is a securities option within the meaning of Chapter 5 of Part 7 of ITEPA 2003 (see section 420(8) of that Act) to which that Chapter applies or would, apart from section 474 of that Act, apply (see section 471 of that Act), and".

(3) In that subsection, in paragraph (*c*) (section 17(1) to apply for calculating consideration for grant of option) after "section 17(1)" insert "of this Act".

(4) The heading of the section accordingly becomes "Employment-related securities options".

Interpretation of TCGA 1992

5— (1) Section 288 of TCGA 1992 is amended as follows.

(2) In subsection (1A) (employment-related securities options) for the second sentence substitute—

"In this subsection "employment-related securities option" means a securities option within the meaning of Chapter 5 of Part 7 of ITEPA 2003 (see section 420(8) of that Act) to which that Chapter applies or would, apart from section 474 of that Act, apply (see section 471 of that Act); and other expressions used in this subsection and that Chapter have the same meaning in this subsection as in that Chapter.".

PART 3
COMMENCEMENT

Commencement

6— (1) The amendments made by paragraphs 1 to 3 have effect in relation to cases where the option in question is exercised on or after 2nd December 2004 (whenever the option was acquired).

(2) The amendments made by paragraphs 4 and 5 have effect in relation to options granted on or after 2nd December 2004.

SCHEDULE 6
ACCOUNTING PRACTICE AND RELATED MATTERS

Section 37

Adjustment on change of accounting basis

1— (1) In Schedule 22 to FA 2002 (adjustment on change of accounting basis: corporation tax), in paragraph 4 (adjustment treated as arising on last day of first period for which new basis adopted), for "last day" substitute "first day".

(2) This amendment has effect for accounting periods ending after 5th April 2005 in relation to periods of account beginning on or after 1st January 2005.

GENERAL NOTE

This confirms the provisions of FA 2005 s 81, which were unintentionally curtailed by the coming into effect of ITTOIA 2005. If a prior year adjustment arises as a result of a fundamental change of accounting practice, it is to be recognised for tax purposes in the accounting period in which it is reported, not in the prior year. For instance, if accounts 31/12/05 report a prior year adjustment on the adoption of IAS, this will be dealt with for tax in the 2005 tax return, not 2004. If the period of account is extended to 30/06/05, the period must be split for tax purposes, and the prior year adjustment will be dealt with in the 2005 return, not the 2006.

2— (1) In section 227 of ITTOIA 2005 (adjustment on change of accounting basis: income tax), for subsection (4) (meaning of "relevant change of accounting approach") substitute—

"(4) A "relevant change of accounting approach" means—

(*a*) a change of accounting principle or practice that, in accordance with generally accepted accounting practice, gives rise to a prior period adjustment, or

(*b*) a change from using UK generally accepted accounting practice to using generally accepted accounting practice with respect to accounts drawn up in accordance with international accounting standards.".

(2) This amendment has effect for the tax year 2005–06 and subsequent tax years in relation to periods of account beginning on or after 1st January 2005.

GENERAL NOTE

FA 2005 s 81 introduced the definition of 'relevant change of accounting approach' specifically covering the adoption of IAS. This paragraph introduces the same definition to ITTOIA 2005 for partnerships and other entities wishing to adopt IAS, effective for the tax year 2005–06.

Meaning of "statutory insolvency arrangement"

3— (1) For section 259 of ITTOIA 2005 (trading income: meaning of "statutory insolvency arrangement") substitute—

"259 Meaning of "statutory insolvency arrangement"

(1) In this Part "statutory insolvency arrangement" means—

(*a*) a voluntary arrangement that has taken effect under or as a result of the Insolvency Act 1986, Schedule 4 or 5 to the Bankruptcy (Scotland) Act 1985 or the Insolvency (Northern Ireland) Order 1989,

(*b*) a compromise or arrangement that has taken effect under section 425 of the Companies Act 1985 or Article 418 of the Companies (Northern Ireland) Order 1986, or

(*c*) any arrangement or compromise of a kind corresponding to any of those mentioned in paragraph (*a*) or (*b*) that has taken effect under or by virtue of the law of a country or territory outside the United Kingdom.".

(2) This amendment has effect for the tax year 2005–06 and subsequent tax years in relation to periods of account beginning on or after 1st January 2005.

GENERAL NOTE

FA 2005 Sch 4 para 8 introduced the definition of 'statutory insolvency arrangement' for purposes of corporation tax. This paragraph introduces the same definition to ITTOIA 2005 for partnerships and other entities, effective for the tax year 2005–06.

Minor corrections

4— (1) In Schedule 4 to FA 2005, omit paragraph 6 (which amended section 109A of ICTA for corporation tax purposes when that section has no such application).

(2) In paragraph 19A of Schedule 9 to FA 1996, in sub-paragraph (4B)(*g*) after "2," insert "4A,".

(3) In paragraph 25A of Schedule 26 to FA 2002, for "section 85B(1)" substitute "paragraph 17B(1)".

(4) In section 103(1) of FA 1996, in the definition of "exchange gain" and "exchange loss", after "(1A)" insert ", (1AA)".

(5) In paragraph 54(1) of Schedule 26 to FA 2002, in the definition of "exchange gain" and "exchange loss", after "(2)" insert ", (2A)".

(6) These amendments shall be deemed always to have had effect.

GENERAL NOTE

These are minor corrections to existing legislation, deemed always to have had effect.

Deemed release of liability on impaired debt becoming held by connected company

5— (1) In Schedule 9 to FA 1996 (loan relationships: special computational provisions), for paragraph 4A substitute—

"Deemed release of liability on impaired debt becoming held by connected company

4A— (1) This paragraph applies—

(*a*) in the case specified in sub-paragraph (2), subject to the exception in sub-paragraph (3), and

(*b*) in the case specified in sub-paragraph (4).

(2) The first case is where—

(*a*) a company ("the debtor company") is party as debtor to a loan relationship,

(*b*) another company ("the creditor company") becomes party as creditor to the loan relationship,

(*c*) the debtor company and the creditor company are connected immediately after the latter becomes party to the loan relationship,

(*d*) there is no connection between the creditor company and the person from whom it acquires its rights under the loan relationship in the period of account in which it does so, and (*e*) the carrying value of the liability under the loan relationship in the accounts of the debtor company exceeds the amount or value of any consideration given by the creditor company for its rights under the loan relationship.

The carrying value referred to in paragraph (*e*) is the amount that would have been the carrying value of the liability under the loan relationship in the accounts of the debtor company if a period of account had ended immediately before the creditor company became party to the loan relationship.

(3) The exception to the first case is where—

(*a*) the creditor company acquires its rights under the loan relationship under an arm's length transaction, and

(*b*) there has been no connection between the creditor company and the debtor company at any time in the period—

(i) beginning four years before the date on which the creditor company acquired those rights, and

(ii) ending twelve months before that date.

(4) The second case is where—

(*a*) a company ("the debtor company") is party as debtor to a loan relationship,

(*b*) another company ("the creditor company") that—

(i) is party to the loan relationship as creditor, and

(ii) is not connected with the debtor company,

becomes connected with the debtor company, and

(*c*) the amount that would have been the carrying value of the asset representing the loan relationship in the accounts of the creditor company if a period of account had ended immediately before the companies became connected would have been adjusted for impairment.

(5) Where this paragraph applies there is deemed to be a release by the creditor company of its rights under the loan relationship.

(6) In the first case the release is deemed to be of the amount of the excess referred to in sub-paragraph (2)(*e*) and to take place when the creditor company acquires its rights under the loan relationship.

(7) In the second case the release is deemed to be of the amount of the impairment adjustment referred to in sub-paragraph (4)(*c*) and to take place when the creditor company becomes connected with the debtor company.

(8) For the purposes of this paragraph there is a connection between a company and another person at any time (subject to sub-paragraph (9)) if at that time—

(*a*) the other person is a company and one of the companies has control of the other, or

(*b*) the other person is a company and both companies are under the control of the same person,

and there is a connection between a company and another person in a period of account if there is a connection (within paragraph (*a*) or (*b*) above) between the company and the person at any time in that period.

"Control" here has the meaning given for the purposes of section 87 of this Act by section 87A.

(9) The provisions of—

(*a*) section 87(4) (companies not regarded as connected by virtue of control by government etc), and

(*b*) section 88 (connection between companies to be disregarded in certain circumstances),

apply for the purposes of this paragraph as they apply for the purposes of section 87.

(10) In determining for the purposes of this section the carrying value of the liability under a loan relationship, or of an asset representing a loan relationship, no account shall be taken of—

(*a*) accrued amounts,

(*b*) amounts paid or received in advance, or

(*c*) impairment losses.".

(2) The amendment in sub-paragraph (1) has effect where the deemed release occurs on or after 16th March 2005.

GENERAL NOTE

This paragraph amends the provisions introduced by FA 2005 Sch 4 para 10, which insert a new para 4A into Sch 9 FA 1996, and is effective from 16 March 2005.

The release of connected party debt is not taxable under FA 1996 Sch 9 para 5(5). In the circumstance where the borrower became connected with the lender after an impaired debt had been written down, the original lender may have recognised the loss, while the borrower was not taxable on the debt released.

These provisions address two circumstances:

1 where a company (the new lender) acquires a debt from an unconnected lender, and immediately afterwards becomes connected with the borrower company (for instance because the new lender already was connected with the borrower); and

2 where a company acquires a debt from an unconnected lender, but then becomes connected with the borrower, for example, by acquiring a majority shareholding.

There is an exception in the first case where the lender acquires its rights under an arm's length transaction, and there had been no connection between the lender and the borrower at any time in the period beginning four years before it acquired the debt and ending 12 months before acquiring the debt.

In both cases, if the new lender pays less for the debt than its original value, there is a deemed release of the debt by the borrower, resulting in a taxable credit for the borrower. This taxable credit will equal the impairment loss realised by the lender, and will give parity of tax treatment between lender and borrower.

There are provisions to ensure that the tax charge does not arise where debt is transferred between companies in a group, nor where the discount on the debt arises solely because the debt was originally issued at the discount. Only impairment losses are affected, not diminution in value of fixed-rate debt as a result of interest rate rises.

For purposes of this section no account is to be taken of accrued amounts, or amounts paid or received in advance, in determining the carrying value.

Adjustment on change to international accounting standards: bad debt debits formerly disallowed

6— (1) In paragraph 19A of Schedule 9 to FA 1996 (loan relationships: adjustment on change of accounting policy), after sub-paragraph (4B) insert—

"(4BA) In determining the accounting value of an asset of the company at the end of the earlier period, no account shall be taken of a debit that in a period of account beginning before 1st January 2005 was disallowed for tax purposes—

(*a*) because of the assumption required by paragraph 5(1) above, or

(*b*) because the exceptions in section 74(1)(*j*) of the Taxes Act 1988 did not apply.".

(2) This amendment has effect for periods of account beginning on or after 1st January 2005.

GENERAL NOTE

This adds a new sub-para to FA 1996 Sch 9 para 19A, supplementing FA 2005 Sch 4 para 31, defining the carrying value of an asset, particularly on the move to IAS. A prior year adjustment will form part of profit and loss for tax. This section makes clear that certain amounts previously disallowed by specific tax legislation do not form part of the carrying value for tax purposes of the end of the accounting period before the change of basis. The effect is therefore to give relief for previously disallowed provisions under the prior year adjustment rules for accounting periods beginning on or after 1 January 2005.

Loan relationships with embedded derivatives

7— (1) Where—

(*a*) a company is subject to old UK GAAP for a period of account beginning on or after 1st January 2005, and

(*b*) it holds assets ("relevant assets") that—

(i) it is not permitted, under old UK GAAP, to treat as mentioned in subsection (1) of section 94A of FA 1996 (loan relationship with embedded derivative treated as two assets), with the result that that section does not apply, and

(ii) it would have been permitted to treat as mentioned in that provision if it had been subject to international accounting standards or new UK GAAP,

the company may elect that Chapter 2 of Part 4 of FA 1996 (loan relationships) and Schedule 26 to FA 2002 (derivative contracts) shall have effect as if section 94A did apply.

(2) Any such election—

(*a*) must be made in writing to an officer of Revenue and Customs,

(*b*) must be made—

(i) on or before 31st December 2005, or

(ii) after that date in accordance with sub-paragraph (3)(*a*) or (*b*), and

(*c*) is irrevocable.

(3) An election may be made after 31st December 2005—

(*a*) if the company does not hold any relevant assets at the beginning of its first period of account beginning on or after 1st January 2005 but subsequently acquires one (or more) and the election is made no later than 90 days after the acquisition (or, if there is more than one, the first of them), or

(*b*) if the company does not have a period of account beginning in the calendar year 2005 and holds one or more relevant assets at the beginning of its first period of account beginning after the end of that year and the election is made no later than 90 days after the beginning of that period of account.

(4) An election under this paragraph has effect in relation to all relevant assets held by the company (including those subsequently acquired).

(5) An election under this paragraph—

(*a*) if made on or before 31st December 2005, has effect from the beginning of the company's first period of account beginning on or after 1st January 2005;

(*b*) if made after 31st December 2005 in accordance with sub-paragraph (3)(*a*), has effect from the beginning of the period of account in which the first relevant asset is acquired;

(*c*) if made after 31st December 2005 in accordance with sub-paragraph (3)(*b*), has effect from the beginning of the company's first period of account beginning on or after 1st January 2005.

(6) Where an election is made under this paragraph the provisions of paragraph 19A of Schedule 9 to FA 1996 and paragraph 50A of Schedule 26 to FA 2002 (adjustments on change of accounting policy) apply as if there were a change of accounting policy (consisting in the company treating its relevant assets as mentioned in section 94A(1) as from the date the election has effect).

(7) In this paragraph "old UK GAAP" means UK generally accepted accounting practice as it applied for periods of account beginning before 1st January 2005 and "new UK GAAP" means UK generally accepted accounting practice as it applies for periods of account beginning on or after that date.

(8) Any election made under paragraph 28(3) of Schedule 4 to FA 2005 before the passing of this Act shall have effect as if made under this paragraph.

GENERAL NOTE

This repeals and replaces FA 2005 Sch 4 para 28, concerning the treatment of embedded derivatives in companies not adopting IAS or FRS 26, and extends the deadline for election from 31/07/05 to 31/12/05. Any election already made under the previous Act continues to have effect.

The company may split securities with embedded derivatives into the host contract dealt with under the loan relationship rules, and the derivative element dealt with under the chargeable gains treatment for derivatives, provided that it is either permitted or required to do so. Chargeable gains treatment reduces volatility in profit for tax in respect of securities that may be of fluctuating value. If a company does not adopt IAS or FRS 26 and remains with 'old UK GAAP', it is neither permitted nor required to split (bifurcate) such securities, and chargeable gains treatment will not apply to derivatives, unless it makes an election.

This paragraph provides for an irrevocable election to be made by 31/12/ 05 (or within 90 days of acquiring its first relevant asset if later) in respect of all relevant securities, effective from the first day of the first period of account beginning on or after 01/01/05, to allow split treatment to continue for tax purposes.

Paragraph 7(6) ensures that no debits or credits on change of accounting policy fall out of account as a result of the election.

8— (1) In section 116(8A) of TCGA 1992 (reorganisations, conversions and reconstructions: application of loan relationships regime in certain cases)—

(*a*) after "shall have effect" insert ", subject to subsection (8B) below,", and

(*b*) for "that subsection" substitute "subsection (6) above".

(2) After that subsection insert—

"(8B) Subsection (8A) above does not apply where the relevant transaction is a conversion of securities occurring in consequence of the operation of the terms of any security or of any debenture which is not a security.

Expressions used in this subsection have the same meaning as they have for the purposes of section 132.".

(3) These amendments have effect in relation to transactions occurring after 26th May 2005.

GENERAL NOTE

TCGA 1992 s 116(8A) provides that the conversion of a qualifying corporate bond to shares is treated as a disposal at market value for the purposes of loan relationships. This may conflict with the specific rules for loan relationships with embedded derivatives, in cases where a security is treated both as a loan relationship and as a derivative. With effect from 26 May 2005 this is resolved by disapplying TCGA 1992 s 116(8A) where a convertible security is converted into shares.

Exchange gains and losses

9— (1) The following provisions shall cease to have effect—

(*a*) section 84A of FA 1996 (exchange gains and losses from loan relationships);

(*b*) paragraph 16 of Schedule 26 to FA 2002 (exchange gains and losses arising from derivative contracts).

(2) These amendments come into force on a day to be appointed by the Treasury by order made by statutory instrument.

(3) The order may contain such transitional provision and savings as appear to the Treasury to be appropriate.

GENERAL NOTE

This section allows the repeal of FA 1996 s 84A for loan relationships, and FA 2002 Sch 26 para 16 for derivatives, which specify the tax treatment of exchange gains and losses. This section will come into effect on a date to be specified by statutory instrument which may contain transitional provisions.

Consultations have identified difficulties in adopting IAS 39 for tax purposes, particularly in the treatment of convertible assets and foreign currency hedging, and in the interaction with SI 2004/3256 (the Disregard Regulations).

The repeal of these regulations may facilitate the adoption of the IAS 39 for tax purposes, particularly as far as convertible assets and foreign currency hedging is affected.

10 In section 103 of FA 1996 (loan relationships: general interpretation), for subsection (1AA) substitute—

"(1AA) The Treasury may make provision by regulations as to the manner in which—

(*a*) exchange gains or losses, and

(*b*) any other profits or gains or losses,

are to be calculated for the purposes of subsection (1A) in a case where fair value accounting is used by the company.

Any such regulations may be made so as to apply to periods of account beginning before the regulations are made, but not earlier than the beginning of the calendar year in which they are made.".

GENERAL NOTE

This section will come into effect on a date to be specified by the Treasury, which may be partly retrospective from 1 January 2005. This section gives the Treasury power to make regulations as to how exchange gains or losses are to be calculated where fair value accounting is used (for instance, financial traders using mark to market). It will replace the definition introduced by FA 2005 Sch 4 para 29. The regulations will be intended to facilitate the adoption of IAS 39 for tax purposes.

11 In paragraph 54 of Schedule 26 to FA 2002 (derivative contracts: general interpretation), for sub-paragraph (2A) substitute—

"(2A) The Treasury may make provision by regulations as to the manner in which—

(*a*) exchange gains or losses, and

(*b*) any other profits or gains or losses,

are to be calculated for the purposes of sub-paragraph (2) in a case where fair value accounting is used by the company.

Any such regulations may be made so as to apply to periods of account beginning before the regulations are made, but not earlier than the beginning of the calendar year in which they are made.".

GENERAL NOTE

This section will come into effect on a date to be specified by the Treasury, which may be partly retrospective from 1 January 2005. This section gives the Treasury power to make regulations as to how exchange gains or losses are to be calculated in the case of derivative contracts. The regulations will be intended to facilitate the adoption of IAS 39 for tax purposes.

SCHEDULE 7

AVOIDANCE INVOLVING FINANCIAL ARRANGEMENTS

Section 39

GENERAL NOTE

The changes Sch 7 makes aim at closing certain tax avoidance schemes disclosed under FA 2004 Part 7.

Rent factoring

1— (1) Part 2 of ICTA (which, at sections 43A to 43G, includes provisions about rent factoring) is amended as follows.

(2) Section 43C(1) (section 43B not to apply where term over which financial obligation is to be reduced exceeds 15 years) shall cease to have effect.

(3) In section 43E (interposed lease: exceptions etc) in subsection (1), omit paragraphs (*a*) and (*b*) (which relate to certain periods exceeding 15 years).

(4) The amendments made by this paragraph have effect in relation to finance agreements entered into on or after 16th March 2005.

(5) But where—

(*a*) a finance agreement was entered into on or after 20th March 2000 and before 16th March 2005, and

(*b*) section 43D of ICTA (interposed lease) would apply in relation to the agreement but for section 43E(1)(*a*) or (*b*) of that Act,

sub-paragraph (6) has effect.

(6) In any such case, any amount of principal in rent paid on or after 16th March 2005 which, apart from this sub-paragraph, would—

(*a*) be deductible as an expense in computing profits charged under Case I of Schedule D, or

(*b*) be deductible under section 75 of ICTA (expenses of management), or

(*c*) fall to be brought into account under section 76 of that Act (expenses of insurance companies) at Step 1 in subsection (7) of that section, shall not be so deductible or brought into account for any accounting period ending on or after 16th March 2005.

(7) If payment of an amount of principal in rent is made on or after 16th March 2005 in respect of a rental period that falls—

(*a*) partly before that date, and

(*b*) partly on or after it,

sub-paragraph (6) has effect in relation to only so much of the payment as relates to the part of the period falling on or after 16th March 2005.

(8) In this paragraph—

"amount of principal in rent" means so much of any amount of rent payable under a lease as, in the case of the finance agreement in question, reduces the amount of the financial obligation mentioned in section 43A(1) of ICTA;

"rental period" means a period in respect of which rent is paid.

GENERAL NOTE

Factoring is the process whereby a person entitled to payment under a commercial contract transfers that right to a factor in return for a payment from the factor. The factor then takes responsibility for recovering the contractual payment.

Factoring can produce a tax saving if it converts a taxable income stream into a capital receipt. These changes achieve this in the case of rent factoring.

Rent factoring can take two forms. By the conventional method, a landlord transfers their entitlement to rent to the debt factor. Alternatively, parties may achieve the same commercial effect by introducing an additional lease between the original arm's length landlord and a tenant, an "interposed lease", granted in return for a premium paid by the interposed tenants.

TA 1988 ss 43A–43G deal with rent factoring. Their broad effect is to treat payments under a debt factoring arrangement as rent.

That treatment was limited to arrangements of less than 15 years. However, this new para removes that limitation. In the case of either type of rent factoring, therefore, arrangements for more than 15 years are now covered.

In the case of interposed leases, the rent paid is not deductible as a trading expense or as a management expense. Nor can insurance companies account for the rent as an expense of their insurance business.

These new rules apply to arrangements made on or after 16 March 2005.

However, special commencement rules apply to interposed leases created between 20 March 2000 and 16 March 2005. If such a lease would have been caught by the interposed lease provisions apart from the 15-year rules that have now been abolished, the rent due in rental periods following budget day is no longer deductible in calculating trading profits, the expenses of management for companies with investment business or the expenses of insurance companies.

The rules apportion the rent due in any rental period straddling Budget day (16 March 2005).

Section 730: restriction to income consisting of distributions in respect of company shares etc

2— (1) Section 730 of ICTA (transfers of income arising from securities) is amended as follows.

(2) In each place where it occurs—

(*a*) for "interest" substitute "distribution";

(*b*) for "securities" substitute "shares".

(3) In subsection (1) (interest deemed to be income of owner etc)—

(*a*) in paragraph (*a*), for "deemed to be" substitute "treated as",

(*b*) in paragraph (*b*), for "deemed to be" substitute "treated as", and

(*c*) omit paragraph (*c*).

(4) For subsection (2) (sale etc where proceeds chargeable to tax by virtue of section 18(3B) of ICTA) substitute—

"(2) This section does not have effect in relation to a sale or transfer if the proceeds of the sale or transfer are chargeable to tax.".

(5) Omit subsection (2A) (loan relationships).

(6) For subsection (3) substitute—

"(3) The proceeds of any subsequent sale or other realisation of the right to receive the distribution shall not, for any of the purposes of the Tax Acts, be regarded as the income of the seller or the person on whose behalf the right is otherwise realised.".

(7) In subsection (4), in the words following paragraph (*b*) after their substitution by paragraph 300(3)(*b*) of Schedule 1 to ITTOIA 2005, for "interest" substitute "distribution".

(8) In subsection (4A), for "interest arising" substitute "distribution".

(9) In subsection (4B), for "interest" substitute "distribution".

(10) For subsection (7) (definitions) substitute—

"(7) In this section—

"distribution", in relation to shares in a company,—

(*a*) has the same meaning as it has in the Corporation Tax Acts (see section 209), but

(*b*) also includes any amount that would be a distribution if the company paying it were resident in the United Kingdom;

"shares" means shares in a company.".

(11) In subsection (8) (information powers) omit from "and for the purpose" to the end of the subsection.

(12) The heading to the section becomes "Transfers of rights to receive distributions in respect of shares".

(13) The amendments made by this paragraph have effect in relation to sales or transfers on or after 2nd December 2004.

GENERAL NOTE

Stripping a security of its right to income might save tax. This is the process of selling the right to the income without selling the underlying security. The relevant income, for these purposes, comprises of interest and dividends.

In response to this potential tax saving, provisions dealing with the treatment of a price differential on sale and repurchase of securities (TA 1988 s 730) provide general rules to prevent it. In addition, FA 1996 Sch 13 provides special rules relating to discounted securities.

The current Finance Act extends the discounted securities rules to all interest-bearing securities (see below). Therefore, the s 730 rules are limited to the sale of any remaining income stream. That is to say, dividends relating to company shares. The new rules apply to transactions on or after to December 2004.

Change in ownership of company with investment business

3— (1) In section 768B(10) of ICTA (Part 4 of Schedule 28A to have effect for restricting the debits to be brought into account in respect of loan relationships) after "debits", where first occurring, insert "and non-trading deficits".

(2) In section 768C(9) of ICTA (Part 4 of Schedule 28A to have effect for restricting the debits to be brought into account in respect of loan relationships) after "debits", where first occurring, insert "and non-trading deficits".

(3) Schedule 28A to ICTA (change in ownership of investment company: deductions) is amended as follows.

(4) In paragraph 7(1)(*b*) (apportionment of excess in paragraph 6(*c*), or of non-trading deficit, to first part of accounting period) after "the whole amount of the excess" insert "or, as the case may be, of the deficit".

(5) After paragraph 9 insert—

"**9A**— (1) This paragraph has effect in any case to which section 768B applies where the non-trading deficit mentioned in paragraph 6(dc) above is apportioned by paragraph 7(*b*) above to the first part of the accounting period being divided.

(2) In any such case, none of that non-trading deficit shall be carried forward to—

(*a*) the accounting period beginning immediately after the change in the ownership of the company, or

(*b*) any subsequent accounting period.".

(6) After paragraph 10 insert—

"**10A**— (1) This paragraph has effect in any case to which section 768C applies where the non-trading deficit mentioned in paragraph 13(1)(ec) below is apportioned by paragraph 16(1)(*b*) below to the first part of the accounting period being divided.

(2) In any such case, none of that non-trading deficit shall be carried forward to—

(*a*) the accounting period beginning immediately after the change in the ownership of the company, or

(*b*) any subsequent accounting period.".

(7) In paragraph 16(1)(*b*) (apportionment of excess in paragraph 13(1)(ec), or of non-trading deficit, to first part of accounting period) after "the whole amount of the excess" insert "or, as the case may be, of the deficit".

(8) The title of Part 4 of the Schedule becomes "Disallowed debits and non-trading deficits".

(9) The amendments made by this paragraph have effect in any case where the change in ownership is on or after 10th February 2005.

GENERAL NOTE

This para corrects a drafting oversight in the provisions relating to the purchase of tax loss companies. The para brings within that regime the purchase of companies with non-trading loan relationship deficits.

The provisions dealing with change in ownership of company and the disallowance of trading losses (TA 1988 ss 768–768E) and computation of offshore income gains (Sch 28) prevent the benefit of buying a company merely for its tax loss. Those provisions define the certain circumstances in which they deem the purchase to be merely for the tax losses. They also define the relevant losses.

The provisions dealing with change in ownership of company with investment business and deductions generally (TA 1988 s 768B) apply to companies with investment businesses and to amounts within the loan relationship rules. However, the provisions did not formerly apply to loan relationship deficits. This para corrects that oversight.

Provisions dealing with the change in ownership of company with investment business and deductions (TA 1988 Sch 28A) provide for the apportionment of losses when there is a change of ownership during an accounting period. However, they did not include a reference to loan relationship deficits. This para corrects that oversight.

The changes apply to a change of ownership on or after 10 February 2005.

Transfers of rights to receive annual payments

4— (1) After section 775 of ICTA (sale by individual of income derived from his personal activities) insert—

"**775A Transfers of rights to receive annual payments**

(1) This section applies in any case where—

(*a*) a person sells or transfers the right to receive an annual payment to which this section applies (see subsection (4)), and

(*b*) the consideration (if any) for the sale or transfer would not, apart from this section, be chargeable to tax.

(2) In any such case, tax is charged—

(*a*) in the case of income tax, under this section; or

(*b*) in the case of corporation tax, under Case III of Schedule D.

(3) Where this section applies—

(*a*) the tax is charged on an amount equal to the market value of the right to receive the annual payment;

(*b*) the tax is charged for the chargeable period in which the sale or transfer takes place;

(*c*) the person liable for the tax is the person who sells or transfers the right to the annual payment.

(4) This section applies to any annual payment other than—

(*a*) an annual payment under a life annuity;

(*b*) an annual payment under a pension annuity;

(*c*) an annual payment to which section 347A applies (annual payments that are not charges on income);

(*d*) an annual payment in respect of which, by virtue of section 727 of ITTOIA 2005 (payments by individuals arising in UK), no liability to income tax arises under Part 5 of that Act.

(5) This section applies in relation to part of an annual payment as it applies in relation to the whole of an annual payment.

(6) For the purposes of this section, a sale or transfer of all rights under an agreement for annual payments, or under an annuity, is a sale or transfer of the rights to each individual payment under the agreement or annuity.

(7) In this section—

"life annuity" means—

(*a*) a life annuity, as defined in section 657(1); or
(*b*) a life annuity, as defined in section 473(2) of ITTOIA 2005;

"pension annuity" means an annuity which is pension income within the meaning of Part 9 of ITEPA 2003 (see section 566(2) of that Act).".

(2) The amendment made by this paragraph has effect in relation to sales or transfers on or after 16th March 2005.

GENERAL NOTE

Following changes made by para 3, these provisions bring back into charge the sales of certain rights to interest and annuities. The new provision does not apply to life annuities, pension annuities or annual payments by individuals that are not charges on income and not chargeable to income tax.

If the relevant sale is not subject to any other tax, then the new TA 1988 s 775A subjects to tax the sale of any right to receive an annual payment. For these purposes, a sale includes a transfer. The charge is under Sch D Case III.

The provisions charge tax based on the market value of the right. The charge can apply to parts of payments and the sales of parts of the rights of an annuity. The transferor is liable for the tax that is due in the relevant period of assessment (that is to say the accounting period or year of assessment) in which the sale takes place.

The new charge applies to sales made on or after a 16 March 2005.

Disposals and acquisitions of company loan relationships with or without interest

5— (1) Section 807A of ICTA is amended as follows.

(2) After subsection (2A) (exclusion of certain tax) insert—

"(2B) Where, in the case of any share, section 91A or 91B of the Finance Act 1996 (shares treated as loan relationships) applies in relation to a company for an accounting period, this section has effect—

(*a*) in relation to a distribution in respect of the share as it has effect in relation to interest under a loan relationship, and
(*b*) in relation to a distribution accruing in respect of the share at a time when the company does not (within the meaning of the section in question) hold the share as it applies in relation to interest accruing under a loan relationship at a time when the company is not a party to the loan relationship.".

(3) The amendment made by this paragraph has effect in relation to shares held by a company on or after 16th March 2005.

GENERAL NOTE

This para makes amendments that follow on from the amendments made by paras 9 and 10 described further below.

Those provisions treat certain shares as loan relationships, in certain circumstances. This provision deals with distributions in relation to those shares. In particular, it concerns distributions paid when the relevant company does not own the shares when the distribution is paid. It treats the distribution in a way equivalent to interest accruing under a loan relationship. In other words, the rules attribute the distribution to the relevant company.

As with paras 9 and 10, these provisions apply to shares held on or after 16 March 2005.

Manufactured interest and the accrued income scheme

6— (1) In Schedule 23A to ICTA (manufactured dividends and interest) paragraph 3 (manufactured interest on UK securities) is amended as follows.

(2) In sub-paragraph (2A) (restriction on relief under sub-paragraph (2)(*c*))—

(*a*) in paragraph (*a*) (receipt of interest or payment representative of it) after "is chargeable to income tax" insert "(and see section 714(5) for the amount so chargeable in a case where section 714(4) applies)", and

(*b*) for paragraph (*b*) (accrued income scheme) substitute—

"(*b*) is, by virtue of section 714(2), chargeable to income tax on annual profits or gains in respect of transfers of securities which are subject to the arrangement giving rise to the payment of manufactured interest; or".

(3) In sub-paragraph (2A), in the paragraph (*b*) so substituted, for "annual profits or gains" substitute "income".

(4) The amendment made by sub-paragraph (3) has effect in relation to payments of manufactured interest made on or after 6th April 2005.

(5) The other amendments made by this paragraph have effect in relation to payments of manufactured interest made on or after 16th March 2005.

GENERAL NOTE

This para amends the interaction between two anti-avoidance provisions; being the accrued income scheme and the provisions dealing with manufactured interest.

The accrued income scheme came into force in 1985. The legislature designed the scheme to prevent the tax saving produced by 'bond washing'. Bond washing is the procedure of selling a security immediately before an interest payment is due and buying it back shortly afterwards. This procedure converts the interest that the rules would tax as income into a capital gain that might bear less or no tax. The accrued income scheme deems the interest on the security to accrue over the period between payment dates and deems that interest to be taxable in the hands of the various owners during that period.

Arrangements transferring securities often generate interest. Examples of such arrangements are: sales with repurchases (a "repo") and stock lending agreements. Tax relief for the interest manufactured under the arrangement is limited to the amount of taxable income that the claimant generates from the arrangement. The manufactured interest regime came into force in 2002.

The changes that this para introduces aim to prevent the claim for manufactured interest relief and a deduction under the accrued income scheme; which deduction is not subject to the limits of the manufactured interest provisions. In other words, they prevent a double relief.

The relief for manufactured interest is now subject to two further limits. First, if the relief under the manufactured interest provisions relates to interest received, which is subject to tax, the taxable amount must take into account any relief under the accrued income scheme. Second, if the relief under the manufactured interest provisions relates to an accrued income scheme charge, the limit under the manufactured interest rules must take into account the relief under the accrued income scheme.

These changes come into effect with effect from 16 March 2005. However, the new rules change the reference to "annual profits or gains" to "income". This reflects the changes made to ITTOIA 2005 with effect from 6 April 2005.

Consideration due after time of disposal: creditor relationships etc

7— (1) Section 48 of TCGA 1992 (consideration due after time of disposal) is amended as follows.

(2) At the beginning insert "(1)".

(3) At the end add—

"(2) Subsection (1) above does not apply in relation to so much of any consideration as consists of rights under a creditor relationship to which a company becomes a party as a result of the disposal.

(3) In the computation of the gain in a case where subsection (2) above has effect in relation to any consideration, the amount to be brought into account in respect of that consideration is the fair value of the creditor relationship.

(4) In this section—

    (*a*) "creditor relationship", and

    (*b*) "fair value", in relation to a creditor relationship,

each have the same meaning as in Chapter 2 of Part 4 of the Finance Act 1996 (see section 103(1) of that Act).".

GENERAL NOTE

The changes that this para makes are closely related to those in para 12 dealing with money debts: discount and profits from interest, see further below.

Paragraph 12 amends the principal legislation (FA 1996 s 100). Paragraph 7 makes consequential amendments to TCGA 1992 s 48, which deals with consideration due after the time of disposal.

The general, previous, rule is now subject to a new exception. The general rule is that tax charged on deferred consideration ignores any discount. For example, if the consideration is a debenture. The new provision is that tax is calculated on chargeable gains arising from rights under a creditor loan relationship and uses the fair value of the creditor relationship.

Corporate strips: manipulation of price: associated payment giving rise to loss

8 In TCGA 1992, after section 151C (strips: manipulation of price: associated payment giving rise to loss) insert—

"151D Corporate strips: manipulation of price: associated payment giving rise to loss

  (1) This section applies if—

    (*a*) as a result of any scheme or arrangement which has an unallowable purpose, the circumstances are, or might have been, as mentioned in paragraph (*a*), (*b*) or (*c*) of section 452G(2) of ITTOIA 2005,

    (*b*) under the scheme or arrangement, a payment falls to be made otherwise than in respect of the acquisition or disposal of a corporate strip, and

    (*c*) as a result of that payment or the circumstances in which it is made, a loss accrues to any person.

  (2) The loss shall not be an allowable loss.

  (3) For the purposes of this section a scheme or arrangement has an unallowable purpose if the main benefit, or one of the main benefits, that might have been expected to result from, or from any provision of, the scheme or arrangement (apart from section 452G of ITTOIA 2005 and this section) is—

    (*a*) the obtaining of a tax advantage by any person, or

    (*b*) the accrual to any person of an allowable loss.

  (4) The reference in subsection (1)(*b*) above to the acquisition or disposal of a corporate strip shall be construed as if it were in Chapter 8 of Part 4 of ITTOIA 2005 (profits from deeply discounted securities) (see, in particular, sections 437 and 452F of that Act for the meaning of "disposal" and section 452E of that Act for the meaning of "corporate strip").

  (5) In subsection (3)(*a*) above "tax advantage" has the meaning given by section 709(1) of the Taxes Act.

  (6) This section applies to losses accruing on or after 6th April 2005.".

GENERAL NOTE

The changes that this para makes are closely related to those in paras 21 and 25, see further below.

Paragraphs 21 and 25 extend the rules on relevant discounted securities ("RDS") to strips of all securities. This para 8 aims to prevent an allowable capital loss arising under any scheme or arrangement in respect of corporate strips. It does so by inserting a new section into TCGA 1992 being an unallowable purpose condition similar to that in para 21.

This para applies to losses accruing on or after 6 April 2005.

Transactions within a group: shares subject to third party obligations

9— (1) Section 171 of TCGA 1992 (transfers within a group: general provisions) is amended as follows.

(2) After subsection (3) insert—

"(3A) Subsection (1) above does not apply—

(*a*) if section 91A of the Finance Act 1996 (shares subject to third party obligations)—

(i) does not apply in the case of the asset in relation to company A immediately before the disposal, but

(ii) does apply in the case of the asset in relation to company B immediately after its acquisition, or

(*b*) if that section—

(i) applies in the case of the asset in relation to company A immediately before the disposal, but

(ii) does not apply in the case of the asset in relation to company B immediately after its acquisition.".

(3) The amendment made by this paragraph has effect in any case where the disposal is on or after 16th March 2005.

GENERAL NOTE

The changes that this para makes are closely related to those in para 10, see further below.

Paragraph 10 relates to shares subject to third party obligations. A share may, therefore, become subject to provisions introduced by para 10 if the holder of the share transfers it without transferring the obligations. If the transferor and transferee were members of the same capital gains tax group, qualifying for intra-group transfer relief, they would avoid a charge to tax.

Paragraph 9 therefore, prevents the intra-group transfer relief applying when there is a transfer that would otherwise be subject to the provisions introduced by para 10.

Shares treated as loan relationships

10— (1) After section 91 of FA 1996 insert the following heading—

"Shares treated as loan relationships"

(2) After that heading insert the following section—

"91A Shares subject to outstanding third party obligations

(1) This section applies for the purposes of corporation tax in relation to a company if at any time in an accounting period—

(*a*) that company ("the investing company") holds a share in another company ("the issuing company"),

(*b*) the share is subject to outstanding third party obligations (see subsection (5)), and

(*c*) the share is an interest-like investment (see subsections (7) and (8)).

(2) This Chapter shall have effect for the accounting period of the investing company in accordance with subsection (3) below as if—

(*a*) the share were rights under a creditor relationship of that company, and

(*b*) any distribution in respect of the share were not a distribution falling within section 209(2)(*a*) or (*b*) of the Taxes Act 1988.

(3) The debits and credits to be brought into account by the investing company for the purposes of this Chapter as respects the share must be determined on the basis of fair value accounting.

(4) No debits are to be brought into account in respect of any transaction (or series of transactions) which (apart from the assumption in subsection (8)(*b*) below) would have the effect of causing the condition in paragraph (*a*) or (*b*) of subsection (7) below not to be satisfied.

(5) For the purposes of this section, the cases where a share is subject to outstanding third party obligations are those cases where—

(*a*) the share is subject to obligations of any description in subsection (6) below, (*b*) the obligations are obligations of a person other than the investing company, and

(*c*) the obligations are yet to be discharged,

and where a share is subject to any such obligations, they are for the purposes of this section the "third party obligations" in the case of that share.

(6) The descriptions of obligation are—

(*a*) an obligation to meet unpaid calls on the share;

(*b*) an obligation (not falling within paragraph (*a*) above) to make a contribution to the capital of the issuing company that could affect the value of the share.

(7) In this section "interest-like investment" means a share whose nature is such that the fair value of the share—

(*a*) is likely to increase at a rate which represents a return on an investment of money at a commercial rate of interest (see section 103(3A)), and

(*b*) is unlikely to deviate to a substantial extent from that rate of increase.

Fluctuations in value resulting from changes in exchange rates are to be left out of account for the purposes of paragraph (*b*) above.

(8) For the purposes of subsection (7) above, it shall be assumed—

(*a*) that any third party obligations will be met in the amounts, and at the time, at which they are due, and

(*b*) that no transaction (or series of transactions) intended to cause the condition in paragraph (*a*) or (*b*) of that subsection not to be satisfied will be entered into.

(9) For the purposes of this section, the fair value of a share that is subject to outstanding third party obligations must include the fair value of the obligations.

(10) For the purposes of this section a company shall be treated as continuing to hold a share notwithstanding that the share has been transferred to another person—

(*a*) under a repo or stock lending arrangement, or

(*b*) under a transaction which is treated by section 26 of the Taxation of Chargeable Gains Act 1992 as not involving any disposal.".

(3) After section 91A insert—

"91B Non-qualifying shares

(1) This section applies for the purposes of corporation tax in relation to a company if at any time in an accounting period—

(*a*) the company ("the investing company") holds a share in another company ("the issuing company"),

(*b*) the share is not one which, by virtue of paragraph 4 of Schedule 10 to this Act (holdings in unit trusts and offshore funds), falls to be treated for that accounting period as if it were rights under a creditor relationship of the investing company, and

(*c*) the share is a non-qualifying share (see subsection (6)),

and at no time in the accounting period does section 91A above apply in relation to the investing company in the case of that share.

(2) This Chapter shall have effect for that accounting period in accordance with subsection (3) below as if—

(*a*) the share were rights under a creditor relationship of the investing company, and

(*b*) any distribution in respect of the share were not a distribution falling within section 209(2)(*a*) or (*b*) of the Taxes Act 1988.

(3) The debits and credits to be brought into account by the investing company for the purposes of this Chapter as respects the share must be determined on the basis of fair value accounting.

(4) In any case where Condition 1 in section 91C below is satisfied, no debits are to be brought into account in respect of any transaction (or series of transactions) which (apart from the assumption in subsection (6) of section 91C below) would have the effect of causing the condition in paragraph (*a*) or (*b*) of subsection (1) of that section not to be satisfied.

(5) In any case where Condition 3 in section 91E below is satisfied—

(*a*) debits and credits shall be brought into account for the purposes of Schedule 26 to the Finance Act 2002 (derivative contracts) by the investing company in respect of any associated transaction falling within section 91E below as if it were, or were a transaction in respect of, a derivative contract (if that is not in fact the case), and (*b*) those debits and credits shall be determined on the basis of fair value accounting.

(6) A share is a non-qualifying share for the purposes of this section if—

(*a*) it is not one where section 95 of the Taxes Act 1988 (dealers etc) applies in relation to distributions in respect of the share, and

(*b*) one or more of the Conditions in sections 91C to 91E below is satisfied.

(7) Subsection (10) of section 91A above (company treated as holding a share) also applies for the purposes of this section.".

(4) After section 91B insert—

"91C Condition 1 for section 91B(6)(*b*)

(1) Condition 1 is that the assets of the issuing company are of such a nature that the fair value of the share—

(*a*) is likely to increase at a rate which represents a return on an investment of money at a commercial rate of interest, and

(*b*) is unlikely to deviate to a substantial extent from that rate of increase.

Fluctuations in value resulting from changes in exchange rates are to be left out of account for the purposes of paragraph (*b*) above.

(2) But Condition 1 is not satisfied if the whole or substantially the whole by fair value of the assets of the issuing company are income producing.

(3) The assets which, for the purposes of this section, are "income producing" are—

(*a*) any share as respects which the conditions in section 91A(1) above are satisfied;

(*b*) any share as respects which Condition 1 above is satisfied or would, apart from subsection (2) above, be satisfied;

(*c*) any share as respects which Condition 2 in section 91D below is satisfied or would, apart from subsection (1)(*c*) of that section (excepted shares), be satisfied;

(*d*) any share as respects which Condition 3 in section 91E below is satisfied;

(*e*) any asset of a description specified in any paragraph of paragraph 8(2) of Schedule 10 to this Act (qualifying investments in relation to a unit trust scheme or an offshore fund);

(*f*) rights under a repo in relation to which section 730A of the Taxes Act 1988 applies;

(*g*) any share in a company the whole or substantially the whole by fair value of whose assets are assets within paragraphs (*a*) to (*f*) above.

(4) The Treasury may by regulations amend this section for the purpose of adding to the assets which are income producing.

(5) The provision that may be made by regulations under this section includes provision for the regulations to have effect in relation to accounting periods (whenever beginning) which end on or after the day on which the regulations come into force.

(6) For the purposes of subsection (1) above, it shall be assumed that no transaction (or series of transactions) intended to cause the condition in paragraph (*a*) or (*b*) of that subsection not to be satisfied will be entered into by the investing company.

(7) This section shall be construed as one with section 91B above.

91D Condition 2 for section 91B(6)(*b*)

(1) Condition 2 is that the share—

(*a*) is redeemable (see subsection (2)),

(*b*) is designed to produce a return which equates, in substance, to the return on an investment of money at a commercial rate of interest, and

(*c*) is not an excepted share (see subsection (3)).

(2) For the purposes of this section, a share is to be regarded as redeemable only if it is redeemable as a result of its terms of issue (or any collateral agreements, arrangements or understandings)—

(*a*) requiring redemption,

(*b*) entitling the holder to require redemption, or

(*c*) entitling the issuer to redeem.

(3) A share is an "excepted share" for the purposes of this section if—

(*a*) it is a qualifying publicly issued share (see subsections (4) and (5)),

(*b*) it is a share that mirrors a public issue (see subsections (6) to (8)), or

(*c*) the investing company's purpose in acquiring the share is not an unallowable purpose (see subsection (9)).

(4) A share is a "qualifying publicly issued share" for the purposes of this section if—

(*a*) it was issued by a company as part of an issue of shares to independent persons, and

(*b*) less than 10% of the shares in that issue are held by the investing company or persons connected with it.

(5) But a share is not a qualifying publicly issued share for those purposes if the investing company's purpose in acquiring the share is an unallowable purpose by virtue of subsection (9)(*a*) below.

(6) The cases where a share mirrors a public issue are those set out in subsections (7) and (8) below.

(7) Case 1 is where—

(*a*) a company (company A) issues shares (the public issue) to independent persons,

(*b*) within 24 hours of that issue, one or more other companies (companies BB) issue shares (the mirroring shares) to company A on the same, or substantially the same, terms as the public issue,

(*c*) company A and companies BB are associated companies (see subsection (11)), and

(*d*) the total nominal value of the mirroring shares does not exceed the nominal value of the public issue,

and in any such case the mirroring shares are shares that mirror a public issue.

(8) Case 2 is where, in the circumstances of Case 1,—

(*a*) within 24 hours of the public issue, one or more other companies (companies CC) issue shares (the second-level mirroring shares) to one or more of companies BB on the same, or substantially the same, terms as the public issue,

(*b*) company A, companies BB and companies CC are associated companies, and

(*c*) the total nominal value of the second-level mirroring shares does not exceed the nominal value of the public issue,

and in any such case the second-level mirroring shares are also shares that mirror a public issue.

(9) For the purposes of this section, a share is acquired by the investing company for an unallowable purpose if the purpose, or one of the main purposes, for which the company holds the share is—

(*a*) the purpose of circumventing section 95 of the Taxes Act 1988 (see subsection (10)), or

(*b*) any other purpose which is a tax avoidance purpose (see subsection (11)).

(10) The purpose, or one of the main purposes, for which the investing company holds a share shall, in particular, be taken to be the purpose of circumventing section 95 of the Taxes Act 1988 (taxation of dealers in respect of distributions etc) if the investing company was an associated company of a bank (see subsection (11)) at the time when the investing company acquired the share, unless the investing company shows that—

(*a*) immediately before that time, some or all of its business consisted in making and holding investments, and

(*b*) it acquired the share in the ordinary course of that business.

(11) In this section—

"associated company", in relation to any other company, means a company which, within the meaning given by section 413(3)(*a*) of the Taxes Act 1988, is a member of the same group of companies as that other company;

"bank" has the meaning given by section 840A of the Taxes Act 1988;

"independent person", in relation to a company, means a person who is not connected with the company;

"tax advantage" has the meaning given by section 709(1) of the Taxes Act 1988;

"tax avoidance purpose", in the case of any company, means any purpose that consists in securing a tax advantage (whether for the company or any other person).

(12) Section 839 of the Taxes Act 1988 (connected persons) applies for the purposes of this section.

(13) This section is to be construed as one with section 91B above.

91E Condition 3 for section 91B(6)(*b*)

(1) Condition 3 is that there is a scheme or arrangement under which the share and one or more associated transactions are together designed to produce a return which equates, in substance, to the return on an investment of money at a commercial rate of interest.

(2) But Condition 3 is not satisfied if—

(*a*) Condition 1 in section 91C above is satisfied as respects the share or would, apart from subsection (2) of that section (income producing assets), be so satisfied, or

(*b*) Condition 2 in section 91D above is satisfied as respects the share or would, apart from subsection (1)(*c*) of that section (excepted shares), be so satisfied.

(3) In this section "associated transaction" includes entering into, or acquiring rights or liabilities under, any of the following—

(*a*) a derivative contract;

(*b*) a contract that would be a derivative contract, apart from paragraph 4(2B) of Schedule 26 to the Finance Act 2002 (trades etc: hedging relationships with shares);

(*c*) a contract having a similar effect to—

(i) a derivative contract, or

(ii) a contract falling within paragraph (*b*) above;

(*d*) a contract of insurance or indemnity.

(4) This section is to be construed as one with section 91B above.".

(5) After section 91E insert—

"91F Power to add, vary or remove Conditions for section 91B(6)(*b*)

(1) The Treasury may by regulations amend this Chapter so as to add, vary or remove Conditions for the purposes of section 91B(6)(*b*) above.

(2) Where the Treasury so add, vary or remove a Condition, they may also by regulations amend any of the following enactments—

(*a*) this Chapter,

(*b*) Chapters 1 to 3 of Part 6 of the Taxes Act 1988 (company distributions),

(*c*) Part 18 of the Taxes Act 1988 (double taxation relief),

(*d*) the Taxation of Chargeable Gains Act 1992,

(*e*) Schedule 26 to the Finance Act 2002 (derivative contracts),

so as to make provision for or in connection with taxation in the case of any asset or transaction that is or was mentioned in the Condition.

(3) The power to make regulations under this section includes power—

(*a*) to make different provision for different cases, and

(*b*) to make such consequential, supplementary, incidental or transitional provisions, or savings, as appear to the Treasury to be necessary or expedient (including provision amending any enactment or any instrument made under an enactment).".

(6) After section 91F insert—

"91G Shares beginning or ceasing to be subject to section 91A or 91B

(1) Where at any time on or after 16th March 2005 the conditions in section 91A(1) or 91B(1) above become satisfied in the case of any share, otherwise than in the circumstances described in subsection (3) below, the investing company shall be deemed for the purposes of the Taxation of Chargeable Gains Act 1992—

(*a*) to have disposed of the share immediately before that time for a consideration of an amount equal to its fair value at that time, and

(*b*) to have immediately reacquired it for a consideration of the same amount.

(2) Where at any time the conditions in section 91A(1) or 91B(1) above cease to be satisfied in the case of any share, the investing company shall be deemed for the purposes of the Taxation of Chargeable Gains Act 1992 and of this Chapter—

(*a*) to have disposed of the share immediately before that time for a consideration of an amount equal to its fair value at that time, and

(*b*) to have immediately reacquired it for a consideration of the same amount.

(3) In any case where—

(*a*) a share is held by a company both—

(i) at the end of 15th March 2005, and

(ii) at the beginning of 16th March 2005, and

(*b*) the conditions in section 91A(1) or 91B(1) above are satisfied in relation to that share at the beginning of 16th March 2005,

subsection (4) below applies.

(4) In any such case, section 116 of the Taxation of Chargeable Gains Act 1992 (reorganisations etc involving qualifying corporate bonds) shall have effect in accordance with—

(*a*) the assumptions in subsections (5) and (6) below, and

(*b*) the provisions of subsections (7) and (8) below.

(5) The first of the assumptions is that the share became an asset representing a creditor relationship of the company (and, accordingly, a qualifying corporate bond) in consequence of the occurrence on 16th March 2005 of a transaction such as is mentioned in section 116(1) of the Taxation of Chargeable Gains Act 1992.

(6) The remaining assumptions are that, in relation to the transaction deemed to have occurred as mentioned in subsection (5) above,—

(a) the share immediately before 16th March 2005 shall be assumed to be the old asset for the purposes of section 116 of the Taxation of Chargeable Gains Act 1992, and

(b) the asset representing a creditor relationship immediately after the beginning of 16th March 2005 shall be assumed for those purposes to be the new asset.

(7) Where—

(a) subsection (3) above has effect in the case of any share, but

(b) the conditions in section 91A(1) or 91B(1) above cease to be satisfied in the case of the share at any time on or before 31st December 2005,

subsection (8) below applies.

(8) In any such case—

(a) the deemed disposal of the share at that time by virtue of subsection (2)(a) above shall not be regarded as a disposal for the purposes of subsection (10)(b) or (c) of section 116 of the Taxation of Chargeable Gains Act 1992, but

(b) the share shall continue to be the new asset for the purposes of that section.".

(7) The amendments made by this paragraph have effect in relation to shares held by a company on or after 16th March 2005.

GENERAL NOTE

Paragraph 10 inserts a number of new sections into FA 1996. The principle new sections are identified here, the remainder being supporting provisions.

New section 91A

This new section applies to shares that are subject to third party obligations and interest-like investments. Interest-like investments are shares whose fair value will probably increase at a rate equivalent to an interest return on money, and is unlikely to deviate substantially from that rate. Those two rates are both considered ignoring any variations arising from variations in exchange rates and assuming no value shifting transactions.

In these circumstances, the share is treated as a creditor loan relationship and any distribution excluded from the definition of "distribution" for the purposes of the corporation tax Acts (TA 1988 s 209(2)(a) or (b)). As a creditor loan relationship, the share will fall under the general loan relationship provisions (FA 1996 Part 4 Chapter 2).

For the purposes of the new section, the fair value of the share is based on the fair value method of accounting reflecting the rights under the outstanding obligations. The rules ignore any debits reflecting the intention to make the share a non-interest-like investment. Outstanding obligations in this context mean any liability to meet undischarged obligations, to meet calls on the shares or to make other form of contribution.

These provisions apply when the share is subject to a repo or stock loan or if the shares have been mortgaged.

New section 91B

This new section applies when an investing company holds shares in an issuing company and the shares are not treated as rights under a creditor loan relationship, s 91A (see above) does not apply and the shares are non-qualifying shares.

In these circumstances, the share is treated as a creditor loan relationship and any distribution excluded from the definition of "distribution" for the purposes of the corporation tax Acts (TA 1988 s 209(2)(a) or (b)).

As a creditor loan relationship, the share will fall under the general loan relationship provisions (FA 1996 Part 4 Chapter 2). That is to say, new s 91B has the same consequences as new s 91A.

The new section defines three circumstances ("conditions") in which a share is a non-qualifying share. However, as a blanket exception, a share is not a non-qualifying share if the rules already bring any distribution or increase in value in respect of that share. For example, if the share is in the hands of dealers in securities or other financial institutions.

As with new s 91A, the tax charge must use a fair value method of accounting. For shares within condition 1, the tax charge ignores any debits intended to make the share a non-interest-like investment. For shares within condition 3, the rules treat any associated transaction as a derivative contract and account for any debits and credits on a fair value basis.

These provisions apply when the share is subject to a repo or stock loan or if the shares have been mortgaged.

The Treasury has exceptionally wide powers to amend the legislation to add, vary or remove a condition.

Condition 1

The first condition applies where the whole or substantially the whole of the assets of the issuing company (based on their fair value) are not income producing (as defined further below). Two other preconditions apply to the shares and are similar to those in new s 91A, namely shares whose fair value will probably increase at a rate equivalent to an interest return on money, and is unlikely to deviate substantially from that rate. Those preconditions are both considered ignoring any variations arising from variations in exchange rates and assuming no value shifting transactions.

The following assets are not income producing.

- Any shares satisfying Condition 1 or that would do so apart from the substantially income producing test.
- Shares satisfying the conditions in new s91A (shares subject to third party obligations which increase in value in an interest-like way).
- Shares satisfying Condition 2 (certain redeemable shares) while ignoring the exception for certain shares in that condition, see further below.
- Shares satisfying Condition 3 (shares increasing in value in an interest-like way in combination with derivatives), see further below.
- Assets within the non-qualifying investments test for the purposes of loan relationships: collective investment schemes (FA 1996 Sch 10 para 8 (2)).
- Certain repo contracts.
- Companies whose assets are, or are substantially, those classes of assets.

The Treasury may, by regulation, add further categories of income-producing assets with effect for any period ending after the date of the regulations.

Condition 2

The second condition applies to a share that is redeemable, designed to produce a return substantially equivalent to the return on an investment of money at a commercial rate of interest (as defined, see below) and not an excepted share.

A redeemable share is one requiring redemption or carrying the entitlement to redemption by the holder or issuer.

Excepted shares are qualifying publicly issued shares, shares mirroring a public issue and shares acquired by an investor without an unallowable purpose. Condition 2 does not cover shares issued within a group of companies moving publicly raised funds to the relevant group member.

A share is a qualifying publicly issued share if the company issued it as part of an issue to independent persons and the investing company, together with persons connected with it, holds less than ten per cent of the issue. However, a share is not a qualifying publicly issued share if the investor had an unallowable purpose in acquiring it. For these purposes, an independent person is a person not connected with the company.

A mirroring issue must happen within 24 hours of the first issue and be on the same or substantially the same terms. The total nominal value of the mirror issue must not exceed the nominal value of the original issue. The legislation describes two cases of mirror issue: mirroring shares (case 1) and second level mirroring shares (case 2). Case 1 applies to shares issued directly to the original issuing company. Case 2 applies to shares issued to associated companies.

An unallowable purpose arises if the main purpose or one of the main purposes of the company in holding the shares is to circumvent the provisions dealing with the taxation of dealers in respect of distributions etc (TA 1988 s 95) or tax avoidance (as defined).

Circumventing TA 1988 s 95 includes a situation where the acquiring company was associated with a bank (within the provisions dealing with banks in TA 1988 s 840A) unless the investing company shows that it was an investment company and held the assets as part of that business.

Condition 3

The third condition applies to schemes or arrangements whereby a party designed the share and one or more associated transactions to produce a return substantially equivalent to a return on investment of money at a commercial rate of interest (as defined, see below).

An asset does not satisfy Condition 3 if Conditions 1 or 2 apply to it or to which those Conditions would apply but for the exceptions that those Conditions make for income-producing assets or excepted shares.

Associated transactions include entering or acquiring the rights or liabilities under: a derivative contract, a quasi-derivative contract, a contract with a similar effect to a derivative or quasi-derivative contract or a contract of insurance or indemnity. For these purposes, a quasi-derivative contract is a contract that would be a derivative contract apart from the provisions relating to contracts excluded by virtue of their underlying subject matter (FA 2002 Sch 26 para 4(2B)).

New section 91G

This new section defines the new charges to tax on shares within new ss 91A and 91B ("the new regime").

In general, if the new regime starts to apply to a share or ceases to apply to the share, then the rules deem that the investing company has sold and reacquired that share. Moreover, the sale price is the fair value of the share at that time.

The rules make an exception of the circumstances when the new regime started applying to certain shares on 16 March 2005. In general, the rules postpone the gain that the rules would have triggered until the shares are disposed of or are no longer within the new regime. Alternatively, if the arrangements are unwound, without a change of ownership, before 31 December 2005 (so that, under the general rules, a charge would be triggered) the rules defer the charge until the owner sells the shares.

Related transactions in relation to right to receive manufactured interest

11— (1) Section 97 of FA 1996 (manufactured interest) is amended as follows.

(2) In subsection (2) (consequences of company having relationship to which the section applies)—

(*a*) paragraph (*b*) (which restricts the debits and credits to be brought into account to those relating to the manufactured interest) shall cease to have effect, and

(*b*) in the closing words, for "paragraphs (*a*)(ii) and (*b*)" substitute "paragraph (*a*)(ii)".

(3) After subsection (2) insert—

"(2A) Where a company—

(*a*) has a relationship to which this section applies, but

(*b*) enters into a related transaction in respect of the right to receive manufactured interest,

then, for the purpose of bringing credits into account by virtue of subsection (2) above in respect of that or any other related transaction, the company shall continue to be treated as having a relationship to which this section applies even though the manufactured interest is not payable to the company.".

(4) Omit subsections (3) and (3A) (which relate to whether debits or credits are trading or non-trading etc and which are unnecessary, in view of the application of sections 82(2) and 103(2) of FA 1996 by virtue of section 97(2) of that Act).

(5) The amendments made by this paragraph have effect in relation to related transactions on or after 16th March 2005.

GENERAL NOTE

The manufactured interest provisions as originally enacted (in FA 1996) applied only to debits and credits "relating to that interest". This meant that the regime did not apply to sales of manufactured interest.

This para amends the provisions relating to manufactured interest (FA 1996 s 97) to bring those other, related, payments within the manufactured interest regime. This applies when the company no longer has the right to the manufactured interest having sold or transferred it.

These provisions apply to related transactions with effect from 16 March 2005.

Money debts etc not arising from lending of money: discounts and profits
from transactions

12— (1) Section 100 of FA 1996 (money debts etc not arising from the lending of money) is amended as follows.

(2) In subsection (1)(*c*) (money debts to which the section applies) after sub-paragraph (iii) insert "or

(iv) as respects which the conditions in subsection (1A) below (discount etc) are satisfied;".

(3) After subsection (1) insert—

"(1A) The conditions mentioned in subsection (1)(*c*)(iv) above are that—

(*a*) the company stands in the position of creditor in relation to the money debt;

(*b*) the money debt is one from which a discount (whether of an income or capital nature) arises to the company;

(*c*) the discount does not fall to be brought into account under section 50 of the Finance Act 2005 by virtue of section 47 of that Act (alternative finance return);

(*d*) if the money debt is some or all of the consideration payable for a disposal of property, the money debt (on the assumption that it will be paid in full) does not fall to be brought into account for the purposes of corporation tax as a trading receipt of the company;

(*e*) if the money debt is some or all of the consideration payable for a disposal of property, the property in question is not any of the following—

(i) an asset representing a loan relationship;

(ii) a derivative contract.".

(4) In subsection (2), as it has effect for periods of account beginning on or after 1st January 2005, in paragraph (*a*), for "matters mentioned in subsection (1)(*c*) above" substitute "matters mentioned in subsection (1)(*c*)(i) to (iii) above or subsection (2ZA) below".

(5) After subsection (2) insert—

"(2ZA) The matters are—

(*a*) in the case of a money debt falling within subsection (1)(*c*)(i) above, profits (but not losses) arising to the company from any related transaction in respect of the right to receive interest;

(*b*) in the case of a money debt falling within subsection (1)(*c*)(iv) above, each of the following—

(i) the discount arising to the company from the money debt;

(ii) profits (but not losses) arising to the company from any related transaction;

(iii) any impairment arising to the company in respect of the discount;

(iv) any reversal of any such impairment.

(2ZB) Where a company—

(*a*) has a relationship to which this section applies by virtue of subsection (1)(*c*)(i) above, but

(*b*) enters into a related transaction in respect of the right to receive interest,

then, for the purpose of bringing credits into account by virtue of subsection (2ZA)(*a*) above in respect of that or any other related transaction, the company shall continue to be treated as having a relationship to which this section so applies even though the interest is not payable to the company.".

(6) After subsection (3) (amounts treated as interest under Schedule 28AA to ICTA) insert—

"(3A) For the purposes of this section, a discount shall, in particular, be taken to arise from a money debt in any case where—

(*a*) there is a disposal of property for a consideration some or all of which is money that falls to be paid after the sale;

(*b*) the amount or value of the whole consideration exceeds what the purchaser would have paid for the property if he had been required to pay in full at the time of the disposal; and

(*c*) some or all of the excess can reasonably be regarded as representing a return on an investment of money at interest (and, accordingly, as being a discount arising from the money debt).

(3B) The credits to be brought into account for the purposes of this Chapter in respect of a discount arising from a money debt must be determined using an amortised cost basis of accounting (see section 103).".

(7) Omit subsections (4) to (6) and (8) (which relate to whether debits or credits are trading or non-trading etc and which are unnecessary, in view of the application of sections 82(2) and 103(2) of FA 1996 by virtue of section 100(2) of that Act).

(8) Omit subsection (13) (express subjection to Schedules 9 and 11 to FA 1996, which is unnecessary in view of the closing words of subsection (2) of the section).

(9) In consequence of the amendments made by this paragraph, paragraph (*c*) of the Case III of Schedule D substituted for the purposes of corporation tax by section 18(3A) of ICTA (tax in respect of discount arising otherwise than in respect of a loan relationship) shall not have effect in relation to any discount arising in an accounting period beginning on or after the commencement date.

(10) Subject to sub-paragraph (9), the amendments made by this paragraph have effect in relation to any money debt to which a company is party as a creditor on or after the commencement date.

(11) Where, on or after the commencement date but in a period of account beginning before 1st January 2005, a company is party to a relationship to which section 100 of FA 1996 applies, then, in the application of that section for that period of account, subsection (2) of it shall have effect as follows—

(*a*) paragraph (*a*) shall have effect in relation to—

(i) any discount arising to the company from the money debt, and

(ii) any profits, impairment of discount, or reversal of impairment of discount, arising to the company as mentioned in subsection (2ZA) of that section,

as it has effect (or would have effect) in relation to interest payable to the company under the relationship,

(*b*) paragraph (*b*) shall have effect as if the reference to interest included a reference to the matters mentioned in paragraph (*a*)(i) and (ii) above, and

(*c*) the closing words shall have effect accordingly.

(12) None of the following shall be brought into account for the purposes of Chapter 2 of Part 4 of FA 1996 by virtue of this paragraph—

(*a*) credits in respect of discount arising from a money debt, to the extent that the discount accrued before the commencement date;

(*b*) credits in respect of profits arising as mentioned in section 100(2ZA)(*a*) or (*b*)(ii) of that Act where the related transaction took place before the commencement date;

(*c*) debits in respect of any impairment arising in respect of discount arising from a money debt, to the extent that the discount accrued before the commencement date;

(*d*) credits in respect of any reversal of any such impairment, to the extent that the discount accrued before the commencement date.

(13) In this paragraph "the commencement date" means 16th March 2005.

GENERAL NOTE

This para amends the provisions relating to money debts etc not arising from the lending of money (FA 1996 s 100). That section deals with loan relationships (money debts etc not arising from the lending of money). It extended the loan relationship rules to interest and exchange gains losses on debts that were not loan relationships. This new para extends those provisions to include profits from disposals of interest and from all discounts.

Certain preconditions apply. Firstly, the company must be the creditor under a money debt being a debt giving rise to a discount. (The discount can be of either income or capital.) Secondly, the discount must not be within the alternative finance arrangements provisions (FA 2005 ss 47 and 50). Thirdly, the discount must not be a trading receipt for the purposes of corporation tax, which could be the case if the debt was the price for the disposal of the company's assets. Nor must the debt be the proceeds of disposing of an asset representing a loan relationship or a derivative contract.

The para goes on to add new categories of benefits derived from relevant assets to the interest and discounts previously covered. One new category is the profits from any related transaction connected to a right to receive interest or affecting the discount. However, losses are not included. The new para also brings into account debits relating to the impairment of a discount and credits when the parties reverse that impairment.

The provisions dealing with debits and credits brought into account (FA 1996 s 84 (5)) define a related transaction.

These charging provisions continue to apply to a company if it enters a related transaction divesting itself of the right to receive interest under a qualifying loan relationship.

The new provision gives as a particular example of where the charge will arise, a sale for a deferred consideration. The charge is subject to a number of preconditions. Firstly, the price must exceed the price that the buyer would have received had the seller paid in full at the time of sale. Secondly, some of the excess must, fairly, reflect a return on the deferred price.

When this provision applies, the credits must be valued on the amortised cost basis of accounting.

These new provisions apply to any money debt that is an asset on or after 16 March 2005. However, transitional provisions apply exempting discounts accrued before 16 March 2005 losses arising from the impairment of a discount or profits from the reversal of such an impairment before that date and profits from related transactions arising before the date.

Meaning of "commercial rate of interest"

13— (1) In section 103 of FA 1996 (interpretation) after subsection (3) insert—

"(3A) For the purposes of this Chapter, a commercial rate of interest, in the case of a company and any asset, is—

(*a*) a rate ("the simple commercial rate") that is reasonably comparable to the rate that the company could obtain by placing on deposit the money it invested in the asset, or

(*b*) in any case where—

(i) the likely rate of increase in the value of the asset is in question, and
(ii) that likely rate is a lower rate than the simple commercial rate, and
(iii) the difference is a result of an expectation that the company would also obtain a tax advantage as a result of investing in the asset,

that lower rate.

(3B) In subsection (3A) above, "tax advantage" has the meaning given by section 709(1) of the Taxes Act 1988.".

(2) The amendment made by this paragraph has effect in relation to assets held on or after 16th March 2005 (whenever acquired).

GENERAL NOTE

This para defines a commercial rate of interest as consisting of two elements. The first is a simple commercial rate being one reasonably comparable to the rate available to the company had it deposited the money it had invested in the asset. The alternative applies if three preconditions apply. Firstly, the rate of increase in value of the asset is uncertain. Secondly, the likely rate is lower than the simple commercial rate of interest, as already defined. Thirdly, the difference in those two rates arises because of an expectation that the company would obtain a tax advantage through its investment in the asset.

Tax advantage is defined by reference to the TA 1988 definition section (s 709 (1)).

Capital redemption policies: removal of exclusion from loan relationships computations

14— (1) Schedule 9 to FA 1996 (loan relationships: special computational provisions) is amended as follows.

(2) In paragraph 1A(1) (credits and debits relating to life policies and capital redemption policies not to be brought into account) paragraph (*b*) (capital redemption policies) shall cease to have effect.

(3) This paragraph has effect in relation to a capital redemption policy on and after 10th February 2005 (whenever the capital redemption policy was effected).

(4) Where a capital redemption policy—

(*a*) is held by a company immediately before 10th February 2005, and
(*b*) on or after that date, is, for the purposes of Chapter 2 of Part 4 of FA 1996, a creditor relationship of the company,

sub-paragraphs (5) and (6) apply.

(5) In any such case, Chapter 2 of Part 13 of ICTA (life policies etc: chargeable events) shall have effect as if—

(*a*) immediately before 10th February 2005, the company had assigned the whole of the rights conferred by the policy for money or money's worth, and
(*b*) the value of the consideration for the assignment had been equal to what the carrying value of the creditor relationship would have been had an accounting period of the company ended on that date;

and Chapter 2 of Part 4 of FA 1996 shall have effect as if, immediately after 9th February 2005, the company had acquired the creditor relationship at a cost equal to that carrying value.

(6) But if—

(*a*) the accounting period in which the assignment is deemed to have happened ("the assignment period"), and
(*b*) the accounting period in which the company ceases to be party to the creditor relationship ("the cessation period"),

are not the same accounting period, any gain which, by virtue of the deemed assignment, would have fallen to be brought into account in accordance with section 547(1)(*b*) of ICTA for the assignment period shall instead be brought into account for the cessation period.

(7) In this paragraph—

"assignment", in relation to Scotland, means an assignation;
"carrying value" has the same meaning as it has for the purposes of paragraph 19A of Schedule 9 to FA 1996, as it has effect for periods of account beginning on or after 1st January 2005.

GENERAL NOTE

If a capital redemption policy ("CRB") is not exempt from capital gains tax, tax planners may use it to create an artificial loss for corporation tax purposes. This para therefore removes CRBs from the capital gains tax regime.

Insurance companies offer CRBs as part of their regulated insurance business. Although they are not conditional on a human life, they are treated as insurance for regulatory purposes, otherwise the companies would not be permitted to issues such business. The tax rules also treat CRBs as policies of insurance for the purposes of taxing offshore funds.

Being removed from the capital gains tax regime, CRBs will now be subject to the loan relationship legislation.

This para deems owners of all CRBs owned from 10 February 2005 to have assigned them on 9 February for an amount equal to the bond's carrying value. The tax provisions use that value as the opening value for the loan relationship rules. The rules postpone the gain arising from that assignment until the accounting period when the policy either matures, is assigned or is surrendered.

The provision dealing with the adjustment on change of accounting policy for the purposes of the loan relationship rules (FA 1996 Sch 9 para 19A(4A)) defines carrying value.

Deemed disposal of assets and liabilities on company ceasing to be resident in UK etc

15— (1) In Schedule 9 to FA 1996 (loan relationships) paragraph 10A is amended as follows.

(2) After sub-paragraph (1) (cases where the paragraph applies) insert—

"(1A) But this paragraph does not apply if—

(*a*) paragraph 12A below (transferee company leaving group) applies in relation to the company, and

(*b*) the cessation in sub-paragraph (1)(*a*) or (*b*) above occurs at the same time as the cessation in sub-paragraph (1)(*b*) of that paragraph.".

(3) In sub-paragraph (2) (Schedule to have effect as if there had been an assignment and reacquisition) for "Schedule" substitute "Chapter".

(4) The amendments made by this paragraph have effect on and after 16th March 2005.

GENERAL NOTE

This para and paras 18 and 24, introduce a charge applicable to degrouping. In particular, this para amends the charge that arises on a company ceasing to be UK resident. It provides that the new provisions (introduced by para 18 (FA 1996 Sch 9 para 12A)) take priority over the provision dealing with the deemed disposal of assets and liabilities on a company ceasing to be resident in the UK etc (FA 1996 Sch 9 para 10A).

Transactions not at arm's length: exceptions relating to groups of companies

16— (1) In Schedule 9 to FA 1996 (loan relationships) paragraph 11 (transactions not at arm's length) is amended as follows.

(2) For sub-paragraph (3) (exceptions relating to groups of companies) substitute—

"(3) Sub-paragraph (1) above does not apply if the related transaction—

(*a*) is a transaction as a result of which paragraph 12 below (groups)—

(i) applies by virtue of sub-paragraph (1)(*a*) of it, or
(ii) would so apply, apart from sub-paragraph (2A) of it (transferor using fair value accounting), or

(*b*) is part of a series of transactions as a result of which that paragraph—

(i) applies by virtue of sub-paragraph (1)(*b*) of it, or
(ii) would so apply, apart from sub-paragraph (2A) of it.".

(3) In consequence, omit sub-paragraph (5) (construction of references to a member of a group).

(4) The amendments made by this paragraph have effect where the related transaction is on or after 16th March 2005.

GENERAL NOTE

This para and 17, 18, 22, 23 and 24, amend the company grouping rules and introduce a charge applicable to degrouping. The aim is to charge any gain on loan relationships and derivative contracts before a company leaves a group.

In particular, this para deals with transactions not at and arm's length (FA 1996 Sch 9 para 11). It corrects an error allowing transfers between members of a group of companies to escape both the no gain no loss provisions and the transfers at fair value provisions. Its effect is that relevant transactions will take place at fair value.

Continuity of treatment of groups etc: treatment of transferee company

17— (1) In Schedule 9 to FA 1996 (loan relationships) paragraph 12 (continuity of treatment of groups etc) is amended as follows.

(2) For sub-paragraph (2) (the credits and debits to be brought into account) substitute—

"(2) For the purpose of determining the credits and debits to be brought into account for the purposes of this Chapter in respect of the loan relationship—

(*a*) for the accounting period in which the transaction or, as the case may be, the first of the series of transactions takes place, the transferor company shall be treated as having entered into that transaction for a consideration equal to the notional carrying value of the asset or liability representing the relationship; and

(*b*) for any accounting period in which it is a party to the relationship, the transferee company shall be treated as if it had acquired the asset or liability representing the relationship for a consideration equal to the notional carrying value of the asset or liability.

For the purposes of this sub-paragraph, the notional carrying value is the amount that would have been the carrying value of the asset or liability in the accounts of the transferor company if a period of account had ended immediately before the date when the company ceased to be party to the loan relationship.".

(3) In sub-paragraph (2A) (paragraph 12 not to apply where transferor uses fair value accounting) for paragraph (aa) (treatment of transferee in respect of the transaction) substitute—

"(aa) paragraph (*b*) of sub-paragraph (2) above shall have effect in relation to the transferee company.".

(4) For sub-paragraph (8) (which applies paragraph 11(5) for construction of references to a member of a group) substitute—

"(8) In this paragraph references to a company which is a member of a group of companies shall be construed in accordance with section 170 of the Taxation of Chargeable Gains Act 1992.".

(5) In sub-paragraph (9) (interpretation) insert the following definition at the appropriate place—

""carrying value" has the same meaning as it has for the purposes of paragraph 19A below;".

(6) Where the period of account mentioned in the second sentence of the sub-paragraph (2) substituted by sub-paragraph (2) begins before 1st January 2005, "carrying value" shall be construed as if the period had begun on or after that date.

(7) The amendments made by this paragraph have effect in any case where the relevant transaction is on or after 16th March 2005.

(8) In this paragraph "the relevant transaction" means—

(*a*) the related transaction mentioned in sub-paragraph (1)(*a*) of paragraph 12 of Schedule 9 to FA 1996,

(*b*) the first of the series of transactions mentioned in sub-paragraph (1)(*b*) of that paragraph, or

(*c*) the transfer mentioned in sub-paragraph (1)(*c*) or (1)(*d*) of that paragraph,

by virtue of which that paragraph applies or would apply apart from sub-paragraph (2A) of it.

GENERAL NOTE

This para and paras 16, 18, 22, 23 and 24, amend the company grouping rules and introduce a charge applicable to degrouping. The aim is to charge any gain on loan relationships and derivative contracts before a company leaves a group.

This para, together with para 22, provides for the continuity of treatment of the transferee company in respect of loan relationships and derivative contracts. In particular, this para deals with the loan relationship rules.

This para provides that the rules use the same value for taxing both the transferee and the transferor in relation to an intragroup transfer in the relevant circumstances. The rules use the amount of the notional carrying value. Previously the valuation put the transferee in the same position as the transferor, which was misleading.

Transferee leaving group after replacing transferor as party to loan relationship

18— (1) In Schedule 9 to FA 1996 (loan relationships) after paragraph 12 insert—

"*Transferee leaving group after replacing transferor as party to loan relationship*

12A— (1) This paragraph applies in any case where—

(*a*) paragraph 12 above applies—

(i) by virtue of sub-paragraph (1)(*a*) of that paragraph ("case A"), or

(ii) by virtue of sub-paragraph (1)(*b*) of that paragraph ("case B"), but

(*b*) before the end of the relevant 6 year period, the transferee company ceases to be a member of the relevant group.

(2) In any such case, this Chapter shall have effect as if the transferee company had—

(*a*) immediately before that cessation, assigned the asset or liability representing the relevant loan relationship for a consideration of an amount equal to its fair value at that time, and

(*b*) immediately reacquired it for a consideration of the same amount,

but only if Condition 1 or 2 below is satisfied and sub-paragraph (5) below does not apply.

(3) Condition 1 is that if sub-paragraph (2) above has effect, a credit would in consequence of paragraph (*a*) of that sub-paragraph fall to be brought into account for the purposes of this Chapter by the transferee company.

(4) Condition 2 is that—

    (*a*) Condition 1 is not satisfied,

    (*b*) the loan relationship is a creditor relationship,

    (*c*) the company has a hedging relationship between a derivative contract and the creditor relationship, and

    (*d*) in consequence of paragraph 30A(2)(*a*) of Schedule 26 to the Finance Act 2002, a credit falls to be brought into account by the transferee company for the purposes of that Schedule in respect of the derivative contract.

(5) Where the transferee company ceases to be a member of the relevant group by reason only of an exempt distribution (see sub-paragraph (8))—

    (*a*) sub-paragraph (2) above does not have effect, but

    (*b*) if there is chargeable payment within 5 years after the making of the exempt distribution, sub-paragraph (6) below applies.

(6) Where this sub-paragraph applies, this Chapter shall have effect as if—

    (*a*) the transferee company had, immediately before the making of the chargeable payment, assigned the asset or liability representing the relevant loan relationship,

    (*b*) the assignment had been for a consideration of an amount equal to the fair value of the asset or liability immediately before the transferee company ceased to be a member of the relevant group, and

    (*c*) the transferee company had immediately reacquired the asset or liability for a consideration of the same amount,

but only if Condition 1 or 2 above, as modified by sub-paragraph (7) below, is satisfied.

(7) The modifications are that—

    (*a*) in Condition 1, the references to sub-paragraph (2) above, and paragraph (*a*) of that sub-paragraph, are to be taken respectively as references to sub-paragraph (6) above and paragraphs (*a*) and (*b*) of that sub-paragraph, and

    (*b*) in Condition 2, the reference to paragraph 30A(2)(*a*) of Schedule 26 to the Finance Act 2002 is to be taken as a reference to paragraph 30A(6)(*a*) and (*b*) of that Schedule.

(8) In this paragraph—

"assignment", in relation to Scotland, means an assignation;

"chargeable payment" has the meaning given by section 214(2) of the Taxes Act 1988;

"exempt distribution" means a distribution which is exempt by virtue of section 213(2) of the Taxes Act 1988;

"the relevant 6 year period" means the period of 6 years following—

    (*a*) in case A, the transaction mentioned in paragraph 12(1)(*a*) above, or

    (*b*) in case B, the last of the series of transactions mentioned in paragraph 12(1)(*b*) above;

"the relevant group" means—

    (*a*) in case A, the group mentioned in paragraph 12(1)(*a*) above, or

    (*b*) in case B, the group mentioned in paragraph 12(1)(*b*) above;

"the relevant loan relationship" means the loan relationship mentioned in paragraph 12(1) above;

"the transferee company" means the company referred to as such in paragraph 12(1) above.

(9) Paragraph 12(14) of Schedule 26 to the Finance Act 2002 (hedging relationships) has effect for the purposes of this paragraph.".

(2) The amendment made by this paragraph has effect where a company ceases to be a member of a group on or after 16th March 2005.

GENERAL NOTE

This para and paras 16, 17, 22, 23 and 24, amend the company grouping rules and introduce a charge applicable to degrouping. The aim is to charge any gain on loan relationships and derivative contracts before a company leaves a group.

This para and paras 15 and 24, introduce a charge applicable to degrouping. In particular, this para deals with loan relationships.

A new charge applies if there has been a transaction between members of a group of companies and, within six years, the transferee leaves the group. Transfers of insurance business are exempt.

The transferee is deemed to have assigned the asset or liability for its fair value immediately before leaving the group and to have reacquired it immediately thereafter at the same value. However, the provision does not apply if it would have either of the following two effects, identified as conditions. Firstly, if the provisions would lead to the transferee company bringing a credit into account. Secondly, if the loan relationship is a creditor relationship the new rule would mean that the transferee company accounted for a debit, or a credit would be brought into account in respect of a hedging derivative.

An alternative charge applies if the company leaves a group and there is an exempt distribution (within the exempt distributions provisions, TA 1988 s 213). In that case, the degrouping charge under the chargeable payments connected with exempt distribution provisions (TA 1988 s 214) does not apply if any party makes a chargeable payment within five years of the departure. Instead, a charge arises immediately before the party makes the chargeable payment.

Avoidance involving repos or stock lending

19— (1) In Schedule 9 to FA 1996 (loan relationships) paragraph 15 is amended as follows.

(2) At the end of sub-paragraph (2) (disposals and acquisitions to which the paragraph applies) add "and as is, in the case of those arrangements, the disposal or acquisition effected by—

(a) the transfer by A to B mentioned in sub-paragraph (3)(a) below, or

(b) any transfer to A that gives effect to the entitlement or requirement described in sub-paragraph (3)(b) below.".

(3) In sub-paragraph (3) (meaning of "repo or stock-lending arrangements")—

(a) in paragraph (a), after "one person" insert "("A")" and after "another" insert "("B")";

(b) in paragraph (b), for "the transferor" substitute "A".

(4) In sub-paragraph (4A) (which states certain consequences of sub-paragraph (1) for each party), omit paragraph (b) (transferee not to be regarded as a party to the loan relationship) and the word "and" before it, and for the words following that paragraph substitute—

"but nothing in sub-paragraph (1) above prevents the person to whom those rights are transferred from being regarded for the purposes of this Chapter as being party to the loan relationship as a result of the transfer.".

(5) The amendments made by this paragraph have effect in any case where the transfer mentioned in paragraph 15(3)(a) of Schedule 9 to FA 1996 is on or after 2nd December 2004, whenever the repo or stock-lending arrangements in question were entered into.

(6) In any case involving an arrangement for the sale and repurchase of securities where the arrangement—

(a) falls within section 737E(1)(b) of ICTA, and

(b) involves securities ("substituted securities") being substituted for other securities,

the substitution of any securities on or after 2nd December 2004 shall be treated for the purposes of sub-paragraph (5) as if it were a transfer falling within paragraph 15(3)(a) of Schedule 9 to FA 1996.

GENERAL NOTE

This para deals with a certain type of avoidance involving repos and stock lending. Paras 6 and 10 also deal with repos and stock lending.

The issue in this case is that the previous provisions allowed the interim holder under a repo or the borrower under a stock lending arrangement to realise the value of the interest. It did so, commonly, by selling the relevant asset to a financial trader. The result from that arrangement was, arguably, that the profit was not taxable because the credit did not relate to interest.

Alternatively, the terms of the repo or stock loan could be such as to allow the interim holder or borrower to transfer the security and to argue that the transfer was in pursuance of the repo or stock loan in which case any profit on disposal was not taxable.

To prevent these arrangements and arguments, this para makes three broad changes. It provides that initial transfer and final transfer are outside the definition of related transactions. It removes the rules preventing the interim holder's, or borrower's, treatment as the interim holder, or borrower, to the underlying loan relationship during the term of the repo or stock loan. It removes the condition that the rules may only impute credits relating to interest to the interim holder or borrower. Therefore, profits, made by the interim holder or borrower, related to a loan relationship under a repo or stock loan may be subject to tax.

Capital redemption policies: computations on the I minus E basis

20— (1) In Schedule 11 to FA 1996 (loan relationships: special provision for insurers) paragraph 1 (I minus E basis) is amended as follows.

(2) After sub-paragraph (1B) insert—

"(1C) In applying the I minus E basis for any accounting period in respect of any life assurance business carried on by an insurance company, no credits or debits shall be brought into account in respect of any debtor relationship that represents a capital redemption policy, within the meaning of Chapter 2 of Part 13 of the Taxes Act 1988.".

(3) The amendment made by this paragraph has effect in relation to a debtor relationship on and after 10th February 2005 (whenever the capital redemption policy was effected).

GENERAL NOTE

The amendments made by this para are connected to those made by para 14.

It disregards the basic life assurance and general annuity business ("BLAGAB") credits and debits arising on a capital redemption policy ("CRB") that is a debtor relationship of an insurance company.

As with para 14, this para these rules come into effect on 10 February 2005.

Relevant discounted securities: corporate strips

21— (1) Schedule 13 to FA 1996 (discounted securities: income tax) is amended as follows.

(2) In paragraph 3 (meaning of "relevant discounted security") in sub-paragraph (1), for "paragraph 14(1)" substitute "paragraphs 13B(1) and 14(1)".

(3) In paragraph 4 (meaning of "transfer")—

(*a*) in sub-paragraph (1), after "Subject to sub-paragraph (2)" insert "and paragraph 13B(4)";

(*b*) in sub-paragraph (5), after "without prejudice to paragraph" insert "13B(2) to (5) or".

(4) In paragraph 5 (redemption to include conversion), in sub-paragraph (3), after "This paragraph does not apply to" insert "—

(*a*) the conversion of an interest-bearing corporate security into corporate strips (see paragraph 13A(2) to (7) below), or

(*b*) ".

(5) After paragraph 13 (excluded indexed securities) insert—

"Meaning of corporate strip and conversion into corporate strips

13A— (1) In this Schedule "corporate strip" means any asset—

(*a*) which is, or has at any time been, one of the separate assets mentioned in sub-paragraph (2) below, and

(*b*) which is not prevented from being a corporate strip by sub-paragraph (9) below.

(2) For the purposes of this Schedule a person converts an interest-bearing corporate security into corporate strips of the security if he has an interest-bearing corporate security ("the converted corporate security") but—

(*a*) as a result of any scheme or arrangements, he comes to have two or more separate assets in place of the converted corporate security,

(*b*) each of those separate assets satisfies condition A,

(*c*) those separate assets, taken together, satisfy condition B, and

(*d*) at least one of those separate assets is not prevented from being a corporate strip by sub-paragraph (9) below, and related expressions shall be construed accordingly.

(3) Condition A is that the asset—

    (*a*) represents the right to, or

    (*b*) secures,

one or more stripped payments.

(4) For the purposes of this paragraph, a "stripped payment" is—

    (*a*) the payment of, or

    (*b*) a payment corresponding to,

the whole or a part of one or more payments (whether of interest or principal) remaining to be made under the converted corporate security.

(5) Condition B is that the assets, taken together,—

    (*a*) represent the right to, or

    (*b*) secure,

every payment (whether of interest or principal) remaining to be made under the converted corporate security (or payments corresponding to every such payment).

(6) Where a person—

    (*a*) has an interest-bearing corporate security, but

    (*b*) sells or transfers the right to one or more payments remaining to be made under it (so that, as a result, there are two or more separate assets which, taken together, satisfy condition B),

this Schedule has effect as if, as a result of a scheme or arrangements, the person had come to have the separate assets in place of the security immediately before the sale or transfer.

(7) For the purposes of this Schedule, sub-paragraphs (2) to (6) above also have effect in relation to each of the separate assets mentioned in sub-paragraph (2) above as if it were itself an interest-bearing corporate security (if that is not in fact the case).

(8) Where sub-paragraphs (2) to (6) above have effect by virtue of sub-paragraph (7) above—

    (*a*) any reference in this Schedule to converting an interest-bearing corporate security into corporate strips of the security shall be construed accordingly, and

    (*b*) sub-paragraph (1) above (meaning of "corporate strip") has effect accordingly.

(9) An asset is not a corporate strip if it—

    (*a*) represents the right to, or

    (*b*) secures,

payments of, or corresponding to, a part of every payment remaining to be made under an interest-bearing corporate security or a corporate strip.

(10) After a balance has been struck for a dividend on an interest-bearing corporate security, any payment to be made in respect of that dividend shall, at times falling after that balance has been struck, be treated for the purposes of this paragraph as not being a payment remaining to be made under the security.

References to payments the right to which a separate asset represents or secures shall be construed accordingly.

Corporate strips deemed to be relevant discounted securities

13B— (1) Every corporate strip is a relevant discounted security.

(2) Where a person converts an interest-bearing corporate security into corporate strips of the security, he shall be deemed to have paid, in respect of his acquisition of each corporate strip, an amount determined in accordance with sub-paragraph (3) below.

(3) The amount is that which bears to the acquisition cost of the converted corporate security the proportion that SMV bears to TMV, where—

    SMV is the market value of the corporate strip, and

    TMV is the total of the market values of all the separate assets resulting from the conversion.

(4) If the converted corporate security is a relevant discounted security—

    (*a*) its conversion into corporate strips is deemed to be a transfer of the security, and

    (*b*) the amount payable on the transfer is deemed to be an amount equal to the acquisition cost of the converted corporate security.

(5) Where corporate strips are consolidated into a single security—

    (*a*) by being exchanged by any person for that security, or (*b*) by being otherwise converted by any person into that security under any arrangements,

each of the corporate strips shall be deemed to have been redeemed, at the time of the exchange or other conversion, by the payment to that person of an amount equal to its market value.

(6) Sub-paragraphs (2) to (5) above have effect for the purposes of this Schedule.

(7) For the purposes of this paragraph, the acquisition cost of the converted corporate security is the amount paid in respect of his acquisition of the security by the person who has it immediately before the conversion (no account being taken of any costs incurred in connection with that acquisition).

(8) References in this paragraph to the market value of a security given or received in exchange for, or otherwise converted into, another are references to its market value at the time of the exchange or conversion.

Corporate strips: manipulation of acquisition, sale or redemption price

13C— (1) This paragraph applies in any case where, as a result of any scheme or arrangement,—

(*a*) the amount paid by a person in respect of his acquisition of a corporate strip is or was more than the market value of the corporate strip at the time of that acquisition,

(*b*) the amount payable to a person on a transfer of a corporate strip by him is less than the market value of the corporate strip at the time of the transfer, or

(*c*) on redemption of a corporate strip, the amount payable to a person, as the person holding the corporate strip, is less than the market value of the corporate strip on the day before redemption,

and the obtaining of a tax advantage by any person is the main benefit, or one of the main benefits, that might have been expected to accrue from, or from any provision of, the scheme or arrangement.

(2) In a case falling within sub-paragraph (1)(*a*) above, the person shall be treated for the purposes of paragraph 1(2)(*b*) above on a transfer of the corporate strip by him as if he had paid in respect of his acquisition of the corporate strip an amount equal to the market value of the corporate strip at the time of that acquisition.

(3) In a case falling within sub-paragraph (1)(*b*) above, the person shall be treated for the purposes of paragraph 1(2)(*b*) above as if the amount payable to him on the transfer were an amount equal to the market value of the corporate strip at the time of the transfer.

(4) In a case falling within sub-paragraph (1)(*c*) above, the person shall be treated for the purposes of paragraph 1(2)(*b*) above as if the amount payable to him on redemption were an amount equal to the market value of the corporate strip on the day before redemption.

(5) The market value of a corporate strip at any time shall be determined for the purposes of this paragraph without regard to any increase or diminution in the value of the corporate strip as a result of the scheme or arrangement mentioned in sub-paragraph (1) above.

(6) For the purposes of this paragraph, no account shall be taken of any costs incurred in connection with any transfer or redemption of a corporate strip or its acquisition.

(7) In this paragraph "tax advantage" has the meaning given by section 709(1) of the Taxes Act 1988.

Corporate strips: manipulation of price: associated payment giving rise to CGT loss

13D— (1) Where—

(*a*) as a result of any scheme or arrangement which has an unallowable purpose, the circumstances are, or might have been, as mentioned in paragraph (*a*), (*b*) or (*c*) of paragraph 13C(1) above,

(*b*) under the scheme or arrangement, a payment falls to be made otherwise than in respect of the acquisition or disposal of a corporate strip, and

(*c*) as a result of that payment or the circumstances in which it is made, a loss accrues to any person for the purposes of capital gains tax,

the loss shall not be an allowable loss for the purposes of capital gains tax.

(2) For the purposes of this paragraph, a scheme or arrangement has an unallowable purpose if the main benefit, or one of the main benefits, that might have been

expected to result from, or from any provision of, the scheme or arrangement (apart from paragraph 13C above and this paragraph) is—

(*a*) the obtaining of a tax advantage by any person, or

(*b*) the accrual to any person of an allowable loss for the purposes of capital gains tax.

(3) In this paragraph "tax advantage" has the meaning given by section 709(1) of the Taxes Act 1988.".

(6) In paragraph 15(1) (general interpretation) insert each of the following definitions at the appropriate place—

""corporate strip" has the meaning given by paragraph 13A above;";

""interest-bearing corporate security" means any interest-bearing security other than—

(*a*) a security issued by the government of a territory;

(*b*) a share in a company;";

""interest-bearing security" includes any loan stock or similar security;".

(7) In paragraph 15(1)—

(*a*) in the definition of "relevant discounted security", after "paragraphs 3" insert ", 13B(1)";

(*b*) in the definition of "strip", after ""strip"" insert ", except in the expression "corporate strip",".

(8) The amendments made by this paragraph have effect in any case where a person acquires a corporate strip on or after 2nd December 2004 otherwise than in pursuance of an agreement entered into before that date.

GENERAL NOTE

The changes that this para makes are closely related to those in paras 8 and 25.

These three paras aim to prevent the tax advantages arising from schemes relating to corporate securities. The schemes involve dealing with various rights under such securities.

Separating those rights and dealing with them separately is called stripping them. Certain of those separate rights will then be sold for less than their redemption value, the difference being a discount.

A special regime applied to strips of government bonds ("gilt strips", referred to in the legislation as relevant discounted securities ("RDS")) aimed at taxing as income the amount of the discount which properly represented interest and not capital (FA 1996 Sch 13 para 3).

Paragraphs 21 and 25 extend the rules on RDS to strips of all securities.

In particular, this para relates to bonds issued by parties other than governments, which are covered by other legislation. It does so by including those bonds in the definition of RDS, and removing a conversion of an interest-bearing corporate security, into a corporate strip, from the provisions treating the conversion of RDS as a redemption.

A corporate strip is a defined term. It arises when a person converts an interest-bearing corporate security into two or more separate assets. Each of these assets must satisfy two conditions: Condition A and Condition B as defined.

The new rules deem the sale or transfer of rights to one or more outstanding payments due under an interest-bearing security to be a conversion of the security into corporate strips and a sale of the relevant rights.

It is possible that a previously stripped interest-bearing corporate security will be stripped again. These new provisions will also extend the charge to apply it in those circumstances.

However, these new provisions do not apply if an interest-bearing security is simply re-denominated into smaller principal amounts.

When there is a corporate strip, the rules deem that the acquisition of each strip is at the appropriate proportion of the acquisition costs based on the relative market values of each strip at that time.

The conversion of an RDS into corporate strips gives rise to a deemed disposal of the RDS for the amount of the acquisition cost. Therefore, the rules will tax the surplus, accrued at the time of conversion, when the strips are later sold or redeemed.

If a number of strips are fused into one security, the rules deem each strip to have been redeemed at its then market value.

When an RDS is changed into corporate strips, the acquisition cost used to calculate the tax charge is the amount paid for the security by the owner for the time being. However, connected costs are not included.

These new provisions also extend the existing anti-avoidance rules relating to gilt strips to apply them to corporate strips. So, if a main benefit arising from a scheme or arrangement is a tax advantage, then the maximum permitted acquisition cost is the relevant market value, and the minimum disposal or redemption proceeds are also market value. In addition, in those circumstances, the rules disregard any capital loss that accrues because of the scheme or arrangement.

These new rules apply to corporate strips acquired on or after 2 December 2004 and not under an agreement made before that date.

Transactions within groups: treatment of transferee company

22— (1) In Schedule 26 to FA 2002 (derivative contracts) paragraph 28 (transactions within groups) is amended as follows.

(2) For sub-paragraph (3) (the credits and debits to be brought into account) substitute—

"(3) For the purpose of determining the credits and debits to be brought into account for the purposes of this Schedule in respect of the derivative contract—

(*a*) for the accounting period in which the transaction or, as the case may be, the first of the series of transactions takes place, the transferor company shall be treated as having entered into that transaction for a consideration equal to the notional carrying value of the contract; and

(*b*) for any accounting period in which it is a party to the contract, the transferee company shall be treated as if it had acquired the contract for a consideration equal to its notional carrying value.

For the purposes of this sub-paragraph the notional carrying value is the amount that would have been the carrying value of the derivative contract in the accounts of the transferor company if a period of account had ended immediately before the date when the company ceased to be party to the contract.".

(3) In sub-paragraph (5), after "In this paragraph" insert the following definition—

""carrying value" has the same meaning as it has for the purposes of paragraph 50A;".

(4) Where the period of account mentioned in the second sentence of the sub-paragraph (3) substituted by sub-paragraph (2) begins before 1st January 2005, "carrying value" shall be construed as if the period had begun on or after that date.

(5) The amendments made by this paragraph have effect in any case where the relevant transaction is on or after 16th March 2005.

(6) In this paragraph "the relevant transaction" means—

(*a*) the related transaction mentioned in sub-paragraph (2)(*a*) of paragraph 28 of Schedule 26 to FA 2002,

(*b*) the first of the series of transactions mentioned in sub-paragraph (2)(*b*) of that paragraph, or

(*c*) the transfer mentioned in sub-paragraph (2)(*c*) or (2)(*d*) of that paragraph,

by virtue of which that paragraph applies or would apply apart from paragraph 30 of that Schedule.

GENERAL NOTE

This para and paras 16, 17, 18, 23 and 24, amend the company grouping rules and introduce a charge applicable to degrouping. The aim is to charge any gain on loan relationships and derivative contracts before a company leaves a group.

This para, together with para 17, provides for the continuity of treatment of the transferee company in respect of loan relationships and derivative contracts. In particular, this para deals with derivative contracts.

This para provides that the same value is used for taxing both the transferee and the transferor in relation to an intragroup transfer in the relevant circumstances. The value to be used is the notional carrying value. Previously the valuation put the transferee in the same position as the transferor, which was misleading.

Transactions within groups: fair value accounting

23— (1) In Schedule 26 to FA 2002 (derivative contracts) paragraph 30 (transactions within groups: fair value accounting) is amended as follows.

(2) In sub-paragraph (1), for paragraph (*b*) (treatment of transferee in respect of the transaction) substitute—

"(*b*) paragraph 28(3)(*b*) shall have effect in relation to the transferee company.".

(3) The amendment made by this paragraph has effect in any case where the relevant transaction is on or after 16th March 2005.

(4) In this paragraph "the relevant transaction" has the same meaning as in paragraph 22.

GENERAL NOTE

This para and paras 16, 17, 18, 22 and 24, amend the company grouping rules and introduce a charge applicable to degrouping. The aim is to charge any gain on loan relationships and derivative contracts before a company leaves a group.

In particular, this para makes consequential amendments following the changes in para 22.

Transferee leaving group after replacing transferor as party to derivative contract

24— (1) In Schedule 26 to FA 2002 (derivative contracts) after paragraph 30 insert—

"Transferee leaving group after replacing transferor as party to derivative contract

30A— (1) This paragraph applies in any case where—

(*a*) paragraph 28 applies—

(i) by virtue of sub-paragraph (2)(*a*) of that paragraph ("case A"), or

(ii) by virtue of sub-paragraph (2)(*b*) of that paragraph ("case B"), but

(*b*) before the end of the relevant 6 year period, the transferee company ceases to be a member of the relevant group.

(2) In any such case, this Schedule shall have effect as if the transferee company had—

(*a*) immediately before that cessation, assigned its rights and liabilities under the relevant derivative contract for a consideration of an amount equal to their fair value at that time, and

(*b*) immediately reacquired them for a consideration of the same amount,

but only if Condition 1 or 2 is satisfied and sub-paragraph (5) does not apply.

(3) Condition 1 is that if sub-paragraph (2) has effect, a credit would in consequence of paragraph (*a*) of that sub-paragraph fall to be brought into account for the purposes of this Schedule by the transferee company.

(4) Condition 2 is that—

(*a*) Condition 1 is not satisfied,

(*b*) the company has a hedging relationship between the relevant derivative contract and a creditor relationship, and

(*c*) in consequence of paragraph 12A(2)(*a*) of Schedule 9 to the Finance Act 1996, a credit falls to be brought into account by the transferee company for the purposes of Chapter 2 of Part 4 of the Finance Act 1996 in respect of the creditor relationship.

(5) Where the transferee company ceases to be a member of the relevant group by reason only of an exempt distribution (see subsection (8))—

(*a*) sub-paragraph (2) does not have effect, but

(*b*) if there is chargeable payment within 5 years after the making of the exempt distribution, sub-paragraph (6) applies.

(6) Where this sub-paragraph applies, this Chapter shall have effect as if—

(*a*) the transferee company had, immediately before the making of the chargeable payment, assigned its rights and liabilities under the relevant derivative contract,

(*b*) the assignment had been for a consideration of an amount equal to the fair value of those rights and liabilities immediately before the transferee company ceased to be a member of the relevant group, and

(*c*) the transferee company had immediately reacquired those rights and liabilities for a consideration of the same amount,

but only if Condition 1 or 2, as modified by sub-paragraph (7), is satisfied.

(7) The modifications are that—

(*a*) in Condition 1, the references to sub-paragraph (2), and paragraph (*a*) of that sub-paragraph, are to be taken respectively as references to sub-paragraph (6) and paragraphs (*a*) and (*b*) of that sub-paragraph, and

(*b*) in Condition 2, the reference to paragraph 12A(2)(*a*) of Schedule 9 to the Finance Act 1996 is to be taken as a reference to paragraph 12A(6)(*a*) and (*b*) of that Schedule.

(8) In this paragraph—

"assignment", in relation to Scotland, means an assignation;

"chargeable payment" has the meaning given by section 214(2) of the Taxes Act 1988;

"exempt distribution" means a distribution which is exempt by virtue of section 213(2) of the Taxes Act 1988;

"creditor relationship" has the same meaning as Chapter 2 of Part 4 of the Finance Act 1996 (see section 103(1) of that Act);

"the relevant 6 year period" means the period of 6 years following—

(*a*) in case A, the transaction mentioned in paragraph 28(2)(*a*), or

(*b*) in case B, the last of the series of transactions mentioned in paragraph 28(2)(*b*);

"the relevant derivative contract" means the derivative contract mentioned in paragraph 28(1);

"the relevant group" means—

(*a*) in case A, the group mentioned in paragraph 28(2)(*a*), or

(*b*) in case B, the group mentioned in paragraph 28(2)(*b*);

"the transferee company" means the company referred to as such in paragraph 28(1).".

(2) The amendment made by this paragraph has effect where a company ceases to be a member of a group on or after 16th March 2005.

GENERAL NOTE

This para and paras 16, 17, 18, 22 and 23, amend the company grouping rules and introduce a charge applicable to degrouping. The aim is to charge any gain on loan relationships and derivative contracts before a company leaves a group.

This para and paras 15 and 18, introduce a charge applicable to degrouping. In particular, this para deals with derivative contracts.

A new charge applies if there has been a transaction between members of a group of companies and, within six years, the transferee leaves the group.

In these circumstances, the transferee is deemed to have assigned the asset or liability for its fair value immediately before leaving the group and to have reacquired it immediately thereafter at the same value.

However, the provision does not apply if it would have either of the following two effects, identified as conditions. Firstly, if the provisions would lead to the transferee company bringing a credit into account. Secondly, if the loan relationship is a creditor relationship the new rule would mean that the transferee company accounted for a debit, and a credit would be brought into account in respect of a hedging derivative.

An alternative charge applies if the company leaves a group and there is an exempt distribution at the same time. In that case, the degrouping charge does not apply if a party makes a chargeable payment within five years of the departure. Instead, a charge arises immediately before the party makes the chargeable payment.

Deeply discounted securities: corporate strips

25— (1) Chapter 8 of Part 4 of ITTOIA 2005 (profits from deeply discounted securities) is amended as follows.

(2) In section 430 (meaning of "deeply discounted security") in subsection (6) (subjections) omit "and" before the entry relating to section 443(1) and at the end of that entry add ", and

section 452A(1) (corporate strips).".

(3) In section 437 (transactions which are disposals) after subsection (4) insert—

"(5) In the case of interest-bearing corporate securities, further provision about occasions counting as disposals is made by section 452F(2)(*a*).

(6) In the case of corporate strips, further provision about occasions counting as disposals is made by section 452F(2)(*a*) and (3)(*a*).".

(4) In section 438 (timing of transfers and acquisitions) for subsection (4) substitute—

"(4) This section is subject to—

section 445(7) (exchanges for and consolidations of strips);
section 452F(4) (conversion into and consolidations of corporate strips).".

(5) In section 440 (market value disposals) for subsection (5) substitute—

"(5) Subsection (4) is subject to—

section 445(8) (exchanges for and consolidations of strips);
section 452F(5) (conversion into and consolidations of corporate strips).".

(6) In section 441 (market value acquisitions) for subsection (3) substitute—

"(3) Subsection (2) is subject to—

section 445(8) (exchanges for and consolidations of strips);
section 452F(5) (conversion into and consolidations of corporate strips).".

(7) Section 444 (meaning of "strip" in Chapter 8) after subsection (5) insert—

"(6) Nothing in this section affects the meaning of the expression "corporate strip" in this Chapter (see section 452E).".

(8) After section 452 insert—

"Special rules for corporate strips

452A Application of this Chapter to corporate strips

(1) All corporate strips are treated as deeply discounted securities for the purposes of this Chapter, whether or not they would otherwise be so.

(2) This Chapter applies to corporate strips subject to the rules in—

(*a*) section 452F (corporate strips: acquisitions and disposals), and
(*b*) section 452G (corporate strips: manipulation of acquisition, transfer or redemption payments).

452B Meaning of "interest-bearing corporate security" in Chapter 8

(1) In this Chapter "interest-bearing corporate security" means any interest-bearing security other than—

(*a*) a security issued by the government of a territory, or
(*b*) a share in a company.

(2) In this section "interest-bearing security" includes any loan stock or similar security.

(3) Section 452D(4)(*a*) gives an extended meaning to references to converting an interest-bearing corporate security into corporate strips (and related expressions).

452C Conversion of interest-bearing corporate securities into corporate strips

(1) For the purposes of this Chapter a person converts an interest-bearing corporate security into corporate strips of the security if he has an interest-bearing corporate security ("the converted corporate security") but—

(*a*) as a result of any scheme or arrangements, he acquires two or more separate assets in place of the converted corporate security,
(*b*) each of those separate assets satisfies condition A,
(*c*) those separate assets, taken together, satisfy condition B, and
(*d*) at least one of those separate assets is not prevented from being a corporate strip by section 452E(2) or (3),

and related expressions shall be construed accordingly.

(2) Condition A is that the asset—

(*a*) represents the right to, or
(*b*) secures,

one or more stripped payments.

(3) For the purposes of this section, a "stripped payment" is—

(*a*) the payment of, or
(*b*) a payment corresponding to,

the whole or a part of one or more payments (whether of interest or principal) remaining to be made under the converted corporate security.

(4) Condition B is that the assets, taken together,—

(*a*) represent the right to, or

(*b*) secure,

every payment (whether of interest or principal) remaining to be made under the converted corporate security (or payments corresponding to every such payment).

(5) Where a person—

(*a*) has an interest-bearing corporate security, but

(*b*) sells or transfers the right to one or more payments remaining to be made under it (so that, as a result, there are two or more separate assets which, taken together, satisfy condition B),

this Chapter has effect as if, as a result of a scheme or arrangements, the person had acquired the separate assets in place of the security immediately before the sale or transfer.

(6) After a balance has been struck for a dividend on an interest-bearing corporate security, any payment to be made in respect of that dividend shall, at times falling after that balance has been struck, be treated for the purposes of this paragraph as not being a payment remaining to be made under the security.

452D Conversion into corporate strips: lower level conversions

(1) For the purposes of this Chapter, section 452C also has effect in relation to each of the separate assets mentioned in subsection (1) of that section as if that separate asset were itself an interest-bearing corporate security (if that is not in fact the case).

(2) In subsection (1), the reference to section 452C includes a reference to that section as it has effect by virtue of this section.

(3) In the application of section 452C by virtue of this section, references to payments the right to which a separate asset represents or secures shall be construed in accordance with subsection (6) of that section.

(4) Where section 452C has effect by virtue of subsection (1)—

(*a*) any reference in this Chapter to converting an interest-bearing corporate security into corporate strips of the security shall be construed accordingly, and

(*b*) section 452E (meaning of "corporate strip") has effect accordingly.

452E Meaning of "corporate strip" in Chapter 8

(1) In this Chapter "corporate strip" means any asset—

(*a*) which is, or has at any time been, one of the separate assets mentioned in section 452C(1), and

(*b*) which is not prevented from being a corporate strip by subsection (2) or (3).

(2) An asset is not a corporate strip if it—

(*a*) represents the right to, or

(*b*) secures,

payments of, or corresponding to, a part of every payment remaining to be made under an interest-bearing corporate security or a corporate strip.

(3) An asset is a corporate strip in the case of any person only if he acquired it—

(*a*) on or after 2nd December 2004, and

(*b*) otherwise than in pursuance of an agreement entered into before that date.

452F Corporate strips: acquisitions and disposals

(1) A person who converts an interest-bearing corporate security into corporate strips of the security is treated as having acquired each corporate strip by the payment of an amount equal to—

$$A \times \frac{B}{C}$$

where—

A is acquisition cost of the converted corporate security;

B is the market value of the corporate strip;

C is the total of the market values of all the separate assets resulting from the conversion.

(2) If the converted corporate security is a deeply discounted security—

(*a*) its conversion into corporate strips is to be treated for the purposes of this Chapter as a transfer of the security, but

(*b*) the amount payable on the transfer is taken to be an amount equal to the acquisition cost of the converted corporate security.

(3) For the purposes of this Chapter—

(*a*) the consolidation of a corporate strip with other corporate strips into a single security is a disposal of the corporate strip by the person consolidating it (whether or not it would be apart from this subsection), and

(*b*) an amount equal to the market value of the corporate strip at the consolidation is treated as payable on the disposal.

(4) Section 438 (timing of transfers and acquisitions) does not apply to a conversion within subsection (1) or a consolidation within subsection (3).

(5) Subsections (1) to (3) apply instead of sections 440(4) (market value on general conversions of deeply discounted securities) and 441 (market value acquisitions).

(6) For the purposes of this section, the acquisition cost of the converted corporate security is the amount paid in respect of his acquisition of the security by the person who has it immediately before the conversion (no account being taken of any costs incurred in connection with that acquisition).

(7) References in this section to the market value of a security given or received in exchange for, or otherwise converted into, another are references to its market value at the time of the exchange or conversion.

452G Corporate strips: manipulation of acquisition, transfer or redemption payments

(1) This section applies if—

(*a*) as a result of any scheme or arrangement, an amount referred to in subsection (2)(*a*), (*b*) or (*c*) differs from the market value of the corporate strip in a way specified in that subsection, and

(*b*) the obtaining of a tax advantage by any person is the main benefit, or one of the main benefits, that might have been expected to accrue from, or from any provision of, the scheme or arrangement.

(2) The ways are that—

(*a*) the amount paid by a person in respect of the acquisition of the corporate strip is or was more than the market value of the corporate strip at the time of that acquisition,

(*b*) the amount payable to a person on transferring the corporate strip is less than the market value at the time of the transfer, or

(*c*) on redemption of the corporate strip the amount payable to a person, as the person holding the corporate strip, is less than the market value on the day before redemption.

(3) In a case within subsection (2)(*a*), for the purposes of section 439(1) on transferring the corporate strip the person is treated as if the person had paid to acquire the corporate strip an amount equal to the market value of the corporate strip at the time of the acquisition.

(4) In a case falling within subsection (2)(*b*), for those purposes the person is treated as if the amount payable to the person on the transfer were an amount equal to the market value of the corporate strip at the time of the transfer.

(5) In a case falling within subsection (2)(*c*), for those purposes the person is treated as if the amount payable to the person on redemption were an amount equal to the market value of the corporate strip on the day before redemption.

(6) The market value of a corporate strip at any time is to be determined for the purposes of this section without regard to any increase or diminution in the value of the corporate strip as a result of the scheme or arrangement mentioned in subsection (1).

(7) For the purposes of this section, no account is to be taken of any incidental expenses incurred in connection with any disposal or acquisition of a corporate strip.".

(9) In Schedule 4 (abbreviations and defined expressions) in Part 2 (expressions defined in the Act or in ICTA) insert each of the following entries at the appropriate place—

"conversion of an interest-bearing corporate security into corporate strips of the security (for the purposes of Chapter 8 of Part 4)	sections 452C and 452D";
"corporate strip (for the purposes of Chapter 8 of Part 4)	section 452E";
"interest-bearing corporate security (for the purposes of Chapter 8 of Part 4)	section 452B".

(10) ITTOIA 2005 shall have effect as if it had been originally enacted with the amendments made by this paragraph.

GENERAL NOTE

The changes that this para makes are closely related to those in paras 8 and 21. Paragraphs 21 and 25 extend the rules on the relevant discounted securities ("RDS") to strips of all securities.

In particular, this para transposes amendments made by para 21 into ITTOIA 2005 so that they apply for income tax purposes from 6 April 2005.

SCHEDULE 8

FINANCING OF COMPANIES ETC: TRANSFER PRICING AND LOAN RELATIONSHIPS

Section 40

INTRODUCTION

Schedule 8 expands the application of transfer pricing rules, to catch (broadly speaking) certain financing provided by persons who act together but do not, individually, control the borrower, which would not previously have been caught by the transfer pricing rules. It is considered to be targeted largely (but not exclusively) at preventing private equity funds from thinly capitalising their acquisitions in order to 'level the playing field' with publicly held companies. It also limits the scope of the statutory override to the 'late interest rule' in the loan relationships regime that was beneficial to debtor companies controlled by private equity funds by enabling them to obtain a deduction on an accruals (rather than a paid) basis for rolled-up interest and accruing discount.

The pre-Finance Act 2005 transfer pricing rules only applied (broadly speaking) to transactions between persons where one person controls the other or both are under common control of another person. For transactions that are 'financing arrangements', control will now additionally be determined by amalgamating the rights and powers of any persons that have "acted together in relation to the financing arrangements".

Each of the persons that have acted together is therefore effectively tainted by the fact that the persons collectively meet the control tests, even if those persons are otherwise unrelated to one another. Loans from third parties that would not previously have been subject to transfer pricing rules are now drawn in.

The consequences for loans that are caught are potentially severe. Interest deductions will be denied to the borrower to the extent that the interest is in excess of the interest that would have arisen on an arm's length basis, ie, were it not for the control relationship. This is the case whether the interest is excessive as a result of the interest rate being too high or the quantum of the loan being more than an arm's length lender would have advanced (known as being "thinly capitalised").

It should be remembered that the transfer pricing rules now apply not only to cross-border transactions but also domestic ones, so the potential impact is quite widespread. In answer to Parliamentary questions, Dawn Primarolo has revealed that "the changes prevent tax avoidance that could otherwise have reduced current and future tax revenues of about £300 million a year".

The new rules may apply to virtually any minority interest that involves "acting together" (like a partnership or joint venture). However, it will in particular ensure that companies controlled by private equity funds are subject to transfer pricing and thin capitalisation principles in relation to their funding from the private equity funds. There is currently a dispute between HMRC and the industry about whether a private equity fund (being one or more limited partnerships) is a "person" for the purposes of deciding if the transfer pricing rules apply. The industry argues that a limited partnership is not a person, so it is necessary to "look through" to the underlying investors, each of whom usually has only a small effective interest in the businesses acquired by the private equity fund, below the normal transfer pricing control thresholds. If this is right, these new rules will clarify that the transfer pricing rules apply in such situations.

With a similar purpose to the extension of the transfer pricing rules, the changes to the loan relationship rules will ensure that companies controlled by private equity funds only obtain a deduction for rolled-up interest and/or accruing discount on a paid basis.

Amendments of Schedule 28AA to ICTA

1— (1) Schedule 28AA to ICTA (provision not at arm's length) is amended as follows.

(2) In paragraph 4 (participation in the management, control or capital of a person), in sub-paragraph (2) (meaning of indirect participation) for "and only if" substitute "and (subject to paragraphs 4A and 6(4C) below) only if".

(3) After that paragraph insert—

"Persons acting together in relation to financing arrangements

4A— (1) A person ("P") shall be treated for the purposes of paragraph 1(1)(*b*)(i) above (but subject to sub-paragraph (7) below) as indirectly participating in the management, control or capital of another ("A") at the time of the making or imposition of the actual provision if—

(*a*) the actual provision relates, to any extent, to financing arrangements for A;

(*b*) A is a body corporate or partnership;

(*c*) P and other persons acted together in relation to the financing arrangements; and

(*d*) P would be taken to have control of A if, at any relevant time, there were attributed to P the rights and powers of each of the other persons mentioned in paragraph (*c*) above.

(2) A person ("Q") shall be treated for the purposes of paragraph 1(1)(*b*)(ii) above (but subject to sub-paragraph (7) below) as indirectly participating in the management, control or capital of each of the affected persons at the time of the making or imposition of the actual provision if—

(*a*) the actual provision relates, to any extent, to financing arrangements for one of the affected persons ("B");

(*b*) B is a body corporate or partnership;

(*c*) Q and other persons acted together in relation to the financing arrangements; and

(*d*) Q would be taken to have control of both B and the other affected person if, at any relevant time, there were attributed to Q the rights and powers of each of the other persons mentioned in paragraph (*c*) above.

(3) It is immaterial for the purposes of sub-paragraph (1)(*c*) or (2)(*c*) above whether P or Q and the other persons acting together in relation to the financing arrangements did so at the time of the making or imposition of the actual provision or at some earlier time.

(4) In sub-paragraph (1)(*d*) or (2)(*d*) "relevant time" means—

(*a*) a time when P or Q and the other persons were acting together in relation to the financing arrangements; or

(*b*) a time in the period of six months beginning with the day on which they ceased so to act.

(5) In determining for the purposes of sub-paragraph (1)(*d*) or (2)(*d*) whether P or Q would be taken to have control of another person, the rights and powers of any person (and not just P or Q) shall be taken to include those that would be attributed to that person in determining under paragraph 4 above whether he is indirectly participating in the management, control or capital of the other person.

(6) In this paragraph "financing arrangements" means arrangements made for providing or guaranteeing, or otherwise in connection with, any debt, capital or other form of finance.

(7) Where the condition in paragraph 1(1)(*b*) above would not be satisfied but for this paragraph, paragraph 1(2) above applies only to the extent that the actual provision relates to the financing arrangements in question.".

(4) After the paragraph inserted by sub-paragraph (3) above insert—

"Financing arrangements: anticipatory provision

4B— (1) To the extent that it applies to provision relating to financing arrangements, this Schedule has effect as if in paragraph 1(1)(*b*) above the words "or within the period of six months beginning with the day on which the actual provision was made or imposed" were inserted immediately before sub-paragraph (i).

(2) In this paragraph "financing arrangements" has the same meaning as in paragraph 4A above.".

(5) In paragraph 6 (elimination of double counting), after sub-paragraph (4) insert—

"(4A) A claim by the disadvantaged person for the purposes of this paragraph shall not be made where—

(*a*) the condition in paragraph 1(1)(*b*) above would not be satisfied but for paragraph 4A above;

(*b*) the actual provision is provision in relation to a security issued by one of the affected persons ("the issuer");

(*c*) a guarantee is provided in relation to the security by a person with whom the issuer has a participatory relationship.

In this sub-paragraph "security" and "guarantee" have the same meaning as in paragraph 1A above.

(4B) For the purposes of sub-paragraph (4A) above, the cases where one person has a "participatory relationship" with another are those where—

(*a*) one of them is directly or indirectly participating in the management, control or capital of the other; or

(*b*) the same person or persons is or are directly or indirectly participating in the management, control or capital of each of them.

(4C) Paragraph 4A above applies for the purposes of sub-paragraph (4B) above as it applies for the purposes of paragraph 1(1)(*b*) above.".

GENERAL NOTE

The broad effect of the amendment in para 1 is to apply transfer pricing rules (Sch 28AA) where parties who collectively could control a business have acted together in relation to the financing arrangements of the business, and to financing arrangements made before a control relationship exists.

Sub-para (2)

This provides, necessary rewording to allow new paragraph 4A, to have effect.

Sub-para (3)

This provides a new para 4A(1) to TA 1988 Sch 28AA, which contains the basic new additional definition of "indirect participation". This is the means by which Sch 28AA determines whether two parties are sufficiently connected for the transfer pricing rules to apply to "provision" made between them. "Participation" is a concept similar to control (usually via shareholdings).

It means that the transfer pricing rules will apply to the terms of any financing arrangements made, or guaranteed, by P for A, if P "acted together" with other persons in relation to the financing arrangements and, at any "relevant time", P plus those other persons could have controlled A.

Actual control is not necessary; the capacity to control is sufficient. But actual "acting together" is required.

P need not have any control of A itself; it can be tainted by others with whom it acts together, if they have the capacity to control.

"Relevant time" is defined in new para 4A(4). It means that the capacity to control is measured at any time when P and the other persons were acting together in relation to the financing arrangements, or for six months after they ceased to act together.

"Financing arrangements" are defined in new para 4A(6). Most commonly, this will mean loans by P to A.

The new wider definition will not apply to transactions that are not financing arrangements (eg, sale of goods, supply of services, royalties will not normally be caught, unless they relate "to any extent" to financing arrangements). Nor will it apply unless A (the person for whom the financing arrangements are made – usually, the borrower) is a body corporate or partnership.

"Provision" is used in Sch 28AA in a way that is difficult to pin down, but it appears to mean that which is brought about by a transaction, or series of transactions (where a transaction includes arrangements, understandings and mutual practices).

New para 4A to TA 1988 Sch 28AA

New paragraph 4A(1) applies to parent-subsidiary relationships. This sub-para has the same effect for sister-sister relationships.

New paragraph 4A(3) makes clear that persons do not have to be "acting together" at the time a provision is made for the tests in new paragraphs 4A(1) or 4A(2) to be satisfied, if they have acted together in relation to the financing arrangements of the business at an earlier time. For instance, if P is not acting together with the "other persons" when it makes a loan to A, the transfer pricing rules will still apply if it did act together with them at some preliminary stage of the financial arrangements of which the loan was a part.

The definition in new para 4A(4) ensures that the tests in new paragraphs 4A(1) or 4A(2) can be satisfied where there is a gap of up to six months between parties ceasing to act together and being in a position where collectively they could control the business (or, where relevant, the other affected person).

Paragraph 4 of Sch 28AA deems a person to have certain rights and powers, for instance, those that it is entitled to acquire in the future or that are exercised on the person's behalf or that are held by certain persons that are connected to the person. The same attribution rules must be used in determining, for P and the "other persons", their collective capacity to control (new para 4A(5)).

The definition in new para 4A(6) is deliberately widely worded. It will include loans, equity, guarantees and other financial instruments.

Sch 28AA adjusts the taxable profits of P and A to what they would have been, had the provision between them been the provision that "would have been made as between independent enterprises", that is, the "arm's length provision". In cases where the participation (control) test is only met by virtue of this new extension to the definition of "indirect participation", the profit adjustment will only apply to the financing arrangements in question, not to transactions unrelated to the financing arrangements.

Sub-para (4)

Generally, the participation (control) tests in Sch 28AA are applied "at the time of the making or imposition" of the provision. This is extended to the previous six months, in the case of the provision of financing arrangements.

This applies not just to financing arrangements newly subject to the transfer pricing rules under this "acting together" extension. It also applies where there is direct control, such as a loan from a parent to its 100%-owned subsidiary.

This six-month look-back for any financing arrangements does not benefit from the two-year grandfathering that is allowed for the new "acting together" test. (See commencement and transitional provisions, Sch 8 para 4, below.)

Sub-para (5)

Broadly speaking, paragraph 6 of Sch 28AA allows for "compensating adjustments" to be claimed in cases where one person has suffered a transfer pricing adjustment that increases its UK taxable profits and the other party to the "provision" that gave rise to the adjustment is a UK taxpayer. The compensating adjustment reduces the UK taxable profits of that other party by a corresponding amount. New sub-para (4A) denies a compensating adjustment in cases where the transfer pricing adjustment would not have been required were it not for the new "acting together" test, above, and the "provision" relates to a security that is guaranteed by a person who has a "participatory relationship" (defined in new sub-para (4B), below) with the issuer of the security. This appears to be intended to prevent "windfall" compensating adjustments for lenders who do not, in any normal sense, control the borrower (but are deemed to control under these "acting together" rules).

New sub-para (4B) provides the same control test as determines whether the transfer pricing rules apply to a provision.

The new "acting together" test will apply in determining whether there is a participatory relationship between guarantor and issuer.

Amendments of Schedule 9 to FA 1996

2— (1) In Schedule 9 to FA 1996 (loan relationships: computational provisions), paragraph 2 (late interest) is amended as follows.

(2) In sub-paragraph (1B)—

(a) omit ", but not a CIS-based close company," and the words after paragraph (c);

(b) in paragraph (a), at the end insert "or a person who controls a company which is such a participator";

(c) in paragraph (b), after "who is" insert ", or who controls a company which is,";

(d) for paragraph (c) substitute—

"(c) a company controlled by such a participator or by a person who controls a company which is such a participator, or

(*d*) a company in which such a participator has a major interest.";
(*e*) at the end insert—
"This is subject to sub-paragraph (1E).".

(3) After sub-paragraph (1D) insert—

"(1E) A case does not fall within sub-paragraph (1B) above if either of the following exceptions applies.

(1F) The first exception applies where—

(*a*) the debtor company is a CIS-based close company at all such times as are mentioned in sub-paragraph (1B) above;

(*b*) the person standing in the position of a creditor as respects the loan relationship is not resident in a non-qualifying territory at any such time; and

(*c*) the debtor company is a small or medium-sized enterprise for the relevant accounting period.

(1G) The second exception applies where—

(*a*) the debt is one that is owed to, or to persons acting for, a CIS limited partnership;

(*b*) no member of that partnership is resident in a non-qualifying territory at any time in the relevant accounting period;

(*c*) the debtor company has received written notice from the partnership containing information from which it appears that the condition in paragraph (*b*) above is satisfied; and

(*d*) the debtor company is a small or medium-sized enterprise for the relevant accounting period.".

(4) In sub-paragraph (6), at the appropriate places insert—

""non-qualifying territory" has the meaning given by paragraph 5E of Schedule 28AA to the Taxes Act 1988;";

""resident" has the meaning given by paragraph 5B(6) of Schedule 28AA to the Taxes Act 1988;";

""small or medium-sized enterprise" has the meaning given by paragraph 5D of that Schedule.".

GENERAL NOTE

Where parties to a loan relationship are connected (within the meaning of FA 1996, s 87) and the accounts of the company paying the interest are drawn up on an amortised cost basis of accounting, FA 1996 Sch 9 para 2 provides that a debit for interest paid more than 12 months in arrears is not given in the period in which it accrues but is deferred to the period in which it is paid. This rule is subject to certain statutory overrides, one of which is where amounts are payable to certain types of collective investment vehicles. The changes made to the "late interest" rules, by the addition of sub-paras (1E), (1F) and (1G), restrict the override in para 2 (1B) so that it will only apply where the debtor company is a "small or medium-sized enterprise" and the lender is not "resident" in a "non-qualifying territory" such as a tax haven.

Paragraphs 2(2)(b)–(d) amend para 2(1B) to add to the list of creditors who are connected with the debtor company the following:

– a person who controls a company participator (para 2(2)(b));
– an associate of a person who controls a company participator (para 2(2)(c)); and
– a company controlled by a person who controls a company participator (para 2(2)(d)).

3— (1) Paragraph 18 of that Schedule (discounted securities of close companies) is amended as follows.

(2) In sub-paragraph (1), omit paragraphs (aa) and (*c*).

(3) In sub-paragraph (1)(*b*)—

(*a*) in sub-paragraph (i), at the end insert "or a person who controls a company which is such a participator";

(*b*) in sub-paragraph (ii), after "an associate of" insert "a person who is, or who controls a company which is,";

(*c*) for sub-paragraph (iii) substitute—

"(iii) a company controlled by such a participator or by a person who controls a company which is such a participator.".

(4) After sub-paragraph (1) insert—

"(1ZA) But for any such accounting period this paragraph shall not apply in relation to that debtor relationship if any of the following exceptions applies.".

(5) In sub-paragraph (1A), for the words before paragraph (*a*) substitute "The first exception applies where—".

(6) After that sub-paragraph insert—

"(1B) The second exception applies where—

(*a*) the issuing company is a CIS-based close company;

(*b*) at all times in the period when there is such a person as is described in sub-paragraph (1)(*b*) above, that person is not resident in a non-qualifying territory; and

(*c*) the issuing company is a small or medium-sized enterprise for the period.

(1C) The third exception applies where—

(*a*) the debt is one that is owed to, or to persons acting for, a CIS limited partnership;

(*b*) no member of that partnership is resident in a non-qualifying territory at any time in the period when there is such a person as is described in sub-paragraph (1)(*b*) above;

(*c*) the debtor company has received written notice from the partnership containing information from which it appears that the condition in paragraph (*b*) above is satisfied; and

(*d*) the issuing company is a small or medium-sized enterprise for the period.".

(7) In sub-paragraph (4), at the appropriate places insert—

""CIS-based close company" and "CIS limited partnership" have the meaning given by paragraph 2(6) above;";

""non-qualifying territory" has the meaning given by paragraph 5E of Schedule 28AA to the Taxes Act 1988;";

""resident" has the meaning given by paragraph 5B(6) of Schedule 28AA to that Act;";

""small or medium-sized enterprise" has the meaning given by paragraph 5D of that Schedule.".

GENERAL NOTE

These changes replicate the changes in para 2(2)(b)–(d) in respect of discount securities.

Amendments similar to those made to Sch 9 para 2 are made to the discounted securities rules in Sch 9 para 18 which limit the deduction of debits for accruing discount unless the exceptions in para 18(1A), new paragraph 18(1B) or new paragraph 18(1C) apply. The new paragraphs 18(1B) and 18(1C) are broadly the same as sub-paras (1F) and (1G) of para 2.

Commencement and transitional provisions

4— (1) Except where sub-paragraph (2) or (3) applies, the amendments made by this Schedule have effect in relation to accounting periods beginning on or after 4th March 2005.

(2) As regards any actual provision that constitutes, or gives rise to, a debtor relationship entered into in pursuance of a contract—

(*a*) made before 4th March 2005, and

(*b*) not varied after that date, or not varied until after that date,

the amendments made by paragraph 1(2), (3) and (5) apply only in relation to accounting periods beginning on or after 1st April 2007 or, in a case where the contract is varied before 1st April 2007, in relation to accounting periods beginning on or after the date of the variation.

(3) As regards a debtor relationship entered into in pursuance of a contract—

(*a*) made before 4th March 2005, and

(*b*) not varied after that date, or not varied until after that date,

the amendments made by paragraph 2(2)(*a*) and (*e*), (3) and (4) and paragraph 3(2) and (4) to (7) apply only in relation to accounting periods beginning on or after 1st April 2007 or, in a case where the contract is varied before 1st April 2007, in relation to accounting periods beginning on or after the date of the variation.

(4) In the case of a company's accounting period ("the straddling period") that begins before and ends on or after a relevant date, for the purposes of sub-paragraph (1) or (where it applies) sub-paragraph (2) or (3) the amendments made by this Schedule have effect as if the straddling period consisted of—

(*a*) one accounting period beginning with the straddling period and ending with the day before the relevant date, and

(*b*) a second accounting period beginning with the relevant date and ending with the straddling period,

and the company's profits and losses are to be computed accordingly for tax purposes.

(5) A reference in sub-paragraph (2) or (3) to a variation of a contract does not include a reference to a variation that does not affect the terms of the debtor relationship in question.

(6) Sub-paragraph (3) is not to be read as allowing or requiring a debit to be brought into account under Chapter 2 of Part 4 of FA 1996 for an accounting period beginning on or after 1st April 2007, or the date of the variation, in respect of any amount of interest or discount in respect of which a debit is so brought into account for any earlier accounting period.

(7) In the application of this paragraph to a person within the charge to income tax—

(*a*) a reference to an accounting period is to be read as a reference to a period of account;

(*b*) a reference in sub-paragraph (4) to a company is to be read as a reference to such a person.

(8) In this paragraph—

"actual provision" has the same meaning as in Schedule 28AA to ICTA;

"debtor relationship"—

(*a*) in relation to a company, has the meaning given by section 103(1) of FA 1996;

(*b*) in relation to a person other than a company, has a corresponding meaning;

"relevant date" means—

(*a*) 4th March 2005 for the purposes of sub-paragraph (1);

(*b*) 1st April 2007, or (as the case may be) the date of the variation, for the purposes of sub-paragraph (2) or (3).

GENERAL NOTE

The basic rule is that the new "acting together" test and the accompanying loan relationships changes apply from 4 March 2005, which is when they were first announced in a press release.

Subparagraph (2) is a two-year grandfathering clause, to delay the application of the new rules provided under a contract entered into before 4 March 2005 that is not varied after that date until 1 April 2007.

Subparagraph (3) replicates the grandfathering for the loan relationships changes.

Subparagraph (4) provides that accounting periods that straddle 4 March 2005 or 1 April 2007 must be split for the purposes of commencing application of these new rules and cessation of the grandfathering, respectively. "Relevant date" is defined in sub-para (8), below.

Subparagraph (5) provides that a change to the terms of a contract which does not change the terms of a debtor relationship is not a variation for the purposes of the grandfathering provisions.

Subparagraph (6) prevents a debtor company from claiming a deduction on or after 1 April 2007 under the new rules if a deduction has already been claimed for the same interest/discount which would have been disallowed but for the grandfathering provisions.

SCHEDULE 9

INSURANCE COMPANIES ETC

Section 42

Expenses of insurance companies

1— (1) Section 76 of ICTA is amended as follows.

(2) In subsection (8) (expenses attributable to basic life assurance and general annuity business for the purposes of Step 1 are to be those so attributable under proper internal accounting practice) in the second sentence (meaning of "proper internal accounting practice") at the end of paragraph (*b*) insert ", or

(*c*) the Integrated Prudential Sourcebook.".

(3) The amendment made by this paragraph has effect in relation to periods of account ending on or after 31st December 2004.

Interpretative provisions relating to insurance companies

2— (1) Section 431(2) of ICTA is amended as follows.

(2) Insert the following definition at the appropriate place—

""the Integrated Prudential Sourcebook" means the Integrated Prudential Sourcebook made by the Financial Services Authority under the Financial Services and Markets Act 2000;".

(3) For the definition of "liabilities" substitute—

""liabilities", in relation to an insurance company, means—

(*a*) the mathematical reserves of the company as determined in accordance with chapter 7.3 of the Integrated Prudential Sourcebook, and
(*b*) liabilities of the company (whose value falls to be determined in accordance with chapter 1.3 of that Sourcebook) which arise from deposit back arrangements;

and for this purpose "deposit back arrangements" has the same meaning as in that Sourcebook;".

(4) Omit the definition of "long-term liabilities".

(5) For the definition of "value" substitute—

""value", in relation to an asset of an insurance company, means the value of the asset as determined in accordance with chapter 1.3, as read with chapter 3.2, of the Integrated Prudential Sourcebook;".

(6) The amendments made by this paragraph have effect in relation to periods of account ending on or after 31st December 2004.

GENERAL NOTE

Paras 1 and 2 make consequential changes to the existing legislation that are necessary following the enactment of parts of the FSA's Integrated Prudential Sourcebook relating to insurers. Since the tax regime for life insurers is tied directly to the regulatory framework, these changes are necessary to ensure that the tax definitions remain on all fours with those used for regulatory purposes. The legislation is amended to include a definition of the Integrated Prudential Sourcebook and terms used in it are then imported into TA 1988 ss 76 and 431. It is also made explicit by use of the term "mathematical reserves" that the liabilities to be used in tax computations are those calculated on a regulatory basis rather than on the realistic basis separately required for companies with large with-profits funds. This is important to achieve consistency with the rest of the life insurance tax regime as well as to ensure equality of treatment between companies.

Schedule 9 contains a number of similar amendments that are separated from paras 1 and 2 merely by virtue of the fact that the paragraphs of the Schedule follow the order in which the provisions that they amend appear in the Taxes Acts.

Amendment of Chapter 1 of Part 12 of ICTA etc

3 For section 431A of ICTA substitute—

"431A Amendment of Chapter etc

(1) The Treasury may by order amend any insurance company taxation provision where it is expedient to do so in consequence of the exercise of any power under the Financial Services and Markets Act 2000, in so far as that Act relates to insurance companies.

(2) Where any exercise of a power under that Act has effect for a period ending on or before, or beginning before and ending after, the day on which an order containing an

amendment in consequence of that exercise is made under subsection (1) above, the power conferred by that subsection includes power to provide for the amendment to have effect in relation to that period.

(3) The Treasury may by order amend any of the following provisions—

    (*a*) sections 432ZA, 432A, 432B to 432G and 755A and Schedule 19AA;

    (*b*) sections 83A, 85, 88 and 89 of the Finance Act 1989;

    (*c*) section 210A of the Taxation of Chargeable Gains Act 1992.

(4) An order under subsection (3) above may only be made so as to have effect in relation to periods of account—

    (*a*) beginning on or after 1st January 2005, and

    (*b*) ending before 1st October 2006.

(5) The Treasury may by order amend subsection (4)(*b*) above by substituting for "1st October 2006" a date no later than 1st October 2007.

(6) Any power conferred by this section to make an order includes power to make—

    (*a*) different provision for different cases or different purposes, and

    (*b*) incidental, supplemental, consequential or transitional provision and savings.

(7) In this section "insurance company taxation provision" means any of the following—

    (*a*) a provision of this Chapter;

    (*b*) any other provision of the Tax Acts so far as relating to insurance companies.".

GENERAL NOTE

Paragraph 3 replaces TA 1988 s 431A in its entirety. The regulation making powers that existed under the old version of s 431A are retained in new sub-s 1. These powers allow the Treasury to amend the insurance company taxation provisions following changes introduced by the FSA under its own legislation. These powers are necessary because of the direct relationship between the tax and regulatory regimes and to require HMRC to introduce amendments by way of primary legislation would deny it the flexibility to react to changes in the regulatory framework. Subsection 2 extends the powers so that it is made explicit that the tax changes may have effect "in year" so as to match the effective date on which the FSA rules change.

New subsections 3 to 5 introduce further regulation making powers allowing the Treasury to amend certain specified tax rules relating to the apportionment of, and rate of tax applicable to, a life insurer's income and gains as well as the new rules for fund recognition (discussed under paragraph 13 below). Unlike the regulation making powers above, these changes are not dependent on changes having first been introduced by the FSA. HMRC has long had concerns that insurers were avoiding tax by ensuring that a disproportionate part of their income and gains were allocated to the exempt categories such as pension business. As a related issue, HMRC also believed that some companies that had identified excess assets that did not belong to the current generation of policy holders were retaining those assets in their long-term insurance funds rather than distributing them to shareholders and were thus benefiting both from the apportionment to exempt business as well as the lower policy holders' rate of tax.

The original proposals to counter these perceived abuses were announced at the time of the pre-Budget Report in December 2004 and were to be introduced by way of regulations laid under the previous version of TA 1988 s 431A. Because of the tight timescale needed for the regulations to have effect for the year ended 31 December 2004, only three days were allowed for consultation. There was considerable disquiet in the industry and among its representative bodies about the short period for consultation on what were far-reaching regulations and it was also pointed out that TA 1988 s 431A as it then stood probably did not include the *vires* necessary for the laying of the proposed regulations. HMRC therefore shelved the plans announced in the pre-Budget Report and entered a period of consultation with interested parties to arrive at a solution that would address the industry's concerns. It has still not been possible to arrive at a consensus view of the best way forward, so the regulation making powers in sub-ss 3 to 5 allow the consultation process to continue with a view to regulations being laid later this year to deal with HMRC's concerns as expressed at the time of the pre-Budget Report while also addressing some of the industry's criticisms of the new rules. As a result of lobbying since the original publication of draft legislation following the March Budget, the primary legislation now contains a "sunset clause" in sub-s 4 so that any regulations will lapse for periods of account ending after 1 October 2006 although this period may be extended by a year if circumstances dictate. Ultimately any regulations laid under new TA 1988 s 431A(3) will be replaced by primary legislation, probably in Finance Act 2006.

Apportionment of income and gains

4— (1) Section 432A of ICTA is amended as follows.

(2) In subsection (9A) (meaning of "net value") for "long-term liabilities" substitute "liabilities".

(3) The amendment made by this paragraph has effect in relation to periods of account ending on or after 31st December 2004.

GENERAL NOTE

Paragraph 4 is a consequential amendment arising from the changes brought about by the enactment of the Integrated Prudential Sourcebook discussed under paragraphs 1 and 2 above.

Section 432B apportionment: participating funds

5— (1) Section 432E of ICTA is amended as follows.

(2) In subsection (2A) (increase in amount determined under subsection (2) where amount is taken into account under subsection (2) of section 83 of FA 1989 by virtue of subsection (2B) of that section) in the opening words—

(*a*) for "an amount is" substitute "an amount or amounts are";

(*b*) after "subsection (2B) of that section" insert "or by virtue of section 444ACA(2) of this Act".

(3) In that subsection, for the definition of "RP" substitute—

"RP is the amount or the aggregate of the amounts taken into account under subsection (2) of section 83 of the Finance Act 1989 by virtue of any of the following provisions—

(*a*) subsection (2B) of that section;

(*b*) section 444ACA(2) of this Act.".

(4) The amendments made by this paragraph have effect in relation to insurance business transfer schemes (within the meaning given by section 444AC(11) of ICTA) taking place on or after 2nd December 2004.

GENERAL NOTE

Many of the changes to life insurance taxation in recent years have been aimed at preventing tax avoidance on the transfer of business from one insurance company to another. HMRC has seen a number of examples of companies extracting assets free of tax using legislation that in broad terms is designed to achieve tax neutrality and it has sought to prevent these attempts to exploit the rules. A significant number of changes were introduced by FA 2003 Sch 33 and additions and amendments to that legislation were brought in by FA 2004 Sch 7. F(N0 2)A 2005 Sch 9 now adds further complexity. As well as introducing legislation to address HMRC's concerns about tax avoidance, the Schedule makes changes to the existing provisions since it has become apparent that in practice certain of them do not work as originally intended.

With one minor exception, the changes relating to insurance transfer schemes all have effect for transactions taking place on or after 2 December 2004.

Paragraph 5 is a consequential amendment following the introduction of TA 1988 s 444ACA (see para 8 below). Because amounts taken into account under FA 1989 s 83(2) and (2B) do not actually feature in a revenue account, there needs to be a mechanism for including them in the amount that must be apportioned between the various categories of business. Paragraph 5 amends TA 1988 s 432E(2) to ensure that any amount taken into account under TA 1988 s 444ACA(2) is included in the amount to be apportioned.

Transfers of business: deemed periodical return

6— (1) Section 444AA of ICTA is amended as follows.

(2) At the end insert—

"(7) Where this section applies in relation to a transfer in a case in which the transferor continues, after the transfer, to carry on insurance business which is not long-term business—

(*a*) references in this section to the last period covered by a periodical return (or deemed periodical return) of the transferor shall be taken to be references to the last period covered by a periodical return (or deemed periodical return) of the transferor containing entries relating to long-term business;

(*b*) subsection (4) above is to be read as if after "other than" there were inserted "the purposes of sections 444BA to 444BD and".".

(3) The amendment made by this paragraph has effect in relation to insurance business transfer schemes (within the meaning given by section 444AA(6) of ICTA) taking place on or after 30th June 2005.

GENERAL NOTE

Paragraph 6 is one of the clarificatory measures and deals with composite insurance companies that transfer the whole of their long-term insurance business while continuing to carry on other insurance business. In such circumstances references in TA 1988 s 444AA (which deals with the preparation of a deemed regulatory return in the context of a transfer of business) are amended so that it is clear that the last actual or deemed return referred to in that section is the one containing long-term business.

This provision is the exception to the general rule that the changes relating to insurance business transfer schemes have effect from 2 December 2004 insofar as it applies to transfers on or after 30 June 2005.

Transfers of business: modification of section 444AC of ICTA

7— (1) Section 444AC of ICTA is amended as follows.

(2) In subsection (2) (excess of element of the transferee's line 15 (or 31) figure representing the transferor's long-term insurance fund over amount specified in paragraph (*b*) not to be regarded as other income of transferee) in paragraph (*b*) (amount of liabilities to policy holders and annuitants transferred to transferee)—

(*a*) for "the amount" substitute "the aggregate amount";

(*b*) at the end insert "and of any relevant debts".

(3) After that subsection insert—

"(2A) Subject to subsections (2C) and (2D) below, subsection (2B) below applies if—

(*a*) the aggregate amount of the liabilities to policy holders and annuitants transferred to the transferee and of any relevant debts, exceeds

(*b*) the element of the transferee's line 31 figure representing the transferor's long-term insurance fund.

(2B) Where this subsection applies—

(*a*) the excess is to be taken into account as a receipt of the transferee in computing in accordance with the provisions of this Act applicable to Case I of Schedule D the profits of its life assurance business for the period of account of the transferee in which the transfer takes place ("the relevant period of account"); and

(*b*) the relevant proportion of the excess is to be taken into account as a receipt of the transferee in so computing the profits of each category of its life assurance business for the relevant period of account;

and, for this purpose, "the relevant proportion", in relation to a category of the transferee's life assurance business, is the proportion that the liabilities of that category that are transferred bear to the total liabilities transferred.

(2C) Subsection (2B) above does not require the excess to be taken into account as a receipt of the transferee in so computing the profits of its life assurance business for the relevant period of account if—

(*a*) transferred liabilities of an aggregate amount equal to the excess are not taken into account in so computing those profits for that period of account, and

(*b*) the amount of the closing liabilities of that period of account is taken into account as opening liabilities in so computing those profits for the next period of account.

(2D) Subsection (2B) above does not require the relevant proportion of the excess to be taken into account as a receipt of the transferee in so computing the profits of a category of its life assurance business for the relevant period of account if—

(*a*) transferred liabilities of an aggregate amount equal to the relevant proportion of the excess are not taken into account in so computing those profits for that period of account, and

(*b*) the amount of the closing liabilities of that period of account is taken into account as opening liabilities in so computing those profits for the next period of account.

(2E) In subsections (2C)(*a*) and (2D)(*a*) above "transferred liabilities" means—

(*a*) liabilities to policy holders or annuitants at the end of the relevant period of account that were transferred to the transferee, and

(*b*) payments made to discharge, during that period of account, liabilities to policy holders or annuitants that were transferred to the transferee.".

(4) After subsection (3) insert—

"(4) In this section "relevant debts" means debts which become debts of the transferee's long-term insurance fund as a result of the transfer.

(5) But if—

(*a*) the fair value, as at the date of the transfer, of the assets which become assets of the transferee's long-term insurance fund as a result of the transfer, exceeds

(*b*) the element of the transferee's line 31 figure representing the transferor's long-term insurance fund,

the amount of any relevant debts for the purposes of this section is to be reduced (but not below nil) by the excess.

(6) In determining the amount of the liabilities transferred for the purposes of this section, there is to be disregarded any reduction in the transferee's liabilities resulting from reinsurance under a contract of reinsurance which is a relevant financial reinsurance contract (within the meaning of section 82C of the Finance Act 1989).

(7) But where—

(*a*) such a reduction results from reinsurance under a contract which was entered into by the transferor as cedant before the day on which the transfer takes place, and

(*b*) the transferor's rights and obligations under the contract are transferred to the transferee under the transfer,

the amount of the reduction that would (apart from this subsection) be disregarded under subsection (6) above shall be reduced (but not below nil) by the amount given by subsection (8) below or, if less, the amount given by subsection (9) below.

(8) The amount given by this subsection is the amount by which the liabilities at the end of the closing period which fell to be taken into account in computing in accordance with the provisions of this Act applicable to Case I of Schedule D the profits of the transferor's business for that period were reduced as a result of reinsurance under the contract.

(9) The amount given by this subsection is the amount given by paragraph (*a*) below reduced (but not below nil) by the amount given by paragraph (*b*) below—

(*a*) the amount given by this paragraph is the aggregate of the relevant amounts for any accounting period, and for this purpose the relevant amount for an accounting period is the amount in sub-paragraph (i) or (ii) below or, where applicable, the aggregate of those amounts—

(i) the amount by which the profits of the transferor's business, computed in accordance with the provisions of this Act applicable to Case I of Schedule D, were increased for that accounting period as a result of reinsurance under the contract;

(ii) the amount by which the losses of the transferor's business, so computed, were reduced for that accounting period as a result of reinsurance under the contract; and

(*b*) the amount given by this paragraph is the aggregate of the relevant amounts for any accounting period, and for this purpose the relevant amount for an accounting period is the amount in sub-paragraph (i) or (ii) below or, where applicable, the aggregate of those amounts—

(i) the amount by which the profits of the transferor's business, so computed, were reduced for that accounting period as a result of a reduction in reinsurance under the contract;

(ii) the amount by which the losses of the transferor's business, so computed, were increased for that accounting period as a result of a reduction in reinsurance under the contract.

(10) In subsections (8) and (9) above—

"the closing period" means the accounting period of the transferor ending with the day on which the transfer takes place;

"the transferor's business" means—

(*a*) the transferor's life assurance business, and

(*b*) any category of its life assurance business to which the liabilities relate.

(11) For the purposes of this section and section 444ACA—

"fair value" has the meaning given by section 444AB(6);

"insurance business transfer scheme" includes a scheme which would be such a scheme but for section 105(1)(*b*) of the Financial Services and Markets Act 2000 (which requires the business transferred to be carried on in an EEA State).".

(5) The heading of the section accordingly becomes "Transfers of business: excess of assets or liabilities".

(6) The amendments made by this paragraph have effect in relation to insurance business transfer schemes (within the meaning given by section 444AC(11) of ICTA) taking place on or after 2nd December 2004.

(7) But in relation to a period of account beginning before 1st January 2005, section 444AC(2A)(*b*) and (5)(*b*) of ICTA shall have effect as if for "line 31 figure" there were substituted "line 15 figure".

GENERAL NOTE

Paragraph 7 amends TA 1988 s 444AC by reinstating proposed legislation that was dropped following industry lobbying at the time of the section's enactment by FA 2003. TA 1988 s 444AC as it currently stands is a relieving provision designed to ensure that any excess of assets over liabilities of the transferor that has been declared as surplus, and hence taxed, is not taken into account as a receipt of the transferee and taxed again. HMRC has, however, seen examples of companies using a transfer of excess liabilities to avoid tax and has therefore looked to reinstate the original symmetry to the legislation, albeit with two modifications to mitigate the effects of the changes on transfers with no tax planning motive.

The legislation treats the excess of policy holder liabilities plus any relevant debts over the value of the transferor's long-term insurance fund shown at line 31 of the transferee's revenue account as a trading receipt (new TA 1988 s 444AC(2A)). In addition to being brought into the Schedule D Case I computation, that excess is also apportioned to the various categories of business of the transferee in the ratio that the liabilities of each category of business transferred bear to the total liabilities transferred (new TA 1988 s 444AC(2B)). However there is an exception to this rule in that the excess is not charged to tax on the transferee if transferred liabilities equal to the excess are disallowed for the purposes of either the Schedule D Case I computation (new subsection 2C) or the Schedule D Case VI computation for a particular category of business (new subsection 2D), provided in both cases that the full amount of the liabilities is taken into account as opening liabilities of the next period of account. In this context transferred liabilities are taken to mean not only liabilities to policy holders shown in the return of the transferee at the end of the period of account in which the transfer occurred, but also any sums paid as claims to discharge the liabilities transferred. Companies involved in insurance business transfer schemes will need to be alert to the possibility of double taxation arising from the interaction of these new rules and the charge on retained assets in the transferor under TA 1988 s 444AB.

The changes in the legislation from the form in which it was published in 2003 are twofold and both are designed to deal with shortcomings that could have resulted in a deemed receipt even if there was no actual excess of liabilities.

Firstly, the excess of liabilities is now calculated by reference to relevant debts as well as policy holder liabilities so that genuine commercial liabilities transferred do not automatically trigger the application of the new rules. However, relevant debts taken as a reduction are themselves reduced by any excess of assets transferred which exceed the transferor's long-term insurance fund thus preventing a double deduction. The definition of relevant debts will ensure that non-insurance liabilities such as borrowings from third parties are taken into account in performing the calculation.

Secondly, liabilities are now stated net of reinsurance rather than gross. This is, however, subject to the fact that a reduction in liabilities under a financial reinsurance contract within the meaning of FA 1989 s 82C is not taken into account (new TA 1988 s 444AC(6)) unless the contract was entered into by the transferor before the day of the transfer and the transferor's rights under it are transferred to the transferee (new

TA 1988 s 444AC(7)). In such cases, the reduction in liabilities that would be disregarded is itself reduced by the lesser of the reduction in the transferor's liabilities taken into account in computing its Schedule D Case I profits for the period ending with the transfer as a result of the reinsurance (new sub-s 8) or the net amount by which its Schedule D Case I profits were increased (or losses reduced) by the reinsurance in previous accounting periods (new sub-s 9).

Like TA 1988 s 444AA and FA 1989 s 82C, these new rules apply to all insurance business transfer schemes whether carried on within the EEA or not.

Transfers of business: transferor shares are assets of transferee's long-term insurance fund etc

8— (1) After section 444AC of ICTA insert—

"444ACA Transfers of business: transferor shares are assets of transferee's long-term insurance fund etc

(1) This section applies where an insurance business transfer scheme (see section 444AC(11)) has effect to transfer long-term business from one company ("the transferor") to another ("the transferee").

(2) If—

(*a*) immediately before the transfer, the assets of the long-term insurance fund of the transferee comprise or include relevant shares or an interest in such shares, and

(*b*) the fair value (see section 444AC(11)) of the relevant shares, or of that interest, is reduced (whether or not to nil) as a result of the transfer,

an amount equal to that reduction in fair value is to be taken into account under section 83(2) of the Finance Act 1989 as a receipt of the transferee of the period of account of the transferee in which the transfer takes place.

(3) But if—

(*a*) the assets transferred to the transferee under the transfer comprise or include assets ("the relevant assets") which, immediately before the transfer,—

(i) were assets of the transferor, but

(ii) were not assets of the transferor's long-term insurance fund, and

(*b*) in respect of the transfer of the relevant assets, an amount is—

(i) brought into account by the transferee as other income of the transferee of the period of account of the transferee in which the transfer takes place, and

(ii) taken into account in computing in accordance with the provisions of this Act applicable to Case I of Schedule D the profits of the transferee's life assurance business and any category of its life assurance business to which the amount is referable,

the amount taken into account under section 83(2) of the Finance Act 1989 by virtue of subsection (2) above shall be reduced (but not below nil) by an amount equal to the amount referred to in paragraph (*b*) above.

(4) In subsection (2) above "relevant shares" means—

(*a*) some or all of the shares in the transferor, or

(*b*) some or all of the shares in a company (whether or not an insurance company) which owns, directly or indirectly,—

(i) some or all of the shares in the transferor, or

(ii) an interest in some or all of those shares.

(5) In subsection (4) above "shares", in relation to a company, includes any interests in the company possessed by members of the company.".

(2) The amendment made by this paragraph has effect in relation to insurance business transfer schemes (within the meaning given by section 444AC(11) of ICTA) taking place on or after 2nd December 2004.

GENERAL NOTE

Paragraph 8 introduces a new TA 1988 s 444ACA to deal with those insurance business transfer situations in which the shares of the transferor are held (whether directly or indirectly) as assets of the long-term insurance fund of the transferee and the fair value (defined as the amount which would be obtained from an independent purchaser) of those shares is reduced as a result of the transfer. This will typically happen because the transfer of the subsidiary company's assets as consideration for the assumption of its liabilities will cause a reduction in the value of its shares which in broad terms will equate to the excess value of those assets over its liabilities, which excess represents the value of its in-force business.

Any part of the loss on the shares as a result of the reduction in value attributable to basic life assurance general annuity business (BLAGAB) would be subject to the rules for depreciatory transactions in TCGA 1992 s 176 but no such general rule exists for the purposes of Schedule D Case I or the Case VI computations based on those principles so that, in the absence of legislation to the contrary, the loss would be an allowable expense in those computations. To counter this, an amount equal to the reduction in value is brought into account as a receipt of the transferee thus cancelling out the loss on the shares. There is an exception to this rule if assets of the transferor that were not assets of its long-term insurance fund are brought into account by the transferee as other income and charged to tax under Schedule D Case I. In such cases the deemed receipt is reduced, but not below nil, by the amount brought into account in respect of those assets thus preventing a double charge.

In this context new TA 1988 s 444ACA(5) makes it clear that "shares" can also include the interests of members in a mutual insurance company.

Equalisation reserves for general business

9— (1) Section 444BA of ICTA is amended as follows.

(2) In subsection (11) (meaning of "equalisation reserves rules") for "Chapter 6 of the Prudential Sourcebook (Insurers)" substitute "chapter 7.5 of the Integrated Prudential Sourcebook".

(3) The amendment made by this paragraph has effect in relation to periods of account ending on or after 31st December 2004.

Unappropriated surplus on valuation

10— (1) Section 82B of FA 1989 is amended as follows.

(2) In subsection (1) (section to apply where insurance company has unappropriated surplus on valuation and has not made an election in accordance with Rule 4.1(6) of the Prudential Sourcebook (Insurers) for the period of account in question) in paragraph (*b*), for "Rule 4.1(6)" substitute "Rule 9.10(*c*)".

(3) The amendment made by this paragraph has effect in relation to periods of account ending on or after 31st December 2004.

GENERAL NOTE

Paragraphs 9 and 10 contain further minor changes to definitions resulting from the enactment of the Integrated Prudential Sourcebook discussed under paragraphs 1 and 2 above.

Relevant financial reinsurance contracts

11— (1) Section 82C of FA 1989 is amended as follows.

(2) In subsection (1) (cases where section applies) in paragraph (*b*), for "either condition A or condition B" substitute "condition A".

(3) Omit subsections (4), (5), (8) and (9) (provisions relating to condition B).

(4) The amendments made by this paragraph have effect in relation to insurance business transfer schemes (within the meaning given by section 82C(9) of FA 1989) taking place on or after 2nd December 2004.

GENERAL NOTE

Paragraph 11 amends FA 1989 s 82C which was introduced as part of a package of anti-avoidance measures in FA 2004. One of the reasons for the original introduction of FA 1989 s 82C was that HMRC had seen instances of transfers of business in which a deficit of assets transferred was made good by use of a financial reinsurance contract ("Condition B" defined in FA 1989 s 82C(4)) while the assets not transferred were extracted from the transferor free of tax. This particular planning technique is now countered by new TA 1988 s 444AC(2A) discussed at para 7 above so that FA

1989 s 82C is now partly redundant. The redundant provisions are removed for the future although they will still apply to transactions occurring before 2 December 2004.

Receipts to be taken into account

12— (1) Section 83 of FA 1989 is amended as follows.

(2) In subsection (2A) (amounts not required to be taken into account by subsection (2)) for paragraph (*a*) (amounts which are entirely notional) substitute—

"(*a*) comprises notional income for the period of account (see subsections (2AA) and (2AB)),

(aa) represents an inter-fund transfer (see subsections (2AC) and (2AD))),".

(3) After that subsection insert—

"(2AA) For the purposes of subsection (2A)(*a*) above, an amount brought into account as mentioned in paragraphs (*a*) to (*d*) of subsection (2) above for a period of account is to be regarded as notional income for the period of account if—

(*a*) it represents income which has not been received, and is not receivable, from another person, and

(*b*) a corresponding notional expense of the same amount is brought into account in the period of account;

and where particular income falls to be regarded as notional income under this subsection, the notional expense by virtue of which that income falls to be so regarded may not be taken into account for determining whether any other income is to be so regarded.

(2AB) In subsection (2AA) above "notional expense" means an expense which has not been paid, and is not payable, to another person and which—

(*a*) is not deductible in computing the profits of the company in respect of its life assurance business in accordance with the provisions of the Taxes Act 1988 applicable to Case I of Schedule D, but

(*b*) had it represented an amount paid or payable to another person, would have been so deductible.

(2AC) For the purposes of subsection (2A)(aa) above, where—

(*a*) one or more inter-fund transfers ("transfers-in") are made into a fund and one or more inter-fund transfers ("transfers-out") are made out of the fund, and

(*b*) the amount brought into account for the period of account as other income in respect of the transfers-in represents the amount by which—

(i) the amount or aggregate amount of the transfers-in, exceeds

(ii) the amount or aggregate amount of the transfers-out,

only the amount of that excess shall be taken to represent the transfers-in.

(2AD) In this section "inter-fund transfer" means a transfer between two funds which in the company's periodical return is shown in, or included in amounts shown in, line 14 or 33 of the Forms 58 for the funds.".

(4) In subsection (2B) (assets of long-term insurance fund transferred out of fund but transfer not brought into account as part of total expenditure) after paragraph (*b*) insert—

"For the purposes of this subsection "total expenditure", in relation to a period of account of an insurance company, includes any expenses brought into account in line 12 of Form 40 (the revenue account) in the periodical return of the company for the period of account.".

(5) The amendments made by sub-paragraphs (2) and (3) have effect in relation to periods of account ending on or after 2nd December 2004.

(6) The amendment made by sub-paragraph (4) has effect in relation to periods of account beginning on or after 1st January 2005.

GENERAL NOTE

Paragraph 12 makes changes to the rules in FA 1989 s 83 that determine which receipts of a life insurance company are to be taken into account in calculating its profit in accordance with the principles applicable to Schedule D Case I. That section was substantially recast by FA 2003 Sch 33 to deal with what HMRC saw as shortcomings in the previous rules, in particular by providing a mechanistic approach to defining the income to be brought into account by reference to certain lines in the revenue account of an insurer's regulatory return.

The section recognised, however, that it was not appropriate to tax purely notional income (in the sense that it was not actually paid away but rather represented an internal allocation of costs balanced by a corresponding notional expense elsewhere) and hence excluded that income from the definition of receipts to be taken into account. An example of this would be notional rents charged by one sub-fund of the long-term insurance fund for use of its properties to another sub-fund. HMRC has apparently seen instances of companies arguing that certain sums, which it regards as real income, are notional and has accordingly extended the definition to put the matter beyond doubt. Going forward new FA 1989 s 83(2AA) and (2AB) make it clear that notional income and expenses can only be amounts neither received nor paid and there is symmetry between the tax treatment in that, while the notional income will not be taxable, the notional expense will not be available for relief. A notional expense can only match one corresponding amount of notional income and must be of a type that it would have been an allowable expense in a Schedule D Case I computation if it had been paid.

In a similar vein, net transfers between different funds of the same company are not brought into account merely by virtue of being included on line 15 of the receiving fund's revenue account. In such instances the net amount of the transfer as shown at line 14 or 33 on form 58 of the regulatory return will not be brought into account in computing taxable profits.

Both of the above changes take effect for periods of account ending on or after 2 December 2004 which for most companies with a calendar year-end will be the period ending on 31 December that year.

Finally, it is made clear that expenses that are netted off against investment income shown at line 12 of the revenue account (the most typical of which will be costs associated with investment properties since Schedule A income is normally included in line 12 net of such costs) are not to be regarded as not having been brought into account as part of total expenditure. If this were not the case, companies could technically find themselves in the position of having to record an additional Case I receipt equal to the netted expenses by virtue of FA 1989 s 83(2B) and hence suffer effective double taxation. In practice it is not certain that HMRC would have taken this point and although the new rules have effect only for periods of account beginning on or after 1 January 2005, Inspectors have been advised not to pursue the issue for earlier periods.

Meaning of "brought into account"

13— (1) Section 83A of FA 1989 is amended as follows.

(2) In subsection (2) (accounts which are recognised for the purposes of sections 82A to 83AB)—

(*a*) in paragraph (*b*) (separate revenue account prepared under Chapter 9 of the Prudential Sourcebook (Insurers) in respect of a part of the company's long-term business to be a recognised account) for "part of that business" substitute "with-profits fund (see subsection (6))";

(*b*) omit the words from "Paragraph (*b*) above" to the end of the subsection.

(3) After subsection (3) insert—

"(3A) Where, in the case of any with-profits fund in respect of which there is prepared such a separate account ("the sub-fund"),—

(*a*) the sub-fund forms part of another with-profits fund ("the wider fund") in respect of which such a separate account is also prepared,

(*b*) in the case of a company whose life assurance business is mutual business, the sub-fund and each other with-profits fund which forms part of the wider fund are 100:0 funds, and

(*c*) the wider fund—

(i) does not form part of another with-profits fund in respect of which such a separate account is also prepared, or

(ii) forms part of another with-profits fund in respect of which such a separate account is also prepared and that separate account is treated by this subsection as not being a recognised account for the purposes of those sections,

the account in respect of the wider fund shall not be a recognised account for the purposes of those sections.

(3B) Where, in the case of such a separate account prepared in respect of a with-profits fund,—

(*a*) the account is not prevented from being a recognised account for the purposes of those sections by virtue of subsection (3A) above, but

(*b*) if paragraph (*b*) of that subsection were to be omitted, the account would be prevented from being such a recognised account by virtue of that subsection,

no such separate account prepared in respect of a with-profits fund forming part of that fund shall be such a recognised account.

(3C) In subsection (3A) above "100:0 fund" means a fund in the case of which—

(*a*) the policy holders of the fund are entitled to participate in all the profits of the fund, and

(*b*) no other persons are entitled to participate in any of the profits of the fund.

(3D) Subsection (3E) below applies where there is prepared such a separate account ("the with-profits account") in respect of a with-profits fund—

(*a*) of which no other with-profits fund forms part, but

(*b*) of which a non-profit fund (see subsection (6)) forms part.

(3E) Where this subsection applies—

(*a*) the with-profits account shall not be a recognised account for the purposes of those sections, but

(*b*) there shall be treated as having been required and prepared a further separate revenue account covering so much of the items brought into account in the with-profits account as remains after excluding the items brought into account in that account in respect of the non-profit fund.".

(4) For subsection (4) substitute—

"(4) If—

(*a*) a company prepares a revenue account in respect of the whole of its long-term business ("the main account"),

(*b*) it prepares one or more such separate accounts as are mentioned in subsection (2)(*b*) above, and

(*c*) the total of the items brought into account in the separate accounts—

(i) excluding any such accounts which by virtue of subsection (3A), (3B) or (3E)(*a*) above are not recognised accounts for the purposes of those sections, but

(ii) including any such accounts which by virtue of subsection (3E)(*b*) above are treated as having been required and prepared,

is not equal to the total amount brought into account in the main account,

there shall be treated as having been required and prepared a further separate revenue account covering the balance.".

(5) At the end of the section insert—

"(6) In this section "with-profits fund" and "non-profit fund" have the same meaning as in the Integrated Prudential Sourcebook.".

(6) The amendments made by this paragraph have effect in relation to periods of account beginning on or after 1st January 2005.

GENERAL NOTE

The calculations of a life insurance company's profits under Schedule D Case I and Case VI rely on entries brought into account in the various revenue accounts in the regulatory return. FA 1989 s 83A previously was written so that the only revenue accounts recognised for tax were those also recognised by the regulator but HMRC has been concerned for some time that companies have been manipulating this provision by preparing revenue accounts that are not strictly required by the regulator. Paragraph 13 deals with these concerns by restricting the revenue accounts recognised for tax purposes to either an account for the whole long-term insurance fund or, in the majority of cases, a separate with-profits fund and a residual fund comprising the balance of the company's long-term business. In this context the definition of a with-profits fund and a non-profit fund matches that given in the Integrated Prudential Sourcebook.

Needless to say, the legislation has to cater for those companies whose fund structure does not sit on all fours with the default position referred to above and three different circumstances are specifically addressed.

1   In the case of a with-profits fund that sits within another with-profits fund, the wider fund is ignored. This provision also applies to multiple nestings of funds and works to ensure that there is no double counting. It also applies in the case of the

with-profits funds of mutual companies in which only the policy holders are entitled to participate in profits (a "100:0 fund").

2   In the case of a mutual company which has a with-profits fund that is not a 100:0 fund within its wider with-profits fund, the nested fund is not recognised resulting in the recognition of the wider fund. This situation can arise if a mutual company takes over a proprietary company and transfers the latter's business into its own long-term insurance fund.

3   If a with-profits fund includes a non-profit fund which prepares a separate revenue account, then the wider with-profits fund is ignored for tax purposes and instead the company is required to prepare a balancing revenue account excluding the non-profit business.

As noted above, any balance left is amalgamated into one residual deemed revenue account.

Changes in recognised accounts: attribution of amounts carried forward under s.432F of ICTA

14— (1) After section 83A of FA 1989 insert—

"83B Changes in recognised accounts: attribution of amounts carried forward under s.432F of Taxes Act 1988

(1) This section applies to a company where any revenue account that is recognised for a period of account (the "new period of account") relates to funds or business which is different from the funds or business to which a revenue account that was recognised for the preceding period of account relates.

(2) Any subsection (2) excess (within the meaning of section 432F(2) of the Taxes Act 1988) which would have been available under section 432F(3) or (4) of that Act to reduce a subsection (3) figure (within the meaning of section 432F(1) of that Act) of the company in the new period of account shall be attributed between the revenue accounts that are recognised for that period of account in such manner as is appropriate.

(3) In this section "recognised" means recognised, by virtue of section 83A, for the purposes of sections 82A to 83AB.".

(2) The amendment made by this paragraph has effect in relation to new periods of account (within the meaning given by section 83B(1) of FA 1989) beginning on or after 1st January 2005.

GENERAL NOTE

Paragraph 14 deals with a possible consequence of the changes introduced by paragraph 13. If there is a change in fund or funds recognised for tax purposes as a result of the operation of the new FA 1989 s 83A, any excess calculated under TA 1988 s 432F(2) for a previously recognised fund is apportioned to the now recognised funds in such manner as is appropriate. This essentially ensures that no excess from prior years is lost as a result of the changes. How the appropriate manner is to be calculated is not entirely clear but Inspectors will presumably accept reasonable methods suggested by an affected company.

Charge of certain receipts of basic life assurance business

15— (1) Section 85 of FA 1989 is amended as follows.

(2) In subsection (2) (receipts excluded from charge under Case VI of Schedule D in respect of receipts referable to company's basic life assurance and general annuity business) after paragraph (*e*) insert "; or

(*f*) any payment received under the Financial Services Compensation Scheme to enable the company to meet its obligations to policy holders.".

(3) In subsection (2C) (rules as to whether receipt is referable to company's basic life assurance and general annuity business for the purposes of subsection (1)) after paragraph (*a*) insert—

"(aa) in the case of a repayment or refund of expenses other than acquisition expenses, the expenses—

      (i) were attributable to basic life assurance and general annuity business for the purposes of Step 1 in subsection (7) of the new section 76 (see subsection (8) of that section), or

      (ii) fell to be deducted by virtue of subsection (1) of the old section 76;

and for this purpose, "the new section 76" and "the old section 76" have the same meaning as in section 44 of the Finance Act 2004 (see subsection (8) of that section),".

(4) The amendments made by this paragraph have effect in relation to accounting periods ending on or after 16th March 2005.

GENERAL NOTE

Paragraph 15 removes a potential mismatch in the taxation treatment of compensation payments to policy holders under the Financial Services Compensation Scheme. Such compensation can reach the policy holder by one of two routes. Under the first, the compensation is paid directly to the policy holder and it has no impact on the insurance company's tax position. Under the second route, the compensation is first paid to the insurance company which then passes it on to the policy holder by way of an increase in policy benefits. Under the legislation as it previously stood, such payments to the insurance company would be taxable in the income less expenses (I-E) computation under FA 1989 s 85 as miscellaneous receipts but there would be no corresponding relief for the payment to the policy holder resulting in an asymmetry. It is now made clear by the amendments to FA 1989 s 85(2) that such receipts are excluded from the I-E computation.

Paragraph 15 also makes a minor correction to the rules in FA 1989 s 85 for refunds of expenses. That section, as redrafted by FA 2004, did not provide a mechanism for apportioning refunds between the classes of business with the result that a refund of expenses clearly referable to, say, pension business and which had been relieved in the appropriate Case VI computation might be apportioned to BLAGAB. The additional sub-para now attributes such refunds to BLAGAB only if they were previously deductible under either the old or new versions of TA 1988 s 76.

Corporation tax: policy holders' fraction of profits

16— (1) Section 88 of FA 1989 is amended as follows.

(2) In subsection (3A) (meaning of "income and gains of the company's life assurance business" in subsection (3)) after paragraph (*a*) insert—

      "(aa) receipts of the company chargeable under Case VI of Schedule D by virtue of section 85(1) above,

      (ab) income of the company treated as referable to basic life assurance and general annuity business by section 441B(2) of the Taxes Act 1988 (treatment of UK land),

      (ac) amounts treated as accruing to the company and charged to tax under Case VI of Schedule D by virtue of section 442A of that Act (taxation of investment return where risk reinsured), and".

(3) The amendment made by this paragraph has effect in relation to periods of account beginning on or after 1st January 2005.

GENERAL NOTE

Paragraph 16 tidies up a number of anomalies to the definition of relevant profits in FA 1989 s 88 following changes introduced in FA 2004 which altered the definition of BLAGAB income and gains to include only those apportioned to that category under TA 1988 s 432A. This change overlooked the fact that, notwithstanding the amendment of TA 1988 s 432A by FA 2004 sch 7, there still remained certain types of income which were not referable to BLAGAB by the application of that section. As a result, on a strict interpretation of the law, those income and gains could not benefit from the policy holders' rate of tax. These changes correct this problem for periods of account beginning on or after 1 January 2005 although Inspectors are being advised not to raise the point for prior periods.

Overseas life insurance companies

17— (1) Section 156 of FA 2003 is amended as follows.

(2) For subsection (4) (regulations amending certain provisions relating to overseas life insurance companies may be made with effect from 1st January 2003) substitute—

"(4) Regulations under this section may be made so as to have effect in relation to accounting periods or periods of account (whenever beginning) which end on or after the day on which the regulations come into force.".

GENERAL NOTE

Paragraph 17 ensures that the regulation making powers regarding the taxation of overseas life insurance companies are consistent with those discussed under paragraph 3 above.

Meaning of "pension business"

18— (1) Schedule 35 to FA 2004 is amended as follows.

(2) Paragraph 20 (life assurance: meaning of "pension business") is amended as follows.

(3) In the section 431B of ICTA substituted by that paragraph, in subsection (2)—

(*a*) after "registered pension scheme" (where first occurring) insert "by virtue of the withdrawal of registration of the pension scheme under section 157 of the Finance Act 2004";

(*b*) after "in which the pension scheme" insert "so".

(4) In that section, insert at the end—

"(3) Where—

(*a*) immediately before 6th April 2006 an annuity contract falls within any of the descriptions of contracts specified in subsection (2) of this section as it had effect immediately before that date, but

(*b*) on or after that date the contract does not fall to be regarded for the purposes of this section as having been entered into for the purposes of a registered pension scheme,

the contract is to be treated for the purposes of this section as having been entered into for such purposes.".

(5) Paragraph 22 (friendly societies: meaning of "pension business") is amended as follows.

(6) In sub-paragraph (3), in the subsection (2B) of section 466 of ICTA inserted by that sub-paragraph—

(*a*) after "registered pension scheme" (where first occurring) insert "by virtue of the withdrawal of registration of the pension scheme under section 157 of the Finance Act 2004";

(*b*) after "in which the pension scheme" insert "so".

(7) The preceding provisions of this paragraph come into force on 6th April 2006.

GENERAL NOTE

Paragraph 18 makes changes to the definition of pension business in TA 1988 s 431B as a result of the introduction of the new tax regime for pensions on 6 April 2006 ("A-day"). In particular, it is made clear that neither the winding up of a scheme nor the fact that annuities in payment do not become part of a registered scheme after A-day, alter the fact that they are pension business.

Miscellaneous references to "class" of business

19— (1) In section 432B of ICTA (apportionment of receipts brought into account) in subsection (1), for "class" substitute "category".

(2) In section 444A of ICTA (transfers of business) in subsection (3), for "class" substitute "category".

(3) In Schedule 12 to FA 1997 (leasing arrangements: finance leases and loans) in paragraph 19 (companies carrying on life assurance business) in sub-paragraph (2), for "class" substitute "category".

(4) In Schedule 29 to FA 2002 (gains and losses of a company from intangible fixed assets) in paragraph 138 (interpretation provisions relating to insurance companies) in sub-paragraph (3), for "class" substitute "category".

(5) The amendments made by this paragraph have effect in relation to periods of account beginning on or after 1st January 2005.

GENERAL NOTE

Paragraph 19 substitutes the word "category" for "class" when referring to different types of insurance business in certain parts of the tax legislation. In general, the former term is used to make distinctions for tax purposes while the latter is used to differentiate for regulatory purposes. In practice the two terms are often used interchangeably and the amendments should have no effect on the tax basis of any company.

Transfers of business: references to accounting period ending with day of transfer

20— (1) Section 12 of ICTA (corporation tax: basis of, and periods for, assessment) is amended as follows.

(2) In subsection (7A), after "(7ZA) above" insert "and subject to subsection (7C) below".

(3) After subsection (7B) insert—

"(7C) Where subsection (1) of section 444AA applies in the case of an insurance business transfer scheme—

(*a*) an accounting period of the transferor shall end for purposes of corporation tax—

(i) with the end of the period covered by the periodical return deemed by virtue of subsection (2) of that section, or
(ii) where the last period covered by an actual periodical return of the transferor ends immediately before the transfer, with the end of that period,

(so that an accounting period will end immediately before the transfer), and

(*b*) an accounting period of the transferor shall end for purposes of corporation tax with the end of the period covered by the periodical return deemed by virtue of subsection (3) of that section (so that the time of the transfer shall be an accounting period of the transferor);

and for this purpose, expressions used in this subsection and in that section have the same meaning in this subsection as in that section.".

(4) In section 444AB of ICTA (transfers of business: charge on transferor retaining assets) in subsection (3), for "ending with the day of the transfer" substitute "ending immediately before the transfer".

(5) In section 444ABA of ICTA (subsequent charge in certain cases within section 444AB of ICTA) in subsection (3), for "ending with the day of the transfer" substitute "ending immediately before the transfer".

(6) In section 213 of TCGA 1992 (spreading of gains and losses under section 212 of TCGA 1992) at the end insert—

"(10) If the transfer is one to which section 444AA(1) of the Taxes Act applies, the references in this section to the accounting period of the transferor ending with the day of the transfer are references to the accounting period ending immediately before the transfer.".

(7) The amendments made by sub-paragraphs (2) to (5) have effect in relation to insurance business transfer schemes taking place on or after 16th March 2005.

(8) The amendment made by sub-paragraph (6) has effect where the accounting period for which the net amount represents an excess of losses over gains is an accounting period beginning on or after 1st January 2003.

GENERAL NOTE

Paragraph 20 introduces clarification by way of minor changes to the rules that determine accounting periods when there is a transfer of business. It is now made explicit by the introduction of a new TA 1988 s 12(7C) that, in cases in which there is a transfer of the whole of the transferor's long-term insurance business, a period of account will end immediately before the transfer and that there will be a period of account covering the time of the transfer. The paragraph also introduces consequential amendments that secure the same effect in TA 1988 ss 444AB and 444ABA as well as TCGA 1992 s 213. All of these changes, with the exception of the latter, have effect for insurance business transfer schemes that take place on or after 16 March 2005. The changes to TCGA 1992 s 213 affect accounting periods beginning on or after 1 January 2005.

SCHEDULE 10
STAMP DUTY LAND TAX: MISCELLANEOUS AMENDMENTS

Section 49

GENERAL NOTE

Schedule 10 is in two parts: Part 1 makes amendments to SDLT provisions, generally with effect from 20 May 2005, and Part 2 makes amendments from Royal Assent. However, amendments under each Part apply to certain provisions such as group and acquisition relief (under FA 2003 Sch 7) and partnership transactions.

Sub-sales

Paragraph 2 excepts from the general provision in s 45(3) (that the substantial performance or completion of the original contract (that has been sub-sold, assigned etc) at the same time as the sub-sold etc contract shall be ignored) where the sub-sold etc contract benefits from relief under FA 2003 s 73 (itself amended by FA 2005). This means that SDLT is imposed on the conveyance of the property under the first contract where the sub-purchaser benefits from relief under s 73 in respect of the sub-sale. This change applies to transactions with an effective date after 19 May 2005.

Group relief

Paragraphs 3–7 mend the group relief provisions where the effective date of the transaction benefiting from relief under Pt 1 of Sch 7 is on or after 20 May 2005. Therefore it does not alter the rules determining clawback where the effective date of the relieved transaction was before 20 May even if the event giving rise to clawback is after 19 May 2005.

Paragraph 19 prevents the application of group relief where a transaction is not for bona fide commercial reasons or forms part of arrangements of which the (or a) main purpose is the avoidance of SDLT, stamp duty, or corporation, income or capital gains tax where a transaction has an effective date on or after Royal Assent. There is a saving for completion of a contract entered into and substantially performed before 17 March 2005 (see para 22(2)(a)). There is a similar saving for contracts entered into before 17 March (see para 22(2)(b)) unless there has been a sub-sale etc after 16 March as described in para 22(3).

Paragraph 3 makes changes to Sch 7 para 1(7) consequential on para 6 of this Schedule.

Paragraph 4 amends the amount by reference to which clawback of SDLT is calculated under Sch 7 para 3. Previously it only had regard to the market value of the property, or the appropriate part of the market value of the property. Now, where relief was obtained from SDLT on rent, it also takes account of the rent payable and previously relieved.

Paragraph 5 restricts the circumstances where group relief is not clawed back as a result of the vendor (but not the purchaser) leaving the group. It is designed to limit the exemption from clawback to where the vendor leaves the group as a result of dealing in the vendor's shares (see Sch 7 para 4(3)(a) – unchanged) or a dealing in the shares in another company which is 'above' the vendor in the group structure (see Sch 7 para 4(3)(b), as amended).

Paragraph 6 inserts a new para 4A into Sch 7 which provides for another trigger for the clawback charge. It requires:

(a) a change of control (using the TA 1988 s 416 test, augmented by there being a change of control when a company is wound up) of the purchaser;

(b) a transaction benefiting from group relief (a later transaction) to have occurred where the effective date was within three years of the change of control or where the effective date was more than three years of the change of control but pursuant to arrangements entered into within that three-year period;

(c) absent para 4A there would have been no clawback charge on the later transaction; and

(d) there to have been a transaction (a 'previous transaction') satisfying para 4A(2).

If so para 4A(1) deems the vendor under the earliest previous transaction to be the vendor under the later transaction.

To satisfy para 4A(2) all of the following four conditions need to be satisfied in respect of the previous transaction, or transactions:

(a) group, reconstruction or acquisition reliefs (under Sch 7, paras 1, 7 or 8) to have been obtained;

(b) the effective date of the previous transaction to have been within three years of the change of control;

(c) there is some link (within para (2)(c)) between the property transferred under the previous transaction and the property the subject of the later transaction; and

(d) there to have been no transaction since the previous transaction involving the property acquired under that previous transaction whereby relief under any of paras 1, 7 and 8 was *not* obtained.

Sub-paragraph 4A(4) provides that where two or more previous transactions were entered into at the same time all the vendors under those transactions are taken into account under para 4A(1). The example given in the Explanatory Notes of transactions entered into at the same time is when A contracts to sell one interest (perhaps a freehold reversion) to C and B agrees to assign its leasehold interest in the same property to C.

The idea behind new para 4A is to attack transactions where relief is available on a series of transactions whereby each transaction sidesteps subsequent clawback by postulating whether the transferee leaves a group as if there had been a group relieved transfer from the vendor (under the earliest previous transaction) to the purchaser under the later transaction. It is not clear whether it will have unexpected effects on bona fide transactions and whether multiple levels of clawback could arise (eg if there is a change of control of a parent company and there had been a previous transfer intra group, whether para 4A could apply to the transaction whereby parent acquired the property *and* the transaction whereby the subsidiary acquired it from the parent, both consequent upon the subsequent change of control of the parent).

In one respect para 4A(2) is retrospective because to the extent that a contract had been entered into prior to 17 March 2005 but was completed after 16 March, one reading of para 16(6)(b) is that such a transaction could be a 'previous transaction'.

Paragraph 7 makes a consequential change to FA 2003 Sch 17A para 11 (which very broadly imposes SDLT on property which had previously benefited from various forms of relief, including group relief, as if a new lease had been granted at the time the relieved property was assigned or otherwise dealt with). It links in to para 4A.

Commencement

Paragraph 16(1) provides for the changes made by paras 3–7 to apply to transactions where the effective date is on or after 19 May 2005. Except as regards the change made by para 4(a) (which applies to transactions effected pursuant to contracts entered into and substantially completed before 20 May), all of the other changes made also apply to transactions pursuant to contracts made and substantially completed prior to 17 March 2005: see para 16(6) and (7). They also apply to completion of contracts made on or before 17 March 2005 (and in the case of contracts affected only by the amendment made by para 4(a), 20 May 2005) provided they are not varied, sub-sold etc: see para 16(7) and (8).

Reconstruction and acquisition reliefs

Paragraph 8 introduces a new para 8(5A) which prevents relief under Sch 7 para 8 unless the, or part of the, undertaking acquired by the transferee company does not consist wholly or mainly of property dealing. It applies to transactions with an effective date after 19 May 2005 unless pursuant to pre-17 March 2005 contracts (which if not substantially completed by 17 March have not been varied, sub-sold etc): see para 16(5), (7) and (8).

Paragraph 9 makes a similar amendment to Sch 7 para 9(2) as is made by para 4(a) in relation to group relief. It has the same commencement date as for para 4(a) above.

Paragraph 20 imposes a further condition for obtaining acquisition relief, namely that the transaction must not form part of arrangements of which the, or one of the, main purposes is tax avoidance. It applies to transactions where the effective date is before Royal Assent or, if after Royal Assent, where the transaction is pursuant to a pre-17 March 2005 contract (which, if not substantially completed on or before 16 March 2005, must not be assigned, varied etc): see para 22.

Partnership transactions

Paragraph 10 introduces a new para 17A into FA 2003 Sch 15 (partnership transactions for SDLT) which imposes a new SDLT charge where there has been an transfer to a partnership which is chargeable under FA 2003 Sch 15 para 10 and there is a withdrawal of capital, or other reduction of partnership interest or cessation of partnership giving rise to money or money's worth within three years of the relevant transfer. It can also apply where there has been a loan to the partnership by the relevant person (broadly transferor or connected person: see para 17A(3)) and within the subsequent three years the loan is repaid or money's worth extracted.

The partners are deemed to have made a land transaction in respect of which they are purchasers and so in accordance with Sch 15, paras 6–8 jointly and severally liable for the SDLT and to make returns. Paragraph 17A(7) limits the charge to the market value of the land or interest in land contributed at the outset, and further reduced by the amount if any on which the transfer to the partnership was liable to SDLT.

The provision applies where the original transfer to the partnership was on or after 20 May 2005, or post-19 May 2005 transfers pursuant to contracts substantially performed before 17 March 2005 and other such contracts which have not been assigned etc: see para 16(3), (6)–(8).

Paragraph 21 amends Sch 15 para 33 (only introduced in FA 2004) which does not reflect what was intended, namely only to charge stamp duty on that proportion of the value of a partnership interest being transferred as is attributable to interests in stock and marketable securities net of debt secured on the stock etc immediately after the transaction (ignoring any such stock etc transferred into the partnership in connection with the transfer of the partnership interest: see new para 33(3A)). The amendments will be effective (although HMRC practice seems already to be to operate para 33 as if it were correctly worded) for post-Royal Assent transactions.

Bare trustees

Paragraph 11 makes an exception from the general rule contained in FA 2003 Sch 16 para 3 that transactions between bare trustee and beneficial owner can be ignored where the transaction is the grant of a lease to or by a nominee. The wording of Sch 16 para 3(3) (ie as amended) is intended to make the transaction as dutiable as if the nominee received or disposed of the beneficial interest in the lease granted. Where nominee and beneficial owner are connected within FA 2003 s 53 market value may be imposed, subject to any available reliefs. The change applies to leases granted after 19 May 2005.

Paragraph 12 makes a consequential amendment to FA 2003 Sch 17A para 11 (which deems there to have been the grant of a lease at the time of an assignment of a lease of property which has previously not been liable to SDLT because of specific reliefs that have not been withdrawn). As with the change made by para 11, the change is effective for transaction with an effective date after 19 May 2005, subject to transitional relief for pre-17 March 2005 contracts: see para 16(4), (6) and (7).

Lease variations

Paragraph 13 amends FA 2003 Sch 17A para 15A by the insertion of a new para (1A) so that now para 15A applies to treat the lessee who has paid for a variation of a lease (other than a variation in the rent or term, already dealt with by para 15A(1) or (2)) as if the payee had received an interest in land. This change is intended to make all lease variations where the lessee pays for the variation liable to SDLT, subject to any applicable reliefs, where the effective date of the transaction is after 19 May 2005: see para 16(5), subject to transitional relief in paras (6) and (7).

Loan and deposits

In an attempt to eradicate perceived avoidance in connection with leases, Sch 10 para 14 inserts a new para 18A(1) into FA 2003 Sch 17A to provide that a deposit or loan to a person (in practice likely to be the grantor of a lease, a person connected with him or with a bank) is treated as consideration provided by the lessee or a connected person even if the deposit or loan may be repayable, where repayment depends upon action taken by or omissions of the lessee. Newly inserted para 18A(2) makes similar provision in connection with assignments of leases.

As a result of representations, new para 18A(3) disapplies sub-paras (1) and (2) where the loan or deposit does not exceed twice 'the maximum relevant rent' determined in accordance with Sch 17A para 17(3), ie broadly the maximum rent payable in the first five years of the lease or of the remaining term of the lease: see para 18A(4). There is still a problem in relation to loans or deposits to secure dilapidations or other expenses exceeding the sub- para (3) carve out.

Paragraph 18A(5) does not give rise to a charge on the deemed premium, just because the £600 per annum rent threshold is exceeded, unless the consideration including deposit exceeds £150,000 for non-residential property or residential property in a disadvantaged area or £120,000 for residential property in a non-disadvantaged area.

To avoid claims that payment of a deposit or loan was contingent consideration such that when the contingency – repayment – occurred, part of the SDLT paid should be refunded, para 14 amends FA 2003 s 80. It inserts a new sub-para (4A) precluding claims to that effect under s 80(4) where either a deposit or loan is repaid or part of the consideration is repaid (under other arrangements contingent on determination or assignment of the lease made at the time the transaction was entered into). The change applies to leases granted or assigned where the effective date is after 19 May 2005: see para 16(5) and the transitional relief in paras 16(6) and (7).

Public bodies

With effect from Royal Assent a more restrictive definition of company (than that contained in FA 2003 s 100(1)) is inserted into s 66 (relief for transactions involving public bodies) by para 18. This is relevant to the definition of public body as extended by s 66(5).

PART 1

AMENDMENTS COMING INTO FORCE IN ACCORDANCE WITH

PARAGRAPH 16

Introduction

1 Part 4 of FA 2003 (stamp duty land tax) is amended in accordance with this Part of this Schedule.

Transfer of rights: exclusion of transaction to which alternative finance provisions apply

2 In section 45 (contract and conveyance: effect of transfer of rights) at the end of subsection (3) insert "except in a case where the secondary contract gives rise to a transaction that is exempt from charge by virtue of subsection (3) of section 73 (alternative property finance: land sold to financial institution and re-sold to individual)".

Group relief

3 In paragraph 1 of Schedule 7 (group relief), in sub-paragraph (7) for "paragraph 3" substitute "paragraphs 3 and 4A".

4 In paragraph 3 of Schedule 7 (withdrawal of group relief)—

(*a*) for sub-paragraph (2) substitute—

"(2) The amount chargeable is the tax that would have been chargeable in respect of the relevant transaction but for group relief if the chargeable consideration for that transaction had been an amount equal to—

(*a*) the market value of the subject-matter of the transaction, and

(*b*) if the acquisition was the grant of a lease at a rent, that rent,

or, as the case may be, an appropriate proportion of the tax that would have been so chargeable.", and

(*b*) at the end of sub-paragraph (5) insert "and paragraph 4A (withdrawal of group relief in certain cases involving successive transactions)".

5 In paragraph 4 of Schedule 7 (cases in which group relief is not withdrawn)—

(*a*) in sub-paragraph (3), for paragraph (*b*) substitute—

"(*b*) another company that—

(i) is above the vendor in the group structure, and

(ii) as a result of the transaction ceases to be a member of the same group as the purchaser.", and

(*b*) in sub-paragraph (5), for "this purpose" substitute "the purposes of sub-paragraphs (3) and (4)".

6 After paragraph 4 of Schedule 7 insert—

"Withdrawal of group relief in certain cases involving successive transactions

4A— (1) Where, in the case of a transaction ("the relevant transaction") that is exempt from charge by virtue of paragraph 1 (group relief)—

(*a*) there is a change in the control of the purchaser,

(*b*) that change occurs—

(i) before the end of the period of three years beginning with the effective date of the relevant transaction, or

(ii) in pursuance of, or in connection with, arrangements made before the end of that period,

(*c*) apart from this paragraph, group relief in relation to the relevant transaction would not be withdrawn under paragraph 3, and

(*d*) any previous transaction falls within sub-paragraph (2),

paragraphs 3 and 4 have effect in relation to the relevant transaction as if the vendor in relation to the earliest previous transaction falling within sub-paragraph (2) were the vendor in relation to the relevant transaction.

(2) A previous transaction falls within this sub-paragraph if—

(*a*) the previous transaction is exempt from charge by virtue of paragraph 1, 7 or 8,

(*b*) the effective date of the previous transaction is less than three years before the date of the event falling within sub-paragraph (1)(*a*),

(*c*) the chargeable interest acquired under the relevant transaction by the purchaser in relation to that transaction is the same as, comprises, forms part of, or is derived from, the chargeable interest acquired under the previous transaction by the purchaser in relation to the previous transaction, and

(*d*) since the previous transaction, the chargeable interest acquired under that transaction has not been acquired by any person under a transaction that is not exempt from charge by virtue of paragraph 1, 7 or 8.

(3) For the purposes of sub-paragraph (1)(*a*) there is a change in the control of a company if—

(*a*) any person who controls the company (alone or with others) ceases to do so,

(*b*) a person obtains control of the company (alone or with others), or

(*c*) the company is wound up.

References to "control" in this sub-paragraph shall be construed in accordance with section 416 of the Taxes Act 1988.

(4) If two or more transactions effected at the same time are the earliest previous transactions falling within sub-paragraph (2), the reference in sub-paragraph (1) to the vendor in relation to the earliest previous transaction is a reference to the persons who are the vendors in relation to the earliest previous transactions.

(5) In this paragraph "arrangements" includes any scheme, agreement or understanding, whether or not legally enforceable."

7 In Schedule 17A (further provisions relating to leases) in paragraph 11(5)(*a*) for the words from "the purchaser" to the end substitute "the event falling within paragraph 3(1)(*a*) of Schedule 7 (purchaser ceasing to be a member of the same group as the vendor), as read with paragraph 4A of that Schedule".

Reconstruction and acquisition reliefs

8 In paragraph 8 of Schedule 7 (acquisition relief)—

(*a*) in sub-paragraph (1)(*b*) for "the first and second conditions" substitute "all the conditions", and

(*b*) after sub-paragraph (5) insert—

"(5A) The third condition is that the undertaking or part acquired by the acquiring company has as its main activity the carrying on of a trade that does not consist wholly or mainly of dealing in chargeable interests.

In this sub-paragraph "trade" has the same meaning as in the Taxes Act 1988."

9 In paragraph 9 of Schedule 7 (withdrawal of reconstruction or acquisition relief) for sub-paragraph (2) substitute—

"(2) The amount chargeable is the tax that would have been chargeable in respect of the relevant transaction but for reconstruction or acquisition relief if the chargeable consideration for that transaction had been an amount equal to—

(a) the market value of the subject-matter of the transaction, and

(b) if the acquisition was the grant of a lease at a rent, that rent,

or, as the case may be, an appropriate proportion of the tax that would have been so chargeable."

Withdrawal of money etc from partnership after transfer of chargeable interest

10 In Schedule 15 (partnerships) after paragraph 17 insert—

"Withdrawal of money etc from partnership after transfer of chargeable interest

17A— (1) This paragraph applies where—

(a) there is a transfer of a chargeable interest to a partnership ("the land transfer");

(b) the land transfer falls within paragraph (a), (b) or (c) of paragraph 10(1);

(c) during the period of three years beginning with the date of the land transfer, a qualifying event occurs.

(2) A qualifying event is—

(a) a withdrawal from the partnership of money or money's worth which does not represent income profit by the relevant person—

(i) withdrawing capital from his capital account,

(ii) reducing his interest, or

(iii) ceasing to be a partner, or

(b) in a case where the relevant person has made a loan to the partnership—

(i) the repayment (to any extent) by the partnership of the loan, or

(ii) a withdrawal by the relevant person from the partnership of money or money's worth which does not represent income profit.

(3) For this purpose the relevant person is—

(a) where the land transfer falls within paragraph 10(1)(a) or (b), the person who makes the land transfer, and

(b) where the land transfer falls within paragraph 10(1)(c), the partner concerned or a person connected with him.

(4) The qualifying event—

(a) shall be taken to be a land transaction, and

(b) is a chargeable transaction.

(5) The partners shall be taken to be the purchasers under the transaction.

(6) Paragraphs 6 to 8 (responsibility of partners) have effect in relation to the transaction.

(7) The chargeable consideration for the transaction shall be taken to be—

(a) in a case falling within sub-paragraph (2)(a), equal to the value of the money or money's worth withdrawn from the partnership, or

(b) in a case falling within sub-paragraph (2)(b)(i), equal to the amount repaid, and

(c) in a case falling within sub-paragraph (2)(b)(ii), equal to so much of the value of the money or money's worth withdrawn from the partnership as does not exceed the amount of the loan,

but (in any case) shall not exceed the market value, as at the effective date of the land transfer, of the chargeable interest transferred by the land transfer, reduced by any amount previously chargeable to tax."

Grant of lease to bare trustee

11 For paragraph 3 of Schedule 16 substitute—

"Bare trustee

3— (1) Subject to sub-paragraph (2), where a person acquires a chargeable interest as bare trustee, this Part applies as if the interest were vested in, and the acts of the trustee in relation to it were the acts of, the person or persons for whom he is trustee.

(2) Sub-paragraph (1) does not apply in relation to the grant of a lease.

(3) Where a lease is granted to a person as bare trustee, he is treated for the purposes of this Part, as it applies in relation to the grant of the lease, as purchaser of the whole of the interest acquired.

(4) Where a lease is granted by a person as bare trustee, he is to be treated for the purposes of this Part, as it applies in relation to the grant of the lease, as vendor of the whole of the interest disposed of."

12 In paragraph 11 of Schedule 17A (cases where assignment of lease treated as grant of lease), for sub-paragraph (1) substitute—

"(1) This paragraph applies where the grant of a lease is exempt from charge by virtue of any of the provisions specified in sub-paragraph (3)."

Variation of lease

13 In paragraph 15A of Schedule 17A (leases: reduction of rent or term)—

(*a*) after sub-paragraph (1) insert—

"(1A) Where any consideration in money or money's worth (other than an increase in rent) is given by the lessee for any variation of a lease, other than a variation of the amount of the rent or of the term of the lease, the variation is treated for the purposes of this Part as an acquisition of a chargeable interest by the lessee.", and

(*b*) for the heading preceding that paragraph substitute "Reduction of rent or term or other variation of lease".

Loan or deposit in connection with grant or assignment of lease

14 After paragraph 18 of Schedule 17A insert—

"Loan or deposit in connection with grant or assignment of lease

18A— (1) Where, under arrangements made in connection with the grant of a lease—

(*a*) the lessee, or any person connected with him or acting on his behalf, pays a deposit, or makes a loan, to any person, and

(*b*) the repayment of all or part of the deposit or loan is contingent on anything done or omitted to be done by the lessee or on the death of the lessee,

the amount of the deposit or loan (disregarding any repayment) is to be taken for the purposes of this Part to be consideration other than rent given for the grant of the lease.

(2) Where, under arrangements made in connection with the assignment of a lease—

(*a*) the assignee, or any person connected with him or acting on his behalf, pays a deposit, or makes a loan, to any person, and

(*b*) the repayment of all or part of the deposit or loan is contingent on anything done or omitted to be done by the assignee or on the death of the assignee,

the amount of the deposit or loan (disregarding any repayment) is to be taken for the purposes of this Part to be consideration other than rent given for the assignment of the lease.

(3) Sub-paragraph (1) or (2) does not apply in relation to a deposit if the amount that would otherwise fall within the sub-paragraph in question in relation to the grant or (as the case requires) assignment of the lease is not more than twice the relevant maximum rent.

(4) The relevant maximum rent is—

(*a*) in relation to the grant of a lease, the highest amount of rent payable in respect of any consecutive twelve month period in the first five years of the term;

(*b*) in relation to the assignment of a lease, the highest amount of rent payable in respect of any consecutive twelve month period in the first five years of the term remaining outstanding as at the date of the assignment,

the highest amount of rent being determined (in either case) in the same way as the highest amount of rent mentioned in paragraph 7(3).

(5) Tax is not chargeable by virtue of this paragraph—

(*a*) merely because of paragraph 9(2) of Schedule 5 (which excludes the 0% band in the Tables in section 55(2) in cases where the relevant rental figure exceeds £600 a year), or

(*b*) merely because of paragraph 5(4)(*b*), 6(6)(*b*), 9(4)(*b*) or 10(6)(*b*) of Schedule 6 (which make similar provision in relation to land which is wholly or partly residential property and is wholly or partly situated in a disadvantaged area).

(6) Section 839 of the Taxes Act 1988 (connected persons) has effect for the purposes of this paragraph."

15 In section 80 (adjustment where contingency ceases or consideration is ascertained) after subsection (4) insert—

"(4A) Where the transaction ("the relevant transaction") is the grant or assignment of a lease, no claim may be made under subsection (4)—

(*a*) in respect of the repayment (in whole or part) of any loan or deposit that is treated by paragraph 18A of Schedule 17A as being consideration given for the relevant transaction, or

(*b*) in respect of the refund of any of the consideration given for the relevant transaction, in a case where the refund—

(i) is made under arrangements that were made in connection with the relevant transaction, and

(ii) is contingent on the determination or assignment of the lease or on the grant of a chargeable interest out of the lease."

Commencement

16— (1) Subject to sub-paragraph (7), paragraphs 3 to 7 have effect where the effective date of the relevant transaction (within the meaning of paragraph 3 or 4A of Schedule 7 to FA 2003) is after 19th May 2005.

(2) Subject to sub-paragraph (7), paragraph 9 has effect where the effective date of the relevant transaction (within the meaning of paragraph 9 of Schedule 7 to FA 2003) is after 19th May 2005.

(3) Subject to sub-paragraph (7), paragraph 10 has effect where the effective date of the transaction transferring the chargeable interest to the partnership is after 19th May 2005.

(4) Subject to sub-paragraph (7), paragraphs 11 and 12 have effect where the effective date of the land transaction consisting of the grant of the lease is after 19th May 2005.

(5) Subject to sub-paragraph (7), the amendments made by the other provisions of this Part of this Schedule have effect in relation to any transaction of which the effective date is after 19th May 2005.

(6) In sub-paragraphs (7) and (8) "the specified date" means—

(*a*) in relation to the amendments made by paragraphs 4(*a*) and 9, 19th May 2005, and

(*b*) in relation to the amendments made by the other provisions of this Part of this Schedule, 16th March 2005.

(7) The amendments made by this Part of this Schedule do not have effect—

(*a*) in relation to any transaction which is effected in pursuance of a contract entered into and substantially performed on or before the specified date, or

(*b*) subject to sub-paragraph (8), in relation to any other transaction which is effected in pursuance of a contract entered into on or before the specified date.

(8) The exclusion by sub-paragraph (7)(*b*) of transactions effected in pursuance of contracts entered into on or before the specified date does not apply—

(*a*) if there is any variation of the contract or assignment of rights under the contract after that date,

(*b*) if the transaction is effected in consequence of the exercise after that date of any option, right of pre-emption or similar right, or

(*c*) if after that date there is an assignment, subsale or other transaction (relating to the whole or part of the subject-matter of the contract) as a result of which a person other than the purchaser under the contract becomes entitled to call for a conveyance to him.

(9) In this paragraph "assignment", "effective date" and "substantially performed" have the same meaning as in Part 4 of FA 2003.

PART 2

AMENDMENTS COMING INTO FORCE IN ACCORDANCE WITH

PARAGRAPH 22

Introduction

17 Part 4 of FA 2003 (stamp duty land tax) is amended in accordance with this Part of this Schedule.

Transfers involving public bodies

18 In section 66 of FA 2003 (transfers involving public bodies) after subsection (5) insert—

"(6) In this section "company" means a company as defined by section 735(1) of the Companies Act 1985 or Article 3(1) of the Companies (Northern Ireland) Order 1986."

Group relief: avoidance arrangements

19 In paragraph 2 of Schedule 7 (restrictions on availability of group relief) after sub-paragraph (4) insert—

"(4A) Group relief is not available if the transaction—

(*a*) is not effected for bona fide commercial reasons, or

(*b*) forms part of arrangements of which the main purpose, or one of the main purposes, is the avoidance of liability to tax.

"Tax" here means stamp duty, income tax, corporation tax, capital gains tax or tax under this Part."

Acquisition relief: avoidance arrangements

20 In paragraph 8 of Schedule 7 (acquisition relief)—

(*a*) for sub-paragraph (5) substitute—

"(5) For this purpose companies are associated if one has control of the other or both are controlled by the same person or persons.

The reference to control shall be construed in accordance with section 416 of the Taxes Act 1988.", and

(*b*) after sub-paragraph (5A) (inserted by paragraph 8 of this Schedule) insert—

"(5B) The fourth condition is that the acquisition is effected for bona fide commercial reasons and does not form part of arrangements of which the main purpose, or one of the main purposes, is the avoidance of liability to tax.

"Tax" here means stamp duty, income tax, corporation tax, capital gains tax or tax under this Part."

(5C) In this paragraph "arrangements" include any scheme, agreement or understanding, whether or not legally enforceable."

Stamp duty on transfers of partnership interests

21— (1) In Schedule 15 (stamp duty land tax: partnerships), paragraph 33 (which relates to stamp duty on transfers of partnership interests) is amended as follows.

(2) For sub-paragraphs (1) and (2) substitute—

"(1) This paragraph applies where stamp duty under Part 1 of Schedule 13 to the Finance Act 1999 (transfer on sale) is, apart from this paragraph, chargeable on an instrument effecting a transfer of an interest in a partnership.

(1A) If the relevant partnership property does not include any stock or marketable securities, no stamp duty shall (subject to sub-paragraph (8)) be chargeable on the instrument."

(3) In sub-paragraph (3)—

(*a*) at the beginning insert "If the relevant partnership property includes stock or marketable securities,",

(*b*) in paragraph (*a*), for the words from "the stock" to "property" substitute "that stock and those securities", and

(*c*) for paragraph (*b*) substitute—

"(*b*) the consideration for the transfer were equal to the appropriate proportion of the net market value of that stock and those securities immediately after the transfer."

(4) After sub-paragraph (3) insert—

"(3A) The "relevant partnership property", in relation to a transfer of an interest in a partnership, is the partnership property immediately after the transfer, other than any partnership property that was transferred to the partnership in connection with the transfer."

(5) Omit sub-paragraph (4).

(6) In sub-paragraph (5), for "That" substitute "The appropriate".

Commencement

22— (1) Subject to sub-paragraph (2), paragraphs 18 to 20 have effect in relation to any transaction of which the effective date is on or after the day on which this Act is passed.

(2) Paragraphs 19 and 20 do not have effect—

(*a*) in relation to any transaction which is effected in pursuance of a contract entered into and substantially performed on or before 16th March 2005, or

(*b*) (subject to sub-paragraph (3)) in relation to any other transaction which is effected in pursuance of a contract entered into on or before that date.

(3) The exclusion by sub-paragraph (2)(*b*) of transactions effected in pursuance of contracts entered into on or before 16th March 2005 does not apply—

(*a*) if there is any variation of the contract or assignment of rights under the contract after that date,

(*b*) if the transaction is effected in consequence of the exercise after that date of any option, right of pre-emption or similar right, or

(*c*) if after that date there is an assignment, subsale or other transaction (relating to the whole or part of the subject-matter of the contract) as a result of which a person other than the purchaser under the contract becomes entitled to call for a conveyance to him.

(4) Paragraph 21 has effect in relation to any instrument executed on or after the day on which this Act is passed.

(5) In this paragraph "assignment", "effective date" and "substantially performed" have the same meaning as in Part 4 of FA 2003.

SCHEDULE 11

REPEALS

Section 70

PART 1

VALUE ADDED TAX

DISCLOSURE OF AVOIDANCE SCHEMES

Short title and chapter	Extent of repeal
Value Added Tax Act 1994 (c. 23)	In Schedule 11A— (*a*) in paragraph 6(1), the word "or" at the end of paragraph (*a*), and (*b*) in paragraph 11(3), the word "and" at the end of paragraph (*a*).

These repeals come into force in accordance with an order under section 6(2) of this Act.

PART 2

INCOME TAX, CORPORATION TAX AND CAPITAL GAINS TAX

(*1*) *Employee Securities: Anti-avoidance*

Short title and chapter	Extent of repeal
Income Tax (Earnings and Pensions) Act 2003 (c. 1)	Section 420(5)(*d*). In section 424(1), paragraph (*c*) and the word "or" before it.
Finance Act 2004 (c. 12)	Section 86(4).

These repeals have effect in accordance with Schedule 2 to this Act.

(*2*) *Scientific Research Organisations*

Short title and chapter	Extent of repeal
Income Tax (Trading and Other Income) Act 2005 (c. 5)	Section 88(4)(*a*). In Schedule 1, paragraph 55(*b*).

[1] The repeal of section 88(4)(*a*) of ITTOIA 2005 has effect in accordance with section 14 of this Act.

[2] The repeal of paragraph 55(*b*) of Schedule 1 to that Act has effect in accordance with section 15 of this Act.

(*3*) *Unit Trusts and Open-ended Investment Companies*

Short title and chapter	Extent of repeal
Income and Corporation Taxes Act 1988 (c. 1)	Section 349B(4)(*b*).
	Sections 468H to 468Q.
Finance Act 1996 (c. 8)	Paragraphs 2A and 2B of Schedule 10.
Finance Act 2002 (c. 23)	Paragraphs 32 and 33 of Schedule 26.
Income Tax (Trading and Other Income) Act 2005 (c. 5)	Section 373(4) and (6). Section 376(4) and (6). Paragraph 151(2) of Schedule 1. Paragraph 350(2) and (3) of Schedule 1.

[1] The repeal of paragraph 350(2) and (3) of Schedule 1 to ITTOIA 2005 comes into force on the day on which this Act is passed.

[2] The other repeals have effect in accordance with section 19(1) of this Act.

(*4*) *Chargeable Gains: Temporary Non-residents*

Short title and chapter	Extent of repeal
Taxation of Chargeable Gains Act 1992 (c. 12)	Section 10A(10).

This repeal has effect in accordance with section 32(7) of this Act.

(*5*) *Chargeable Gains: Options*

Short title and chapter	Extent of repeal
Finance Act 1996 (c. 8)	Section 111(2) and (5).

These repeals have effect in accordance with paragraph 6(2) of Schedule 5 to this Act.

(*6*) *Accounting Practice*

Short title and chapter	Extent of repeal
Finance Act 1996 (c. 8)	Section 84A. Section 85B(6). In Schedule 9— (*a*) in paragraph 11A(4)(*c*), the words ", or would apart from section 84A(2) to (10) of this Act,"; (*b*) paragraph 19(12).
Finance Act 2002 (c. 23)	In Schedule 23, paragraphs 3 and 26(5). In Schedule 26— (*a*) paragraph 16; (*b*) in paragraph 23(9), the words from "which by virtue" to the end.
Finance Act 2004 (c. 12)	In Schedule 10, paragraphs 2 and 48.
Finance Act 2005 (c. 7)	In Schedule 4, paragraphs 6, 10, 28(3) and (4) and 29.

[1] The repeal of paragraph 6 of Schedule 4 to FA 2005 has effect in accordance with paragraph 4(6) of Schedule 6 to this Act.

[2] The repeal of paragraph 10 of Schedule 4 to FA 2005 has effect in accordance with paragraph 5(2) of Schedule 6 to this Act.

[3] The repeals in FA 1996, FA 2002 and FA 2004 have effect in accordance with paragraph 9(2) and (3) of Schedule 6 to this Act.

(*7*) *Charges On Income for Corporation Tax*

Short title and chapter	Extent of repeal

Income and Corporation Taxes Act 1988 (c. 1)	In section 125(1), the words "and shall not be a charge on income for the purposes of corporation tax".
	Section 338A(2)(*a*) and (4).
	Section 338B.
	In section 402(6)(*b*), the words "or a charge on income".
	Section 434A(2)(*a*)(i).
	In section 487(3), the words "or be treated for those purposes as a charge on income".
	In section 494—
	(*a*) in subsection (1), the words "Section 338 of this Act and";
	(*b*) subsection (3).
	In section 494A—
	(*a*) in subsection (2), paragraph (*b*) and the word "or" before it;
	(*b*) in subsection (3), paragraph (*b*) and the word "and" before it.
	In Schedule 28AA—
	(*a*) in paragraph 7A(2)(*b*), the words "or charges on income";
	(*b*) in paragraph 7C(2)(*b*), the words "or charges on income".
Finance Act 1989 (c. 26)	In section 102(7)(*b*), the words "or a charge on income".
Taxation of Chargeable Gains Act 1992 (c. 12)	In section 171A(5)(*b*), the words "or a charge on income".
	In section 179A(11)(*b*), the words "or a charge on income".
Finance Act 2002 (c. 23)	In Schedule 29, in paragraph 71(4)(*b*), the words "or a charge on income".

These repeals have effect in accordance with section 38 of this Act.

(8) Avoidance Involving Financial Arrangements

Short title and chapter	*Extent of repeal*
Income and Corporation Taxes Act 1988 (c. 1)	In section 18, paragraph (*c*) of the Case III of Schedule D substituted by subsection (3A).
	Section 43C(1).
	Section 43E(1)(*a*) and (*b*).
	In section 730—
	(*a*) subsection (1)(*c*);
	(*b*) subsection (2A);
	(*c*) in subsection (8), the words from "and for the purpose" onwards.
Finance Act 1996 (c. 8)	In section 97—
	(*a*) in subsection (2), paragraph (*b*) and the word "but" before it, and
	(*b*) subsections (3) and (3A).
	Section 100(4) to (6), (8) and (13).
	In Schedule 9—
	(*a*) in paragraph 1A(1), paragraph (*b*) and the word "or" before it;
	(*b*) paragraph 11(5);
	(*c*) in paragraph 15(4A), paragraph (*b*) and the word "and" before it.
Finance Act 2000 (c. 17)	In Schedule 29, paragraph 44(3).
Finance Act 2002 (c. 23)	In Schedule 25, paragraphs 13(4) and 51.

Income Tax (Trading and Other Income) Act 2005 (c. 5)	In section 430(6), the word "and" before the entry relating to section 443(1). In Schedule 1, paragraph 300(5).

These repeals have effect in accordance with Schedule 7 to this Act.

(9) *Loan Relationships*

Short title and chapter	Extent of repeal
Finance Act 1996 (c. 8)	In Schedule 9— (a) in paragraph 2(1B), the words ", but not a CIS-based close company,", the word "or" preceding paragraph (c) and the words after paragraph (c); (b) in paragraph 18(1), paragraph (aa), and paragraph (c) and the word "and" preceding it; (c) in paragraph 18(4), the word "and" preceding the definition of "participator".
Finance Act 2002 (c. 23)	In Schedule 25, paragraph 34(4).
Finance Act 2004 (c. 12)	In Schedule 8, paragraphs 2(2) and 6(2) and (3).

These repeals have effect in accordance with paragraph 4 of Schedule 8 to this Act.

(10) *Insurance Companies etc*

Short title and chapter	Extent of repeal
Income and Corporation Taxes Act 1988 (c. 1)	In section 76(8), in the second sentence, the word "or" at the end of paragraph (a). In section 431(2), the definition of "long-term liabilities".
Finance Act 1989 (c. 26)	Section 82C(4), (5), (8) and (9). In section 83A(2), the words from "Paragraph (b) above" to the end of the subsection. In section 88(3A), the word "and" at the end of paragraph (a).
Finance Act 1990 (c. 29)	In Schedule 6— (a) in paragraph 1(2)(b), the definitions of "liabilities" and "value"; (b) paragraph 2.

[1] The repeals in ICTA have effect in relation to periods of account ending on or after 31st December 2004.

[2] The repeals in section 82C of FA 1989 have effect in accordance with paragraph 11(4) of Schedule 9 to this Act.

[3] The repeal in section 83A of FA 1989 has effect in accordance with paragraph 13(6) of Schedule 9 to this Act.

[4] The repeal in section 88 of FA 1989 has effect in accordance with paragraph 16(3) of Schedule 9 to this Act.

[5] The repeals in paragraph 1(2)(b) of Schedule 6 to FA 1990 have effect in accordance with paragraph 2(6) of Schedule 9 to this Act.

[6] The repeal of paragraph 2 of Schedule 6 to FA 1990 comes into force on the day on which this Act is passed.

(11) *Lloyd's Names*

Short title and chapter	Extent of repeal
Finance Act 1993 (c. 34)	Section 173. In section 182(1)(a), "(so far as not provided for by Schedule 19 to this Act)". Schedule 19.

Finance Act 1994 (c. 9)	Section 221.
	In section 229(1)(*a*), "(so far as not provided for by Schedule 19 to the 1993 Act as applied by section 221 above)".
	In Schedule 21, paragraphs 9 and 10.
Finance Act 2001 (c. 9)	In Schedule 29, paragraph 36.

These repeals have effect in accordance with section 45(8) and (9) of this Act.

(*12*) *Energy Act 2004 and Health Protection Agency Act 2004*

Short title and chapter	*Extent of repeal*
Income and Corporation Taxes Act 1988 (c. 1)	Section 349B(3)(*g*) and (*h*).
	Section 512.
Taxation of Chargeable Gains Act 1992 (c. 12)	In section 271(7)—
	(*a*) the words ", the United Kingdom Atomic Energy Authority";
	(*b*) the words "and the National Radiological Protection Board";
	(*c*) the words from "; and for the purposes" to the end of the subsection.
Income Tax (Trading and Other Income) Act 2005 (c. 5)	In Schedule 1, paragraph 199.

These repeals have effect in accordance with section 46 of this Act.

PART 3
STAMP TAXES

(*1*) *Stamp Duty Land Tax: Miscellaneous*

Short title and chapter	*Extent of repeal*
Finance Act 2003 (c. 14)	In Schedule 15, paragraph 33(4).

This repeal has effect in relation to any instrument executed on or after the day on which this Act is passed.

(*2*) *Stamp Duty and Stamp Duty Reserve Tax: Extension of Exceptions*

Short title and chapter	*Extent of repeal*
Finance Act 2002 (c. 23)	Section 117.

This repeal has effect in accordance with section 50 of this Act.

PART 4
EUROPEAN COMPANY STATUTE

Short title and chapter	*Extent of repeal*
Taxation of Chargeable Gains Act 1992 (c. 12)	In section 140A(7) the definition of "securities".
	In section 140C(9) the definition of "securities".

These repeals have effect in accordance with section 59(7) of this Act.

PART 5

MISCELLANEOUS MATTERS

(1) Vehicle Excise Duty

Short title and chapter	Extent of repeal
Vehicle Excise and Registration Act 1994 (c. 22)	Section 7A(4)(*a*).

This repeal comes into force on the day on which this Act is passed.

(2) Abolition of Adjudicator for National Savings and Investments

Short title and chapter	Extent of repeal
National Savings Bank Act 1971 (c. 29)	Sections 10 and 11. In section 27, the definition of "the adjudicator".
National Debt Act 1972 (c. 65)	Section 5.
Friendly Societies Act 1992 (c. 40)	Section 84. In Schedule 21, paragraphs 2 to 4.
Tribunals and Inquiries Act 1992 (c. 53)	In Schedule 1, in the first column, the entry relating to National Savings Bank and National Savings Stock Register, and, in the second column, paragraph 33B.

These repeals have effect in accordance with section 69 of this Act.

FINANCE BILL DEBATES

6 July 2005	Report Stage (Cl 18)
30 June	Standing Committee B (Cl 54, Schs 9, 10)
28 June	Standing Committee B (Cll 28, 31, 32, 33, 35, Schs 4, 5, 6, 7)
23 June	Standing Committee B (Cll 24, 25, 26, 28, Sch 3)
21 June	Standing Committee B (Cll 1, 2, 3, 6, 7, 12)
13 June	Committee Stage (Cl 11, Sch 8)
7 June	Second Reading

Tuesday 7 June 2005—Second Reading

(Col 1137)

The Paymaster-General (**Dawn Primarolo**): ... To counter a number of stamp duty land tax avoidance schemes, clause 49 and schedule 10 will close known loopholes: for instance, limiting artificial group relationships which have been set up purely to avoid clawback of group relief. The definition of "undertaking" will also be restricted in relation to acquisition relief to trades other than property trading, so that only genuine businesses can benefit. The clause that I have just mentioned has been subject to some amendment, which I want to draw to the House's attention, as compared with the legislation originally presented to the House in the first Finance Bill back in March. We have listened, and amendments have been made to ensure that stamp duty land tax measures work as intended for home reversion plans, loans or deposit schemes and to ensure that group relief clawback cannot be avoided by the use of leases. There are a small number of other amendments to clauses in the Bill, which include ensuring that legislation introduced by clause 39 and schedule 7 does not affect routine arrangements concerning preference shares—another matter on which we received representations. They will ensure that other common corporate structures not set up for the purpose of avoidance are not affected. We have also extended the period of transitional protection to some companies allowed by clauses 24 to 31 and schedule 3, and we have time-limited the regulation-making power to amend a number of life assurance company tax provisions granted by clause 42 and schedule 9.

Clause 11 – Gift Aid: donations to charity by individuals

(Col 47)

The Economic Secretary (Ivan Lewis): ... The list of types of property in clause 11 is not exhaustive. Where charities meet the other conditions of the clause, they will be able to use gift aid. I can confirm that the list, in terms of guidelines, will specifically include interactive experiments with an educational purpose. ... Military memorabilia would also be included in the list.

Schedule 8 – Financing of companies ets: transfer pricing and loan relationships

(Col 77)

The Financial Secretary (**John Healey**): ... companies and their investors were being advised by some professional advisers to put in place financing and ownership structures specifically designed to get around the rules so as to achieve an unfair tax advantage. The schedule anticipates such problems on a wider scale and seeks to close the loophole. It will ensure that the transfer pricing rules also apply if two or more parties who together control a business act together in relation to its financing arrangements. In addition, transfer pricing rules are extended to cover financing arrangements put in place after six months before a control relationship between the parties involved. The schedule also tightens loan relationships that regulate deductions for late paid interest and discounts owed to connected parties.

(Col 94)

The Financial Secretary: ... When compensating adjustments were introduced in the Finance Act 2004, their purpose was to ensure that if transactions between members of a group of companies were affected by transfer pricing rules, the position in the group could be balanced out. The compensating adjustments are intended for enterprises such as groups that must apply transfer pricing to different parts of the enterprise. We deliberately limited the scope of the adjustments in 2004 so that they could not be used by third-party lenders. If a company is denied a tax deduction for interest on a guaranteed third-party loan under existing transfer pricing rules, the third party is thus not allowed to claim a compensating adjustment. The restriction on compensating adjustments in the schedule ensures that that policy is maintained under the new rules. If, for example, an independent lender was able to claim a compensating adjustment, the effect would be to enable the lender to receive interest tax-free. A lender should expect to pay tax on the interest received on a loan, whatever the tax treatment of the borrower, so it would be wrong for a lender to receive such a tax benefit.

(Col 100)

The Financial Secretary: ... a business controlled by a private equity limited partnership will be treated in the same way as a business controlled by a company or by an individual, and the SME exemption will operate in exactly the same way as it does under existing transfer pricing rules, using a standard European definition to determine whether a company qualifies as a small enterprise or as a medium-sized enterprise. ... The hon. Member for Cities of London and Westminster also asked what happens when debtors are no longer small or medium-sized enterprises. In that case, such enterprises lose their exemption from late-paid interest or discount rules. The exemption exists to encourage funding in SMEs, which are the businesses that are most likely to grow and to create jobs. The Government put a great deal of policy attention and support behind those businesses, often with the support of the Opposition. When such businesses are no longer SMEs, however, it is difficult to justify the continuation of that protection at the taxpayer's expense.

Clause 1 – Goods subject to warehousing regime: place of acquisition or supply

(Col 6)

The Paymaster-General (Dawn Primarolo): The VAT-free trading of goods within a customs warehouse is a valuable trade facilitation measure that is enjoyed by hundreds of UK businesses. Unfortunately, it has been subject to an abuse by a small number of traders. Therefore, new section 18(1A) of the Value Added Tax Act 1994 will provide Her Majesty's Revenue and Customs with the power to specify circumstances in which the relief from VAT afforded to transactions in a customs warehouse will not apply.

Clause 2 – Cars: determination of consideration for fuel supplied for private use

(Col 7)

The Financial Secretary (John Healey): Clause 2 is modest and straightforward. It is designed to provide the flexibility for the VAT fuel scale charge system to be amended to include a charge based on a vehicle's carbon dioxide emissions. ... The current charge is based on a combination of engine size and type of fuel. Clause 2 gives the flexibility to reform the charge to one based on CO2 emissions, which would align the VAT fuel scale charge with the Government's other reforms to transport taxation in order to support our environmental objectives on climate change and air quality and to encourage a switch to less polluting cars through tax incentives and other measures.

Clause 3 – Credit for, or repayment of, overstated or overpaid VAT

(Col 10)

The Paymaster-General: The clause provides for the extension of the defence of unjust enrichment by the Revenue and Customs to all claims for VAT credit where the tax has been overcharged and over-accounted for in error. Under the existing law, the defence is available only where claims are made for repayment of VAT that was overpaid but was not due. Inevitably, the time limit for such claims begins to run from the date the tax is overpaid, whereas the time limit for correcting errors for the Revenue and Customs to assess in respect of under-declared VAT runs from the end of the prescribed accounting period in which the error occurred.

Clause 6 – Disclosure of value added tax avoidance schemes

(Col 13)

The Paymaster-General: ... Clause 6 and schedule 1 provide for two additional disclosure rules, which follow on from the introduction of the disclosure rules in the Finance Act 2004. ...

(Col 14)

... The first change is to extend the definition of tax advantage to include circumstances in which the scheme is intended to reduce irrecoverable VAT—and a number of avoidance schemes are intended to do that. Those schemes are artificial and provide the business concerned with an unfair competitive advantage over compliant taxpayers. The disclosure rules identify where legislation or changes are particularly required. The second change in clause 6 and schedule 1 is a simplification measure. It provides that a business will not have to disclose a listed scheme if it had previously notified the authorities of the use of the scheme as a hallmark scheme.

Clause 7 – Charge to income tax on lump sum

(Col 25)

The Economic Secretary (Ivan Lewis): ... I am happy to confirm that the rate of tax applied to the lump sum, commonly known as the marginal rate, is the one that applies to total income less all statutory deductions and personal allowances that can be deducted.

Clause 12 – Employee securities: anti-avoidance

(Col 39)

The Paymaster-General: ... A change being made to chapter 4 of the Income Tax (Earnings and Pensions) Act 2003 will remove, where avoidance is involved, the provision that automatically exempts benefits received in connection with securities from a full income tax and national insurance charge, if income tax has been paid elsewhere. I am aware, from representations made directly to me and my Department, that professionals have expressed concern about the possible scope of the change. I want to make it clear that this change does not bring all benefits derived from securities into a tax and national insurance charge. A reference to benefits in the context of the schedule means the employment reward—the passing of value to an employee in return for the employee's labour. Where investors are carrying out their normal investment transaction, this charge will not affect them.

The purpose test introduced in section 447 of the 2003 Act has been carefully designed to target complex, contrived avoidance arrangements that are used mainly to disguise cash bonuses. If taxpayers use contrived arrangements to get round anti-avoidance legislation—to avoid paying the proper amount of tax and national insurance—they cannot expect to be excluded from the charge. However, it will be absolutely clear from what I say about the purpose test that this measure will not affect the taxation of those small businesses that do not use contrived schemes to disguise remuneration to avoid tax and national insurance. ...

(Col 42)

The Paymaster-General: ... Unless a scheme falls within the category of schemes contrived specifically to avoid income tax and national insurance on employment remuneration for an employee, it is not within the scope of clause 12 or schedule 2.

Clause 24 – Arbitrage: deduction cases

(Col 103)

The Paymaster-General: The issue of the notice to the company only requires the company to take the legislation into consideration. If the company receiving the notice believes that HMRC was wrong and that the conditions are not met, it will make a self-assessment on the basis that the arbitrage legislation does not apply. If HMRC agrees, that will be the end of the matter. If HMRC does not agree and the matter ...

(Col 104)

... cannot be resolved by discussion and agreement, it can proceed to the special commissioners for a decision. ...

(Col 123)

The Paymaster-General: ... The hon. Gentleman raised the question of double relief. Rule A addresses a deduction that has been, or may be, deducted. It will prevent the double dips that sit in different time periods, which is what it is designed to achieve. The hon. Gentleman also asked about commercial purpose. The application of the legislation does not depend on whether there is a commercial purpose. It depends on whether there is a main purpose of achieving a UK tax advantage.

Schedule 3 – Qualifying scheme

(Col 129)

Mr. Philip Hammond: In paragraph 3(1), an entity is defined as hybrid if, "under the tax law of any territory, the entity is regarded as being a person".

It has been suggested to me that that is clearly intended to mean" under the tax law of any relevant or pertinent territory" ...

The Paymaster-General: My answer to the hon. Gentleman's first concern is yes, it means any relevant territory. On his second point—that I should reflect on whether that needs to be spelt out in greater detail—I should say that it has not been raised with us as a problem of interpretation. It seems clear from the presentations, the open day and the submissions received by the Department, that the paragraph is understood to mean" relevant" territory.

Clause 25 – Rules relating to deductions

(Col 131)

The Paymaster-General: Clause 25 sets out how the legislation restricts the amount of deductions allowable for corporation tax purposes with deduction rules, where all the conditions in clause 24 are met. The clause contains two rules that can reduce or deny deductions. The first of those—rule A—applies if two deductions are available for the same expense, and limits the amount of the deduction for corporation tax to an amount that is not allowed or deducted elsewhere. Rule A also applies where there would be double deduction but for the fact that another country has similar legislation. As drafted, the rule makes no identification as to the person to whom the deduction rules arise. However, the context of rule A could be construed as requiring that both the deductions must arise in the same country. That is clearly not how rule A should operate and it is not in keeping with the published guidance.

Government amendments Nos. 71 and 72 put the matter beyond doubt by making it clear that the additional deductions can arise for another person. Rule A also refers to the same expense, although it does not directly link that reference to the deduction that is the subject of the rule.

Parliamentary counsel advised on the tabling of amendment No. 70. The advice was provided to the Government on the basis that there was an ambiguity which needed to be removed. As drafted, amendment No. 70 does that.

The second rule—rule B—applies when a payment gives rise to a tax deduction but the matching receipt is not taxable and the receipt is normally taxable on its income or gains. However, where rule B applies, it will reduce the amount of the UK tax deduction to the extent that the recipient is not taxable. Rule B will not apply, however, where the recipient is exempt from tax due to a statutory exemption—for example, charities and pension funds.

The draft guidance issued by HMRC on 16 March 2005 made it clear that rule B also applies where the recipient has reduced their liability by using tax credits or other deductions that may arise under the scheme. The clause as drafted covers that, but it also includes a paragraph that clarifies how the clause will operate in the case of deductions. I give credit to the Law Society, which was very helpful in pointing out to the Government that the explanatory paragraph could be read as restricting the intended operation of the clause. Amendments Nos. 73 and 74 therefore ensure that the clause continues to operate as intended and in accordance with the guidance already issued. ...

Clause 26 – Receipts cases

(Col 140)

The Paymaster-General: ... The clause identifies payments that are allowable as a deduction for the payer which adds the capital value of the recipient, but which would not otherwise be taxable for the recipient. As with deductions, the rules will apply only where a notice has been issued to the company by HMRC. There is an overlap between the operation of those rules and those proposed in clause 39, on financial avoidance. ...

However, the Government also recognise that the existence of a double charge to remedy the avoidance is inappropriate where one charge can be eliminated without putting the other at risk. The elimination of the arbitrage charge where there was already a charge under the financial avoidance legislation was made clear in the statements published when the legislation took effect. However, there is a difference between the two sets of rules, both in method and in terms of the person on whom the charge can fall.

The Government amendments ensure that that difference is correctly identified by the legislation, and that no charge will arise under the arbitrage rules if the financial avoidance rules are in point. Business has asked for certainty on this matter, and the amendments provide that. ...

Clause 28 – Notices under sections 24 and 26

(Col 144)

Amendment made: No. 29, in clause 28, page 26, line 24, leave out 'have been reasonably' insert 'reasonably have been'.—[Mr. Philip Hammond.]

Clause 28 – Notices under sections 24 and 26

(Col 153)

The Paymaster-General: ... I wish to clarify the Hansard record of our sitting last Thursday, which could be capable of a wider interpretation than I had intended. I fear that the problem is down to me, not the Hansard reporters. I stress that point. We were debating Opposition amendment No. 38 and controlled foreign companies. I referred to companies that have been unable to pass any of the exemptions under the controlled foreign company provisions and thus would be caught by the CFC legislation. I regret that, during what was quite a long day, the sentence

"In any case, there can be no justification for treating a CFC, which is by definition set up for tax avoidance purposes, more favourably than other companies"—[Official Report, Standing Committee B, 23 June 2005; c.141.]

potentially has a much wider interpretation. I apologise to the Committee. I was not concentrating as much as I should have been on matters under discussion. I hope that the hon. Member for Runnymede and Weybridge (Mr. Hammond) will accept that that one tiny sentence does not fundamentally change a huge piece of legislation on controlled foreign companies. ... I apologise to the Committee for my inadvertent slip.

Clause 31 – Commencement

(Col 157)

The Paymaster-General: ... Clause 31(3) provides an exemption for schemes with unconnected parties that were in existence on 16 March, provided that they are wound up before 31 August 2005. The purpose of the exemption is to give companies that have entered into a transaction that constitute an arbitrage scheme with an unconnected party—typically, with an unrelated bank—the chance to unwind the transactions without triggering the legislation.

(Col 158)

The exemption is restricted to transactions with unconnected parties, as it recognises that although transactions within the same group of companies can normally be unwound quickly, that process can take longer when third parties are involved. When the first Finance Bill was published, the transitional period lasted until 1 July 2005. As no statement was made on that specific point on Second Reading, the period has been extended to 31 August to take account of the election period and to give companies slightly longer to unwind their existing third party arrangements. ...

(Col 162)

The Paymaster-General: ... I come back to the fundamental point that I have made all the way through our discussions: where an arrangement involving arbitrage is set up for wholly commercial non-tax purposes, it will not be affected by the legislation. ...

Clause 32 – Temporary non-residents

(Col 164)

The Financial Secretary (John Healey): ... In 1998 the Government introduced legislation to counter the widespread use of certain tax avoidance schemes that relied on the fact that in most circumstances the rules for capital gains tax did not generally impose a charge on people who had been non-UK resident for the entire tax year in which they disclosed financial information. Under the rule that was introduced in 1998 the gains of people who leave the UK temporarily are taxed; it applies only if they had a close connection with the UK before they left and they are absent for fewer than five complete tax years. However, some people took advantage of the interaction between the terms of some of our tax treaties and the capital gains tax rules in such a way that they could return to the United Kingdom before the stipulated five years had elapsed without having to pay any UK tax from gains realised while they were resident outside the UK.

(Col 165)

The measure in clause 32 removes this avoidance opportunity. It stops the exploitation of our double taxation treaties and ensures that a charge to capital gains tax is imposed when the individual's absence from the UK is of a temporary nature. It does that by ensuring that the tax treaties cannot have the effect of preventing the UK's rules that were introduced in 1998 from applying.

The measure also deals with a situation in which the individual is regarded as resident in a foreign territory for tax treaty purposes, while simultaneously being resident in the UK. In such cases, the 1998 legislation will have no effect as the individual concerned will not have ceased to be resident in the UK. In certain circumstances, therefore, treaty non-residents could also be exploited by tax planners to enable people to avoid tax on capital gains; this measure closes that opportunity.

The Government are introducing the measure to put beyond doubt the question whether the terms of our tax treaties prevent the application of the 1998 temporary non-residence anti-avoidance rules. Her Majesty's Revenue and Customs has changed its view on that. It no longer accepts that our tax treaties have that effect, but to avoid uncertainty it seems sensible, wise and reasonable for us to legislate in clause 32 so that everyone is clear and individuals cannot seek to avoid capital gains tax in that way. The effect of this measure is to ensure that an appropriate amount of tax is charged in respect of gains made while individuals are temporarily absent from the UK. Whenever foreign tax has been paid, the double taxation relief will be available in line with the normal rules. ...

Clause 33 – Trustees both resident and non-resident in a year of assessment

(Col 168)

The Financial Secretary: The clause introduces an anti-avoidance measure to counter certain tax avoidance schemes that, in tax planning circles, are commonly known as sunset schemes. They have been used by some trustees and settlers of settlements to exploit the gap in our capital gains tax rules that allows trustees to avoid capital gains tax by arranging their affairs so ...

(Col 169)

... that they are both resident and non-resident in the UK in any given tax year. Under the existing rules only gains arising to trustees if they are resident in the UK throughout the year or are non-resident throughout the year are taxed. The schemes take various forms but the common feature is that they exploit the terms of our tax treaties to ensure that no UK tax is chargeable on gains that would otherwise be taxable in the UK and little or no tax is payable on the gains elsewhere. The schemes rely on the broad proposition that at any given moment trustees are resident for capital gains tax purposes in the country where the majority of the trustees reside. ...

The clause ensures that the avoidance device cannot work in respect of disposals made by trustees on or after Budget day. It does so by ensuring that if residence changes during the tax year the terms of our tax treaties do not interfere with our right to tax gains under our existing domestic legislation. It does not affect the foreign country's right to tax that gain, and established mechanisms are in place to prevent double taxation of the trustees ...

Schedule 4 – Location of assets etc.

(Col 172)

The Financial Secretary: ... People who are resident abroad but carry on a business in this country are liable to tax on capital gains only in respect of disposals of business assets that are situated in the UK. The current tax rules for determining where assets are situated do not cover every circumstance. Where there is no specific rule in the tax code, the provisions and principles of common law apply to determine the situation of an asset. People have exploited some gaps in the tax rules to avoid tax on gains arising from the sale of assets abroad. ...

The measure stops exploitation in two ways. First, shares in companies incorporated in the UK will generally be regarded as situated here. Secondly, unless an existing tax rule already specifies their location, intangible assets, such as options or rights over other assets, will now be treated as being situated in the UK for the purposes of tax and capital gains if they are subject to UK law at the time that they are created. The rules for futures and options that are not subject to UK law at the time they are created will take account of the location of the underlying subject matter. ...

Clause 35 and Schedule 5 – Exercise of options etc.

(Col 175)

The Financial Secretary: ... The clause and the schedule introduce another anti-avoidance measure and correct a defect in the capital gains tax rules for assets that are bought or sold under options contracts. That loophole has been exploited to avoid tax, and we announced our intention to close it in the pre-Budget report of 2 December 2004. The defect in the rules might have allowed people to avoid tax on capital gains by using options to dispose of assets at uncommercial prices. For example, someone might want to transfer an asset worth £1 million to their family trust. If they transferred it directly to the trust, they would be taxed by reference to the value of the asset—£1 million. Instead, they could use an option that set the sale price at, say, £1,000. They would then be taxed by reference to the uncommercial option price of £1,000 and not on the true £1 million value of the asset. ...

People might also have been able to use options to buy an asset at an uncommercially high price from, for example, their offshore trust. The trustees would not be liable to capital gains tax because the trust would be offshore. The person who bought the assets from the trustees could sell them and create an artificial tax loss because of the unrealistically high price that they had paid. That, of course, would be used to compute the gain or loss arising on that sale. Alternatively, if that person disposed of the asset after its value had increased, the full increase in value would not be taxed because the gain on the disposal would be computed using the artificially high price paid. The proposed measure puts such cases back on the correct footing. ...

Under these measures, the tax liability will be based on the value of ...

(Col 176)

... the asset bought or sold, instead of on the uncommercial option price. The same position applies for assets given away or sold at an uncommercial price without using an option. The measures are targeted at people who use that device to avoid tax. Companies and individuals who exercise options at arm's length on normal commercial terms will not be affected and will face no additional compliance burden. Employees who participate in approved company share option plans will also be unaffected. ...

Schedule 6 – Accounting practice and related matters

(Col 194)

The Paymaster-General: ... The hon. Member for Wimbledon (Stephen Hammond) referred to the Chartered Institute of Taxation. He was concerned about schedule 9 of the Finance Act 1996 and asked whether it would stop a company from receiving relief for a drop in value of part of a loan relationship, when there is a derivative such as an interest rate swap acting as a cash-flow hedge of interest rate risk elements for the loan relationship. ... my understanding is that officials from HMRC have discussed such issues with a leading tax practitioner at the CIOT and said that, in their view, the legislation will not have the effect that is feared, and the revised guidance that is being prepared on loan relationships and derivative contracts will make that clear. ...

Schedule 7 – Avoidance involving financial arrangements

(Col 220)

The Paymaster-General: ... The amendments arise from consultation and, as I said during the previous debate, they are targeted specifically to deal with contrived disclosed regimes. The 13 amendments in this group mostly narrow the scope of the conditions. However, two of them correct unintended let-outs that were included when the clauses from the original Bill were altered.

Amendments Nos. 78 to 82 would change section 91C, which relates to condition 1. They do three things to amend the income-producing asset test. First, they make it clear that to be let out, the assets of the issuing company have to be wholly, or substantially wholly, income producing. In other words, the company should not be tainted by the presence of a few non-income producing assets.

Secondly, the measure of assets is now by reference to their value rather than their book value. That prevents the accounting manipulation that uses a valuable non-income producing asset with a low book value to get round the test. Thirdly, the amendments add to the categories of income-producing assets to deal with the issue of multiple charges in chains of groups ...

The group of amendments also makes changes to section 91D, which applies to redeemable shares designed to give an interest-like return. The amendments do three things. They ensure that when a public issue of shares is acquired by a company, the shares are subject to the charge if the company is using them to avoid tax on UK dividends. They change the test of when cases will be taken to be avoiding tax on UK dividends and hence having an unallowable purpose. The new test is narrowed to apply only to banking groups, requires that the acquiring company's shares were acquired in the ordinary course of investment business and removes some redundant wording that asks the nonsensical question of whether the company was associated with itself.

(Col 221)

Finally, amendment No. 90 changes condition 3 in section 91E. The amendment simply ensures that a share that by itself gives an interest-like return cannot come within condition 3. That means that condition 3 is mutually exclusive from conditions 1 and 2. We believe that to have been the case all along, but representations suggested that the wording of the original Bill could be read another way, so we thought it best to put the matter beyond doubt, otherwise the shares that gave an interest-like return but were not within condition 1 or 2—because there was no tax avoidance—might be dragged into condition 3 because of the presence of, say, a derivative, which would have nothing to do with the nature of the return on a share. ...

Schedule 9 – Insurance companies, etc.

(Col 257)

Mr. Field: I hope that the Economic Secretary can provide an answer to the following question about mutual companies. Given that mutual insurers have no shareholders, will they be subject to shareholder-type tax?

The Economic Secretary (Mr. Lewis): ... The only conceivable effect on a mutual company will be in certain specified and identifiable circumstances: if it has acquired business from a company that is not mutual, and if that other company has carried out the reattribution exercise, the effect on a mutual company in that position will be to ensure that the income from the excess assets will not be attributed to pension business. Any excess assets held by a mutual in that way will not be taxed at the 30 per cent. rate applying to shareholders' income. ...

(Col 267)

The Economic Secretary: ... paragraph 8 adds a new section— section 444ACA—to the Income and Corporation Taxes Act 1988. It is designed to stop avoidance where business is transferred from one life assurance company to another. Paragraph 8 deals with situations in which company A—the company taking on the business—already owns some or all of the shares of company B, the company that transfers the business. In most cases, the transfer will cause the value of the shares in company B to fall. Under current tax rules, company A gets a tax deduction for that fall in value from either current or future profits. However, it is important to remember that that has happened only because company B transferred the business to company A, so the value of the business has now moved to company A. Therefore, company A has not really suffered a loss in value; the loss on the shares in ...

(Col 268)

... company B is balanced by an increase in the value of its other assets. If we do not make the proposed change, companies such as company A will, in effect, get tax relief for the cost of acquiring business, and that is not an allowable tax deduction in any other circumstances. New section 444ACA stops that by adding an amount equivalent to the loss of the trading profits of company A for tax purposes. This is not a new idea. There are provisions in the capital gains tax code for denying deductions when that happens, and provisions that stop banks, share dealers—and, indeed, non-life assurance companies—getting relief for such losses. This change brings life assurance companies into line. ...

(Col 271)

The Economic Secretary: ... I should like to explain what paragraph 13 does. Like paragraph 3 about inherited estates and the sunset clause—the subject of amendments Nos. 105 and 106, which hon. Members may recall debating this morning—paragraph 13 deals with apportionments of life company income and gains. The aspect that we are concerned with is how many separate apportionments have to be made to allocate investment returns to those categories of business, such as pension business, that are taxed on the basis of their operating profits.

Where a company divides its accounts into separate funds or sub-funds, it can, if certain conditions in tax law are met, carry out separate apportionments for each sub-fund, rather than make a single apportionment for the business as a whole. That can make quite a difference to the end result. I have to tell ...

(Col 272)

... the hon. Gentleman that, unfortunately, some companies have manipulated their fund structures purely for tax purposes, and others have benefited excessively from fund structures created for other reasons. We are amending the rules to restrict the separate funds that can be the subject of separate apportionments. In essence, there will be a separate apportionment for each with profits sub-fund and one for everything else. ...

Schedule 10 – Stamp duty land tax: miscellaneous amendments

(Col 288)

The Economic Secretary: ... paragraph 6 ... extends the circumstances in which stamp duty land tax group relief can be clawed back. The Government's intention has been clear ever since the clawback provisions were introduced in 2002. If group relief is claimed, and the transferee company leaves the group within three years, the relief should be clawed back. In the absence of such a provision, groups would ...

(Col 289)

... be free to wrap a property in a company and sell the shares shortly afterwards without incurring any liability for stamp duty land tax. Although the Government's intention was clear, schemes aimed at frustrating it began to emerge almost as soon as the clawback provisions were published. The schemes work by interposing within the group transfers that have no commercial purpose but that stop the eventual clawback of group relief. Hence the need for paragraph 6, which in effect causes the transfers to be disregarded, and which means that it is the relationship between the earliest transferor and the ultimate transferee in a three-year period that is considered. If, at the end of that period, those two companies are no longer in the same group, then unless stamp duty land tax has been paid on one of the intermediate transactions, the relief is clawed back. ...

... At present, once group relief is withdrawn, the tax can be recovered from the company that originally claimed it, connected companies, or the transferor company. That reflects the fact that if payment has been made for the property the transferor company may still be in possession of the money, whereas the transferee may have been liquidated. As a result of the changes made by paragraph 6, there will be a right of recovery against the earliest transferor in the three-year period before the ultimate transferee leaves the group ... It is worth pointing out that, where there are successive transfers, the earliest transferor may be the only company carrying on a genuine business, with the other companies being inserted for tax reasons and being quickly eliminated. It therefore seems entirely right that HMRC should be able to recover tax from that company. Hon. Members should bear in mind that in most cases paragraph 6 will only affect contrived avoidance schemes ...

(Col 292)

The Economic Secretary: Paragraph 8 of schedule 10 restricts the availability of acquisition relief so that the definition of the undertaking must be a trade, not an investment business, and must not be a property-dealing trade. ... I understand that there have been worries that the concept of dealing in chargeable interests is uncertain, a point made by the hon. Gentleman. It is unclear, for example, whether a property developer or house builder will be caught. While it is ultimately a question of fact what trade a company is carrying on, I can reassure the Committee that property developers and house builders who derive most of their profits from their work, rather than from buying and selling would not be caught by the measure. Companies that want reassurance about that in relation to their specific trade can approach HMRC to seek clarification.

(Col 293)

The Economic Secretary:... Paragraph 11 applies where a lease is granted to or by a nominee. The normal rule is that transactions with nominees are ignored for stamp duty land tax purposes. That reflects the intention that stamp duty land tax should be charged when beneficial ownership changes, not when someone puts their own property into the name of a nominee ... Paragraph 11 disapplies that rule where the transaction is the grant of a lease. The reason for that is to counter avoidance schemes where the grant of a lease to or by a nominee is followed by the assignment of the lease to a third party. Normally, there is a charge on the rental element of a lease when it is granted. However, if transactions with nominees are ignored, that charge will not occur. That will enable leases to be granted without any charge on the rental element. Paragraph 11 therefore provides that where the transaction is the grant of a lease, the fact that a nominee is involved is ignored; in other words, there is the same charge that there would be if there were no nominee arrangements. That ensures that there will be the normal charge on the rental element. In many cases, there is a relief such as group relief, which will prevent a charge to tax from arising at all.

Clause 54 – Loan relationships

(Col 308)

The Financial Secretary (John Healey): ... New paragraph 12B(5) in this clause and new paragraph 30B(5) in clause 55 contain an anti-avoidance rule. New paragraph 12B(6) in this clause and new paragraph 30B(6) in clause 55 both state that the provisions of sub-paragraphs (5) will not have an effect ...

"if before the merger Her Majesty's Revenue and Customs have on the application of the merging companies notified them that Her Majesty's Revenue and Customs are satisfied"

(Col 309)

... that the transaction" is effected for bona fide commercial reasons, and does not form part" of an arrangement to avoid tax. I hope that the hon. Member for Braintree appreciates that both new sub-paragraphs (6) aim to make it clear that HMRC is fully prepared to give pre-transaction clearance to any company or companies that are considering merging to form an SE. However, there is no existing statutory clearance procedure within the loan relationship and derivative contracts regime under which that can be given. The procedures will therefore have to be made clear in guidance.

Clause 18 – Authorised investment funds, etc: specific powers

(Col 392)

The Economic Secretary: ... We recognise that some investors may end up owning 10 per cent. or more of a fund inadvertently. For example, that might happen if a substantial investor redeemed his units. To ensure that investors who find themselves over the limit unwittingly are not affected adversely, the regulations will provide a period of grace for matters to be reversed. ...

INDEX